THINKING ABOUT ART

THINKING ABOUT ART

Critical Essays

by

EDWARD LUCIE-SMITH

Originally published in *The Times*

CALDER AND BOYARS
LONDON

First published in Great Britain 1968
by Calder and Boyars, Ltd.,
18, Brewer Street, London, W.1.

These essays first appeared in *The Times*
with whose permission the author has
arranged them for this edition.

The first one hundred copies of this edition have been signed and numbered by the author and have been specially bound. They are exclusively available from Turret Books, Publishers, 5 Kensington Church Walk, London, W.8.

All royalties earned from these one hundred special copies will be donated by the author to the Defence of Literature and the Arts Fund, 61 Welbeck Street, London, W.1.

Printed in Great Britain by
Unwin Brothers Limited
Woking and London

to
Georg

CONTENTS

INTRODUCTION

Few diarists really enjoy re-reading their own journals. It argues too great a degree of self-complacency if they do. The same reaction is aroused even by a journal that one has kept in public. The inconsistencies, the intellectual failures, stand out all too clearly.

The articles reprinted here were all of them written for the "Things Seen" column in *The Times*. My brief was to think about, and around, the visual arts; sometimes choosing a current exhibition as my starting point, and sometimes not. The result, in a real sense, is a kind of journal, with all the flaws which the use of that term implies. Each article reflects what I was thinking and feeling at a given moment. Over a four-year period, these thoughts and feelings have been changeable. Anyone who wants to look for inconsistencies and self-contradictions in the pages that follow will surely have no difficulty in finding them.

Yet, perhaps strangely, I am not sorry to find that I have been such a weathercock. I might cut a better figure if it wasn't so, yet I'd be further from my own view of the critic's function. A lot of people tend to think of all critics, even art critics, as members of the judiciary. Critics reward the virtuous, and send the guilty off to perdition. The immoral reader welcomes a professional moralist—one, of course, that he can snigger at now and again, behind the back of authority. Let me say at once then that sermons on canvas (like sermons in stones) are not my line. No doubt, just because I'm a critic and writing in English, I occasionally find myself using the language of morality. That, after all, is the tradition of English art criticism, insofar as it has one.

Nor am I going to pretend that moral ideas play no part in my reactions to works of art. Of course they do. The visual arts are so closely linked to the whole structure of society—and this structure, in turn, is necessarily affected by ideas about conduct and ethics—that it would be artificial to avoid the great moral issues. But it is equally artificial to pretend that moral reactions and moral criteria are the only valid ones.

Indeed the art critic—and especially the critic who concerns himself with contemporary art—seems to me to operate on a kind of Tom Tiddler's ground of the intellect. It's for this reason that I tend to value the method of approach more than the conclusion. Looking back over these essays, it seems to me that what I was trying to do, however clumsily, was to think my way through a number of problems, and that these problems are not exclusively the concern of the visual arts. Written under the pressure of events, my articles inevitably contain things that I now disagree with. Occasionally I've added a footnote to say so. But, apart from correcting a few slips of fact and grammar, I've left the text to stand as it was.

But there is something more than this to be said, and a preface is the place to say it. The arts today are not static but dynamic. The idea of "relativity" has a place in criticism as well as in science. It's very tempting for a critic to feel that he's solved a given problem once and for all, and that it need never be thought of again. But then, next week, the string on the parcel unknots itself, the problem leaps down from the shelf where it has been put. The modern situation has been variously defined. But one thing we can perhaps say: modernity is essentially something fluid. Its fluidity is its real identity. Technology alters the world for us, and we have barely adjusted ourselves to one invention before another comes along and supersedes it. Modern society is also in flux. Why should we expect the arts alone to remain in one place?

And yet this is precisely what we do expect. To the layman a work of art is something fixed, immutable, permanently valid. This makes the contemporary critic's task a thankless one. The professional expert has also got to be a professional heretic. The critic must continually test ideas—old ones and new—not always in the hope of finding anything with a quality of absoluteness, but often just looking for what will serve in the circumstances, and for the moment. An awareness that the arts, and individual works of art, have played very different roles in society at different times underlies what I've written. For instance, I am aware that cave-paintings by prehistoric men are still valid to us today, in the sense that they produce a genuine aesthetic reaction. But the "validity" is still something that the artists who made them wouldn't have recognised, because of the difference in the referential framework.

On the other hand, I am not willing to abandon the notion

of standards, and, unlike the libertarians who are now so prevalent in the world of the arts, I do not find the pursuit of definitions either useless or academic. According to the libertarian, the critic is not so much the judge as the jailer. He is the man who says "no", who erects barriers to appreciation. This view causes me as much, indeed perhaps more, irritation than the demand that I, and all critics, should be willing at any moment, appropriate or inappropriate, to deliver judgment *ex cathedra*. The libertarian attitude—a condemnation of all critics of whatever kind—seems to me to be very much the same as its opposite, which asks that critics should be not only authoritative, but authoritarian.

I have already touched on the subject of morality. I should like to say a little more about the relationship between moral ideas and works of art. Libertarianism is itself a system of morality. The command to be "free" contains, just as older moralities do, a series of quite detailed imperatives and prohibitions. Some of these, at first sight, are genuinely in conflict with older notions of what art and art criticism are about. The libertarian is, as he himself declares, in favour of a direct confrontation between the spectator and the work of art. The man who looks at a picture is commanded to open himself to the artist without reserve, to allow another being to mingle with his own being. In fact, the basic metaphor is a sexual one. The sexual revolution—"Make Love not War"—is in fact often equated with current developments in art. And, by virtue of the metaphor, the critic becomes both a pimp and a *voyeur*. He is the unwanted third party, the intermediary who deflects the free flow of communicative emotion and uses its corrupted but still powerful energies to his own profit.

The question of how and where art relates to moral ideas is a real question, but a very delicate one, not to be solved by the leverage of crude slogans. In the essays that follow, I think I may occasionally give the impression that I should like to remove art from the sphere of morality altogether. If so, I am in the wrong. Language seems to me to be essentially a moral instrument—not only English, but all language. Built into the English language, in particular, are all kinds of moral preconceptions, as we see from the shades of meaning to be found in those two common words "good" and "bad". The trouble is that objects, such as paintings and sculptures, are not themselves necessarily either moral or immoral; morality resides only in the concepts that we form about them, and the language with which we clothe these concepts. If the visual arts have a bearing on the world of moral ideas, it's an oblique and ambiguous one. They approach this realm by means of symbol and allegory. The density of most successful works of art lies in their ambiguity, in the layers of meaning that are compacted into one object, in the multitude of slightly different interpretations that one painting or one piece of sculpture will allow us to make.

Libertarianism, like puritanism, seems to me to omit all consideration of the variousness of mankind. It assumes that if the spectator gives himself wholly to the work of art, the end can be foreseen. A spark will be struck; a soul will be illuminated. My assumptions are different. I believe that the work of art is usually more slippery than we suppose. I even measure its power by its ability to evoke a range of reactions—often contradictory—within me or any spectator. If a work of art has a particular effect upon me, I am interested in trying to describe not only the object but the effect. I am interested, too, to see whether my reactions correspond to those of other people.

It seems to me, in fact, that the work of art doesn't illuminate the spectator; it challenges him. The relationship is that between Jacob and the Angel. Or, to change the metaphor, what happens when we look at a work of art is that a dialogue begins—with all those concealments, those shifts of tone, those attempts to gain some momentary advantage, those little manœuvrings, that we find in real and spoken dialogues. And I believe that this dialogue does genuinely take place between man and object, not man and man. The work of art is not the same thing as the artist—it is a crude error to suppose that it is.

The critic's task is bounded by the circumstances I have described. It is his job to sort out the implicit and explicit intentions of the artist, and to relate them to the work. More, the critic must create some kind of pattern, some field of force, which will enable the less practised spectator to align himself with what he sees. And then again, the critic must commit some part of himself, put some part of his own personality at risk, if he is to succeed in the task he has set himself. What should interest the professional art critic is not just a single answer, but all the possible answers, all the possible reactions. But, having explored them, he must choose.

Of course, this is an inhuman demand to make, and art criticism is always more imperfect than the people who write it like to think. A kind of nostalgia for the absolute is probably the thing that has produced the many discussions of classicism in this volume. But then it is easier—much easier—to talk about absolute standards than to create them. The hardest lesson the art critic has to learn is that standards are not only necessary, but they apply to himself, and no-one is likelier to fall short of them. Yet to admit this is also to say something more positive: that a work of art, of whatever sort, is not only a challenge to the emotions, but a challenge to the mind. Basically, we value works of art as emblems of the richness and variety of the human spirit and the human intellect; though, on second thought, "emblem" is perhaps the wrong word, as it suggests something thin and impoverished. Because of their riches, criticism must respond to the visual arts with a flexibility which may often amount to waywardness. But perhaps it is better to be wayward than to be doctrinaire. The problem is to combine waywardness and honesty. It's the critic's business to argue, and the tone in which he argues is his own affair: frivolously or solemnly as the mood takes him. But he must at least be prepared to accept the consequences of argument, and more important still, the consequences of experience.

The best art critic is the man who is changed, even if only a little, by every new work of art he sees. How can such a man pretend that his judgments are absolute and his opinions not to be questioned? And yet there are still standards, of a kind. The determination to search and go on searching (knowing finality to be a mirage) is the thing I most admire in other critics. I hardly dare to claim such persistence for myself. And yet here is the morality of criticism I recognise—this untiring search. For the rest, it's probable that I'm simply a puritan who disapproves of puritanism and a libertarian who takes a gloomy view of liberty. Those in a similar situation are invited to read on.

Edward Lucie-Smith

PART I

1. ART AND THE INQUIRING SPIRIT

Critics often ask themselves: "What is going on in the painting?" It seems to me that, where modern art is concerned, the correct question is not this, but: "What is going on in the spectator?" The whole point of modern painting often seems to be not what takes place on the canvas itself, but the event which the painting generates within the onlooker. Hence those strange disconnections which we notice in modern art, those gaps in logical organization. The hiatuses are bridged not externally and physically, but somewhere within the psyche. When painters talk, as they sometimes do, about the need to invent a new pictorial language, they mean, I think, a language which takes account of the interior event.

All of this is not entirely unique in the long history of art. If we accept the thesis put forward by the Reverend Gervase Mathew in his brilliant recent book, *Byzantine Aesthetics*, then something very similar happened to art in Byzantium. The difference is that modern art does not usually have the tight intellectual control which we find in Byzantine painting. And this lack of precision has led, in turn, to embittered arguments about the exact relationship between artist and spectator, artist and critic.

One difficulty—a major one—is due to the difficulty which we have in finding a terminology in which to describe the "interior event" which I referred to above. The language we choose is most often that of the emotions. We say that the spectator "feels" what the painter is trying to do. We say, going farther, that the artist's aim is to generate "emotion", or, rather, to communicate it. And this leads us directly to the assumption that the artist must feel deeply himself and must pour this feeling into the picture, otherwise he is not being "sincere". All the key words carry strong moral overtones. They are the vocabulary, not only of discussions about modern art but of modern anxiety. "The true voice of feeling" is, so it seems, the voice which assures us that modern technology, modern society and its demands, have not yet succeeded in cutting us off from the basic sources of our humanity.

But is the language of feeling really of much help when we

are discussing pictures? The answer to this question depends on another—is aesthetic emotion the same thing as personal emotion? If, for example, we decide to judge emotion by the crude yardstick of its physical effects, then we do sometimes find that works of art produce in us physical symptoms which resemble those which we experience at moments of crisis in our own lives. The accelerated heart-beat of the lover can be paralleled by that catch of the breath which comes to most people on seeing the sculptures in the Medici Chapel for the first time. Yet we must admit that these physical sensations are not primary. We could, I think, discard them, and find no fundamental difference in our response to the work of art. The sensuality of the man who stands in front of a Titian *Venus* is rather different from that of the bridegroom on his wedding-night.

There are many and complex explanations of what does really happen to us when we become truly "engaged" by a work of art, but most of them seem to suggest that what takes place is a complex interaction of the mental and the physical. It is almost as if the artist enabled us to explore our own senses in a detached way, and then persuaded us to carry the exploration forward from the purely physical level to something far more all-embracing and therefore more satisfying.

The anti-intellectual trend of modern art, however, encourages the artist to think that what matters is the instantaneous communication rather than the complete one. The critic is regarded as a barrier to communication because he "intellectualizes", therefore corrupting the first freshness of feeling. Now, while it is quite true that works of art ought to be seen through the spectator's own eyes, and not through someone else's, this doctrine seems to me to be nonsense. And I say this in the slightly despairing consciousness that "nonsense" is just what many artists set out to achieve. In their distrust of the intellect, in their concentration on emotion (which they define very crudely), they try to banish all trace of the logical.

Yet here, again, there is a dangerous confusion of ideas. For those "hiatuses" which I referred to originally are not, I think, by any means the same thing as mere deliberate jumblings and *non-sequiturs*. Indeed, one could go so far as to say that it is one of the signs of bad modern painting that the *non-sequiturs* seem to matter more than the possible communication. The extreme narcissists among modern painters defend themselves by saying that, after all, communication itself is irrelevant, and the artist must simply "express himself". I confess that I fail to see the difference. It seems to me that what communicates is, *ipso facto*, expressed.

But even if we admit that the definition of "feeling" employed by modern artists and their supporters is sometimes so crude as to be laughable, what about the critic's function? The critic's job is not only to experience the work of art. It is to analyse the experience, and to communicate his conclusions to others. This does not rule out the presence of emotion—the best criticism is usually that which is emotionally engaged. But it does demand that the critic should look at his emotions and try to see them for what they are. This, however, is only a beginning. I have said modern painting is what happens inside the spectator. This description implies that a painting is no longer a single event, but rather an infinity of separate events, each divided from all the others. And here, I suppose, is the most sensible argument against critics. Why should we, where an infinite number of different sensibilities are involved, attach so much weight to the evidence of one?

The answer is, of course, that critics are no more pure sensibility than painters are pure emotion. Sensibility is only the critic's guide, and even so, it will take him no more than the first part of the way. The strident claims to total individuality which we hear from modern artists have to be reconciled with the increasingly tight mesh which society weaves about every individual, be he artist or not. The critic's job—fallible as he necessarily must be—is to examine the problem, and other problems with it. Part judge, part lover, part intermediary, he represents the inquiring spirit which is the real bridge between art and humankind, and the prime cause of art itself.

2. CRISIS IN THE AVANT-GARDE

The respectability of *avant-garde* art in England is currently being confirmed by the success of one exhibition after another. Rauschenberg, Johns, the Peggy Guggenheim Collection, Bruce Lacey's robots, various showings of Kinetic Art—all of these have been acclaimed. I sometimes wonder if advanced artists wholly relish the situation in which they now find themselves. Success is sweet—but it is part of the philosophy of avant-gardism to stay ahead of the public taste. What will happen when the race with eager acceptance is finally lost, when total permissiveness at last prevails?

Let me be the first to admit that this is a mischievous question. But it is still one which (once asked) has to be answered. The reason why it calls for a reply lies buried in the history of the *avant-garde* itself. It has often been fashionable to pretend that the violent artistic experiments of this century are things which were created in isolation. The most superficial examination of events will prove that this is untrue. If modern art in one sense owes its birth to Cézanne, in another it is the product of social discontents, and especially of society as it existed before the First World War. The upheaval in the arts was then a warning of the blood-letting to follow. Thus, among the Russian Futurists, we find a feverish artistic activity closely linked to a sense of the sickness of tsarist Russia. Until recently it was forgotten how many of the experiments we see today were foreshadowed by the work of such artists as Malevitch, Tatlin, Larionov, and Gontcharova. Again, many critics have remarked how closely Pop art is modelled upon the activities of the Dadaists during the early twenties. And Dada in its original form was unmistakably a product of social conditions. It is a despairing response to the ruin and misery created by the war.

If we ask ourselves whether conditions today resemble those which produced Futurism and Dada, the answer must surely be no. There may, perhaps, be much to complain of in the society in which we find ourselves, but it is incomparably freer, and incomparably better organized, than pre-1914 Russia. It is also incomparably more prosperous (and also more optimistic) than the Germany of 1920. *Avant-garde* art, if we insist on looking at it through our old spectacles, becomes a curious and unlikely phenomenon indeed. It seems as if the urgent gestures of protest and revolt are being directed at something which no longer deserves them, and which ought not, therefore, to provoke such actions. The usual reply to this point, on the rare occasions when it is raised, is to say that the artist is now in revolt against modern materialism, against the smugness which has replaced the old oppression. Alternatively, there is the view that the artist is forced to make violent gestures of revolt in order to assert the previous quality of individuality, which the modern state, with all its "improvements", threatens to squeeze out of him.

I think that we ought to look at these claims with an exceedingly wary eye. First of all, if the situation (though still oppressive) is now different, why doesn't the protest take on a different guise? One of the most interesting aspects of today's *avant-garde* is its tendency to recapitulate yesterday's experiments in almost identical form. Much that we accept as "new" is, in essence, entirely lacking in novelty. This might not matter so much if the main line of development had been through Cubism. The Cubists envisaged this kind of recapitulation. As Lipchitz once said, "Cubism was essentially a search for a syntax". But it is things which once seemed very much "of the moment" that have enjoyed the longest life. We still subscribe to the religion of "anti-art". The acts of demolition are endlessly repeated.

What we are confronted with is a paradox—nothing less than the existence of an *avant-garde* tradition. How this came about can only be explained with reference to the social pattern which the Futurists and Dadaists created. They did not conquer—at least not in the way that they meant to do. Neither did they wholly lose. What happened in the arts was a kind of fission. The *avant-garde* began to draw a limited audience to itself, and it began to make demands upon the loyalties of that audience. Being still, in a sense, beleaguered, it was perhaps entitled to do so. The result was that advanced art, having failed to change society at large, set up a society of its own. Like all societies, this small band of supporters and admirers began to look for means of self-definition. These were found, naturally enough, in *avant-garde* art itself. The audience fastened upon the most obvious aspects of what it admired. It accepted gleefully, and encouraged, the violent and negative side of the new painting and sculpture. The hysterical gestures acquired a ritual significance, and in so doing lost at least a part of their original meaning. They were now made for their own sake, as much as in the hope of achieving a positive result. In particular, the audience which *avant-garde* art had made for itself became fascinated by the very idea of novelty. And here, again, the tendency towards ritual intervened. If novelty was sacred, it was essential that it should take on recognizable and immediately identifiable characteristics. In doing so, it very often ceased to be "new" in any but a very special sense. The new art had spawned its own academy.

Yet I must not paint too gloomy a picture. The initial impetus of the pre-First War discoveries in art had been so tremendous that the *avant-garde* conquered many of the difficulties which lay in wait for it. There were many reasons why the new public, itself created by the changed social conditions for which many of the original *avant-garde* had striven so passionately, could be fascinated by modernity in painting and sculpture. Not the least of these reasons was the fact that the "mass arts" —such as advertising and packaging—were themselves the bastard descendants of the original Futurist and Dada experiments. This new public, more nearly classless than the public for art had been before, was ripe for the doctrine of the "switched on" and the "with it". The artists responded, and the era of popular success was at hand.

But can the *avant-garde* now survive in anything like its old form? Are the attitudes, the styles, and even the methods, which took root 50 years ago adequate to meet the challenge of the new audience? I, for one, am beginning to doubt it. Ritual novelty seems an inadequate answer.

3. ART CRITICS AND LEGEND-MAKERS

I concluded my last article on this page by saying that, so far as modern art was concerned, ritual novelty had begun to seem an inadequate answer. Perhaps the moment has come to consider the ways in which novelty of this kind is sustained and propagated. This means that I must talk about the function of the critic. What is an art critic for? What should his attitudes be, especially when he has to deal with work which is consciously—or perhaps self-consciously—*avant-garde*? The answer is not easy. Even after sixty triumphant years, modern art still has to encounter powerful hatreds, and these hatreds centre as much upon the critic as upon the artist. For example, every critic receives the occasional anonymous letter, and these are invariably both sick and nasty. For the crime of saying this, I shall myself probably receive several prime specimens of the genre. Yet they are not to be taken seriously—anonymity is the sure sign that the writers of these letters feel themselves to be on the losing side.

Far more dangerous to the cause of modern art are its advocates. Not only is there the fact that much art criticism is of very poor quality, and is written in English so turgid that "art critics' prose" has become a by-word. There is the sadder and subtler fact that many writers about art who think of themselves as critics hardly deserve that title in the old sense at all. These are the often eloquent, often powerful, often convincing advocates—the self-appointed defenders of a faith which one would have thought was already triumphant, and therefore in no need of their services.

It has often struck me, both in connection with poetry and with the visual arts, that the mythopoeic faculty has shifted its sphere of activity. It is the painters and poets who are the new saints. About them the legends gather, and to certain of them religious homage is paid. None have been more active in creating the climate for this than the advocates of whom I have just spoken. If we examined the public history of modern art in England—the history, not of what goes on in the studios, but of exhibitions and publicity, and prestige—we find that it can best be characterized by its crazes. For a moment, a certain artist, or even a certain school of artists, can do no wrong; whether it be Bacon, or the Abstract Expressionists, or (currently) Rauschenberg and Johns. New saviours are constantly being hailed, but after a while they are—if not precisely discarded—allowed to sink back on to a secondary plane of interest. About this process there is something both generous and a little ridiculous. Generous because, in their varying degrees, most of the artists singled out in this way deserve to be praised. Ridiculous because, despite the strides made by British painting in the past 10 years, Britain remains from the artistic point of view a provincial country, and these excessive and exclusive celebrations are the sign of our provincialism.

Yet this is perhaps too kindly a view. At each successive paean of praise, at each blare of television trumpets, each triumph in the colour supplements, it becomes more and more apparent that works of art are treated merely as adjuncts to personality. The heroes pass by us in a steady procession, and one can see the advocates already drawing breath to fill a fresh set of sails. They remain constant, whatever else changes, and the epiphany is their natural element. Such unwearying enthusiasm is touching to behold.

Enthusiasm—this word brings me to the nub of my argument. It can be the critic's duty to be enthusiastic, whatever else changes. Then he has a unique privilege; he must find words for a new experience, a new extension of himself. He must *share*. But share what? He cannot cut the painter up in slices and hand him round, in a kind of secular communion (which bit of Picasso will you have, Sir, breast or wing?). The critic's business is not with the artist, but with the individual work of art, and his own experience of it. He writes in the margin; he speaks as a spectator to other spectators.

But this is to make, even now, the error of assuming that the main business of the art-critic is to be enthusiastic, and to propagate enthusiasm. Nothing of the kind—the business of the critic is to judge. What he judges is again not the artist (his morals, physical beauty, intellectual eminence, sphinx-like demeanour, wife, children, and eating habits) but simply the picture on the wall. Said thus, it sounds arrogant, and indeed there is a certain arrogance about all criticism which parallels the arrogance of the artist in setting himself up as a creator in the first place.

The act of judgment which the critic performs is a lonely one, and every conscientious critic must be aware of this. But the critic does not, and cannot, take the work of art in isolation. He has to work from accumulated knowledge as well as from sensitivity. He consults his experience of other works of art; he may even (though cautiously) consult his knowledge of the artist himself and what he knows of the artist's intentions. He will try to see the work before him both in context, imbedded in the circumstances of its time, and completely outside of it. This kind of engagement, this kind of grappling is both pleasurable and painful. Every work of art which we see inevit- the works of art which we have previously seen. A crude able, if it works, brings about a tiny shift in our attitude to all example of this is the way in which an addition to the *oeuvre* of a famous Old Master can quite substantially alter our attitude towards all his other pictures. It tells us something new, and we hasten to apply the knowledge we have gained to pictures which we thought we had solved already.

What the critic cannot do, in the case of an *avant-garde* artist, is to judge the work of art before him in terms of what *will* happen, later. In a situation where the artist relies upon his capacity to astonish, the spectator is worse than foolish if he tries to predict the nature of the astonishment. And this, to my mind, is the counterargument to the cry which the advocate (not the critic) so often makes to us. "Trust the artist", he says. "If you don't like his new work, you will when future developments have justified it." A touching plea—but is the critic to trust his own trustingness, or somebody else's? It seems that here the arrogance of advocacy outruns the arrogance of criticism. The critic, after all, is content to judge what he sees before him, according to his own lights, however inadequate. Yet the "trust" which the legend-makers urge can simply be a corruption of judgment, a fear to speak out against fashion. It goes without saying that the critic who tells lies to himself will finish by telling them to others. His punishment will be that legends and personalities come to mean more to him than paintings.

4. COMMITMENT AND ISOLATION

As a result of my article about the critic's position, I received an impressive post. Two of my correspondents raised points which are so interesting that I would like to discuss them here. One asks me whether the critic should not commit himself firmly to those artists he finds congenial, in fact, whether he should not renounce the effort to look at everything with an equally sympathetic eye. The other asks me if the critic can truly communicate what he sees, if one man's reaction isn't as good as another's. The answer to these queries, as to all truly interesting questions, is at once "yes" and "no".

Perhaps I can explain myself more clearly if I take a current exhibition for my text—the large show of "Brazilian Art Today" which is now on at the Royal College of Art. It was immensely enterprising of the people concerned to mount this exhibition, but it does present the critic with certain special problems. Chief of these is the fact that (while we may know something about modern Brazilian architecture) modern Brazilian painting is almost unknown to us in England. There is, one might think, a great opportunity facing the critic, and a great challenge. Yet, as one looks round the walls, one begins to despair. The exhibition suits the large gallery it is shown in quite admirably. Anyone who goes to it will receive an impression of great vitality unleashed. But what happens when the visitor begins to look at the pictures in detail? The truth is that he finds them very difficult to see as individual works of art. It is the *coup d'oeil* which counts, to look at the pictures one by one is almost too demanding.

It is demanding because there is so little to guide the spectator. For the most part, these pictures are abstract. Many are in the cousinage of Abstract Expressionism. If one knew all about these artists—their development, their influence one upon the other—one might be ready to attempt an interpretation of these enigmatic works. Most of all, what one lacks is not specific knowledge of the modern Brazilian painters, but knowledge of the context. How are these pictures used? What are the aesthetic assumptions behind them? We may make an informed guess, on the basis of what we know about modern art in general. But we cannot be certain about our conclusions. Above all, we cannot hope to be very specific. The pictures stare us out of countenance. It is as if we had gone to see Siena before the art-historians got there.

As it happens—and still sticking to the theme of modern Brazilian art—London was treated to an entirely different approach to the whole problem in an exhibition which has just closed. This was the show devoted to the Brazilian sculptor Camargo at the Signals Gallery in Wigmore Street. This enterprising gallery exists to promote a particular cause: that of kinetic art. On this occasion it devoted a whole issue of the news bulletin which it runs to an explanation of Camargo's work. The bulletin spoon-feeds us. It gives us not only all the details we need about the artist's career, but helpful hints as to what he is about. A photograph of a cloud formation is set beside a photograph of a white relief which resembles it. There is an article on "Modern Physics in Brazil" to help to nudge us in the right direction. There is even a little poem by José Garcia Villa, which runs as follows: "*Hush*! (snow-verb)." After all this it would be difficult to refuse to form some kind of judgment of Camargo's work—perhaps without even seeing the sculptures themselves. In fact, conclusions are a little too insistently demanded of us, and we arrive at the conclusion before we have really absorbed the impact of the work of art.

And this brings me back to the point at which I started—my two correspondents and their questions. I will take the second question first—the matter of judging, and the communication of judgment—because it is a trifle the easier to deal with. On this occasion my correspondent seemed to hold the view that all communication was difficult, and that the communication of pleasure was impossible. The critic, he felt, had no right to assume that his judgment was of greater worth than anyone else's. All reactions to a given work of art were to be regarded as equally valid. This point of view has not been without its distinguished supporters. A first experience of the exhibition at the Royal College of Art would seem to bear him out.

With nothing to get hold of but the work of art itself, the critic is helpless to communicate his reactions, or even to define them. He is reduced to the level of pure sensibility. And this is very often the level of the ordinary gallery-goer—the man who has just wandered in to the National Gallery to see a few pictures. How, for example, will the "Baignade" by Seurat strike him, if he knows nothing about Poussin, and nothing about Seurat's later development into Pointillism?

Yet is the critic really as helpless as this, even among a host of unfamiliar Brazilians? As soon as we think of it, we realize that he cannot be. It is not only that he has a certain amount of general knowledge to fall back on—he also has something else: the habit of organizing what he sees so that it becomes knowledge. And knowledge, by hook or by crook, can always be communicated. The critic's expertise lies not in his sensibility, but in his way of using it—his way of disciplining it, if you like. He is able to differentiate. This is a power which exists in all of us, but it is one which needs to be trained. If you add to this organizing faculty a certain amount of brute fact, the critic is already beginning to draw away from the man-who-doesn't-know-about-pictures-but-knows-what-he-likes.

The question of communicating the results is more difficult—some would say that it remains impossible. Yet here, I think, we ought at least to consider the social function of art, the fact that all works of art are used, if not always in the way we expect. What the critic tries to get across is how—he tries to tell the spectator beside him what this particular work of art can do, specifically, for the man who looks at it. In fact, what enlargement it has to offer him. And this involves, as I have said, not only explanation, but judgment. Until the critic has formed his judgment, he cannot explain. The explanation proceeds directly from the process of judging, making distinctions.

And this, in turn, brings me to the question of sympathies. How far should the critic deliberately limit himself? Should he set up standards, and admire only those artists who conform to them? In a sense, this is just what he must do. A critic needs his points of reference—his absolutes. Yet one of these absolutes must certainly be the demand for flux, for growth, for change. The trained sensibility is, above all, trained to register how much we have been altered by experiencing the work of art before us. The greater the change, the greater the work of art is likely to be. This does not mean that the critic becomes simply the recorder of his own inconsistency. We respect those critics who are not afraid to modify their opinions (Bernard Berenson was one of them). But we expect these changes to be part of a continuous, steady process. The critic's real absolute is not a single fixed point, but the line along which he moves. In this case, to move also means to expand.

5. KEEPING UP WITH ART'S PROTEAN TRANSFORMATIONS

On Wednesday last, when I was taking part in the three-night series of conversations arranged by the B.B.C. Third Programme on the subject of the avant-garde, I found myself looking for an image which would describe the relationship between the spectator and modern art. The one which sprang to mind came from the ballad of "Tam Lin". The story has reached the point where the fairy knight is instructing his lover to bring him back into the mortal world again. She is to wait, he says, till the cavalcade approaches, and then she is to pull him off his horse:

They'll turn me in your arms, lady,
  Into an esk and adder;
But hold me fast, and fear me not,
  I am your bairn's father.

They'll turn me to a bear sae grim,
  And then a lion bold;
But hold me fast, and fear me not
  As ye shall love your child.

Again they'll turn me in your arms
  To a red het gaud of airn;
But hold me fast, and fear me not,
  I'll do to you nae harm.

And last they'll turn me in your arms
  Into the burning gleed;
Then throw me into well water,
  O throw me in wi speed.

And then I'll be your ain true-love,
  I'll turn a naked knight;
Then cover me wi your green mantle,
  And cover me out of sight.

The verses are so beautiful that of course I have been unable to resist quoting them at length. But I would not quote them at all unless I thought they made a valid point. It seems to me that, where the visual arts are concerned, this restless, dangerous process of metamorphosis has been one of the characteristics of our century. Some people may raise their eyebrows a little at the second adjective. How can a work of art be "dangerous"? The answer is—very easily, if it seems to threaten our psychological equilibrium, to interfere in some way with thoughts and feelings which we once thought were private to ourselves.

More than this: it is our most Protean artists who have caused the greatest uproar, who have seemed the most threatening. The stock example is Picasso. Critics have not been slow to remark the element of aggression which is present in so much of Picasso's work, and which seems to supply the motivation for his many changes of style. Picasso is not only a maker of images but a breaker of them. His *oeuvre* is a vast shambles, style after style lies there, weltering in its own gore. When Picasso chooses to paraphrase the work of another artist—Cranach, for example, or Delacroix, we are aware that what he is doing is at once an act of demolition and a sincere tribute.

But it is not only artists who are Protean, but the whole evolution of art itself. One style devours another. This process has been particularly marked in the years since the war. Abstract Expressionism was gobbled up by "Pop" Art, which is now itself in the process of being devoured by the new Optical painting. The spectator can, perhaps, disapprove of this rapid succession of styles, but he can hardly hope to bring it to a halt. The critic is in an even more difficult situation.

Critics tend to attach themselves to a particular style. It is a professional malady. But when styles prove to be ephemeral things, what is the critic to do? If he switches his allegiance suddenly and whole-heartedly, he may perhaps make nonsense of all his former arguments. He will seem like a hired advocate, defending the cause which pays him best. On the other hand, few spectacles are more pathetic than that of a critic whom time and fashion have passed by. The critic who has been closely associated with a particular style, who may indeed (such is the way of critics) have come to feel that he invented it, is left stranded, like some wretched castaway who has found his way to a rock in the middle of a tide-race. He may wave his arms and shout, but the roar of the waters drowns his voice.

At this point someone will want to point out that I am taking a very shallow view of criticism. So I am—it is the shallow view which critics seem to take of themselves. For what makes the process of transformation in modern art frightening rather than exhilarating is the lack of any firm faith in its purposes. To go back to the quotation with which I began—the lady in the ballad is prepared to embrace her knight whatever fearsome shape he takes, because she is convinced that in the end he will become merely his naked self. I would not like to promise, or even seem to promise, that painting will return to its old path, that out of all our twentieth-century experiments another Raphael will arise, confident and golden haired, to decorate another set of *stanze* in a new extension of the United Nations building in New York. But I would like to think, and to have others think with me, that the world will recover its shaken faith in the purposes of the arts. Certainly the fact that the artists' own faith is shaken does not make things any easier—it's like trying to worship in a church where the priests are all atheists, or so it may seem in our more despairing moments.

What I think we ought to consider is the nature of art itself in the twentieth century. On the whole, the great overall change has been the way in which the artist has abandoned the outer for the inner world—he has transferred his attention from nature to the psyche. And this, in itself, has led him to deal in images of change. For the first thing we learn about our own inner selves is the fact of changeability and instability. In this respect, twentieth-century artists have often been both courageous and honest. Our best painting is the record of change—in it all images are in a state of flux, one image is perpetually becoming another. We find this wherever we look—in the Cubists, the Surrealists, the rapid images of "Pop", the perpetually changing patterns of the optical painters. There is also the fact that we have all of us, whether we admit it or not, begun to grapple with an entirely new concept of time and of our own relationship to the idea of time, and the more successfully we do this, the easier it becomes for us to see the visual arts for what they are.

Till quite recently, the spectator assumed that he watched the development of the visual arts, and noted the changes which took place, from a fixed stand-point. We perceive this very clearly if we read the great critics of the past. We notice it in Vasari and we notice it in Ruskin. Each of these has a system of rules, and by applying these rules, he hoped to arrive at judgments and answers. The only trouble is that these two sets of absolutes—the sixteenth-century set and the nineteenth-century one—do not correspond. The old explanation for this was that a gradual process of refinement was taking place, with the gradual elimination of errors. Now we are both bolder and more cautious, we accept that everything exists in a state of flux, that the spectator is carried forward on the stream of time as helplessly as the artist, though perhaps at a different rate. And once we have learnt to accept this, the restless transformation which we see around us becomes not only easier to accept and enjoy, but far easier to evaluate.

6. HOW ABSTRACT ART CAN INFLUENCE THOUGHT AND VISION

After reading my article of three weeks ago on this page a correspondent writes to ask if I will expand some of the things I said in it. In particular, she asks me to give a more elaborate explanation of the reasons why I think that abstract art has taught us to think abstractly, and how it has helped us to see things in nature which were previously invisible to us. A tall order, some may think. Yet the subject is undoubtedly fascinating. What's more, it has a direct bearing on our own daily lives and on the way in which we experience not merely modern painting but the whole world around us.

The first thing to say is that pattern is something which happens in the head. When we see a pattern in nature, it is because the mind has selected certain objects, certain aspect of objects, and has set to work to impose an order upon them. This ordering faculty is a very important one. We protect ourselves with it, and make the world safe. We build a wall against chaos. The lack of it is one of the things which divides the mad from the sane.

Let me go a little further than this. Language, as most of us are willing to recognize, is a code which we have learnt to decipher. It is only an agreed convention that this sound shall stand for *that* object. As the traveller finds to his cost, the code is subject to almost endless variations. Sight, too, is a code, though one which does not vary so much. The impulses which fall upon the retina are interpreted by the brain. Once we learn the rules, we can begin to play games; we can, to some extent, make a rearrangement of the conventions. The ability to "see" in several different ways is one of the marks of visual sophistication. The deliberate exploitation of this ability is something we often find in modern art.

In particular, the progress of civilization has been marked by an increase in the generalizing faculties of mankind. Gradually, we have learnt to make a sum of particular instances, and to draw general conclusions from them. In the field of the visual arts, this leads us, very often, directly to abstraction. If we take a number of similar visual experiences, and look for what they have in common, we often discover that this common factor is not something which can be shown as a representation, but only as a pattern. The waves breaking on a beach, for example, and the blown sand in the desert, and the pattern of terraces descending a hill: all of these three things have elements in common, though the physical embodiment is in each case quite different. What links them together is a rhythm, or pattern. If we draw this pattern on a piece of paper, it will not be a picture of any one of the three, though it may suggest each of them in turn. In fact, thanks to the ordering faculty inherent in the mind, these three things have given birth to a fourth.

One of the best ways to think about pattern and abstraction and what they are is to think of those instances where the handiwork of man and the purely natural (which is to say the accidental) seem to meet and collaborate. As it happens, the Museum of Modern Art in New York has just published a book which supplies a number of apt examples. The book, by Bernard Rudofsky, is called *Architecture without Architects*. Dr Rudofsky has brought together a fascinating collection of photographs showing architecture which has been made spontaneously, and often in response to specific natural conditions. He shows us, for example, the underground villages of China, which are cut into the soft loess. He shows us Marrakesh from the air. He shows us the *Ciudad Encantada*, 120 miles east of Madrid, with its fantastic rock formations. Only the last of these shows no sign of human intervention. But this is not quite the point. It is the *way* in which we look at the photographs which is interesting. In each case, we see something which is made of simple elements—solid and void. These elements are repeated, though not quite regularly. The eye takes pleasure in finding in them an underlying order. This order is not necessarily symmetrical, but some principle of order or harmony lies within it. Yet, visibly it is not complete. It requires the effort of our own minds for its completion, and if the mind refuses the task then the pattern is no longer there—it ceases to exist.

There are, of course, various ways of defining the word "pattern". From what I've already said, it will be clear that I'm using it here in a fairly broad sense. Nevertheless, not so broad as to lose the underlying meaning of order, regularity, rhythm. Modern painting of a certain sort brings these characteristics forcibly to mind. By discarding the particular references which are required by representation, it leaves us to contemplate them in almost pure state. But it also does something else. Once we have absorbed the idea of pure pattern into our system of visual coding, once our eyes and minds have acquired the ability to handle abstract shapes and forms, we begin to "feed back" the new information to other and more familiar kinds of visual experience. When we do this, we alter, even if by ever so little, the quality of that experience.

That is, we begin by saying, when we see the ripples on the surface of a stream, that the pattern of lines is like the pattern of lines which we have just seen in a particular abstract painting. But it is unlikely that we will be able to keep the two moments in strict quarantine, with an impassable barrier between them. When this resembles that, then this is well on the road to becoming that. The simile becomes the metaphor. The stream is no longer *like* the painting; it *is* the painting.

Every change in style which we see in art, every alteration of vision, enlarges—if we are able to absorb it thoroughly—our capacity to deal with the chaos which surrounds us. Paintings supply a kind of mould; they shape the way we look at things. The Impressionists are a celebrated example of this. When their pictures were first shown the spectators had great difficulty in deciphering them. Claude, with his golden tones, had provided them from a completely different visual code for the interpretation of landscape. The adjustment made, we wonder at the initial difficulty. We have forgotten the time when eyes could not speak the language of pure colour, which had to be blended on the retina. Abstract paintings are in the midst of accomplishing a similar revolution. They are teaching our eyes a different dialect. Nature has already begun to talk it.

*

N.B. *The reader had better be warned that this, even more than most of the pieces here reprinted, tries to deal with a large topic in a small space. The view of abstract art which I put forward here would, I suspect, be considered very debatable by the majority of academic aestheticians.*

7. SURREALISM NOW AND TO COME

Having written about abstract art in my last article, it seems a logical step to turn to surrealism. How rash! For, where movements in modern painting are concerned, logic has a thin time of it. Having said this, I realize that it sounds a little unfortunate. I don't mean, of course, that I think modern painting is an inexplicable and barbarous phenomenon. What I do mean is that I dread having to find a new set of terms. The terms in which abstraction can be discussed are not, somehow, very useful when one begins to talk about surrealism. And this discontinuity presents the critic with a real difficulty, for, naturally enough, he wants to present these two phenomena—abstraction and surrealism—as part of the same order.

But, instead of rushing off towards some possibly unattainable synthesis, let me turn to one of the prime documents of surrealism (choosing, now, to treat the term in a way which is narrowly historical). I am thinking of André Breton's *First Surrealist Manifesto*. In it Breton says this: "We still live beneath the sway of logic—here, indeed, is what I want to get away from. But logical procedures, in our own time, can only be applied to the solution of problems of secondary interest. The absolute rationalism which is still in fashion permits us to consider only those facts which are narrowly relevant to our experience. On the other hand, logical ends escape us. There is no point in adding that experience itself has had limits assigned to it. It paces a cage which it is more and more difficult to bring it out of. It, too, founds itself upon immediate utility and is guarded by common sense. Upon the pretext of civilization and of progress, we have come to banish from our minds everything which might be accused, justly or unjustly, of being superstitious or chimerical; we have come to proscribe all methods of searching for the truth which do not conform to accepted custom." Immediately after this outcry, Breton goes on to pay tribute to Freud.

And here, perhaps, is the beginning of the difficulty. Abstract art encourages us to discuss things in terms of absolutes. Surrealism, on the other hand, immediately sends us chasing off down historical perspectives. One notes, for example, that

Breton was writing in 1929. One even notes that the style he uses—which I have rendered very imperfectly—catches an echo of romantic writers such as Chateaubriand.

Even when we turn to those actual works of painting which can be called surrealist, we find outselves in much the same difficulty. Surrealist art covers a very wide spectrum—it can be full of immediately recognizable imagery, or it can retreat towards the abstract. Both Dali and Magritte present us with art which forms a kind of rebus. The separate images are not in themselves transformed; but the meaning which they bear is transformed because of the way in which the artist puts them together on the canvas. We do not absorb these images as a whole; we read them, rather as we read the words and phrases which go to make up a complete sentence. Nor does the physical embodiment of these images on the canvas do much to modify their meaning. Dali's glossiness, Magritte's use of *trompe l'oeil*—these (paradoxically) argue that the artist has a certain distrust of the whole process of painting. If he could bring the actual objects before us, instead of just representing them, then he would.

The tension to be found in their painting springs from the juxtaposition of forms, and not from the forms themselves. The process has been carried much further in our own day. Pop art is so clearly the child of surrealism that one scarcely needs to argue the point. But surrealism has contrived to have other children as well.

Instead of turning our attention to Magritte and Dali, let us look at such painters as Ernst and Matta. Ernst is an artist who has often made experiments with the actual handling of materials. His *frottages*—rubbings made from various textures and small objects—have enabled him to achieve some extraordinarily suggestive effects. Matta, a less talented and less various painter, is even more interesting if we look at his work from the historical point of view. Matta's forms are often rendered in a calligraphic way which makes them resemble those of Arshile Gorky, whom he in fact influenced. From Gorky, in turn, we can trace the direct descent of Abstract Expressionism. Abstract Expressionism is, indeed, only the ruthless application of surrealist tenets. The unconscious layers of the mind are encouraged to embody themselves, not in images which are afterwards mechanically transferred to canvas, but *on* the canvas. The liberation thus achieved is—supposedly—truer to itself.

The position therefore is that a great deal of post-1945 painting, much of it superficially very unalike, can quite justifiably be regarded as surrealism of the second and even of the third generation. But this does not quite explain my title. Why should I want to talk of the *future* of surrealism, as well as of its past and its present?

It is here, perhaps, that the demon of explanation enters with horns and tail fully revealed. One can talk, as I have done in my previous article, about looking at abstract art as a kind of technique which the spectator can deliberately set himself to acquire. Where surrealist painting and its main derivatives are concerned, one is faced with a less comfortable alternative. Either one is driven back on a too-simple explanation of Freudian doctrine (a doctrine which the original surrealists themselves tended to misinterpret). Or else one is left urging people to "commit themselves"—not, somehow, a very dignified position for an art critic.

Yet committed we all are, willy-nilly. The mode of thinking and feeling which surrealism represents is very evidently the mode which is characteristic of our century. The introverted involvement with the self somehow becomes mixed up with social commitments—Freud marries Marx in a shotgun wedding. Nineteen twenty-nine is, after all, a date significant for more than M. Breton's manifesto, and the epoch it began was one in which all men, and especially the artists, were to become much more acutely aware of politics than they had been in the previous decade.

But now I am talking in historical terms again. Basically, perhaps, one ought to define things thus—abstract art represents the great groundswell, the direction in which modes of perception are moving. Surrealist painting (some of which is also abstract) gives us art as it meshes with the historical event.

8. NEW NOTIONS—FROM ASSEMBLAGE TO ENVIRONMENT

"Does he paint?" says Browning, "he fain would write a poem. Does he write? he fain would paint a picture." For me these words have taken on a meaning somewhat different from the one which Browning meant to give them. Any critic of modern art must necessarily be astonished, as he looks about him, by the sheer heterogeneity of the objects he is called upon to examine. It is not only that paintings often contain captions which must be read, that a piece of sculpture can turn out to be, in fact, a poem-writing machine—to be judged, presumably, by what it produces as well as by what it looks like. It is, quite simply, that artists are frantic to escape from conventional formats, and conventional materials, that they use anything and everything that comes to hand.

The explanation that sculptures made from crushed automobiles, and a painting/object whose main ingredient is a large and baleful stuffed goat, are things created merely from a puerile desire to shock, will hardly hold water—because no one is shocked, though they may of course dislike the objects themselves. Things of precisely this sort are on show at the Tate in the Gulbenkian Exhibition, and surprisingly little stir has been caused by them. There were far fiercer protests about Mr. Reg Butler's "Unknown Political Prisoner" of some years ago.

The reason is not merely the apathy of a public which has been outraged too often. It is that unconsciously, and without really examining the change, we have begun to accept entirely new notions about art—notions which perhaps take us back to the very beginnings of the artistic impulse. Since the Middle Ages has been in the process of secularizing itself. By the eighteenth century works of art had adapted themselves very successfully to a new role. They became adornments of everyday living, objects of private pleasure, instead of being (as they so usually were in earlier times) religious totems and symbols. If we examine the art of our own time we see, I think, that the process has gone into reverse. It is customary to complain about the decline of private patronage. But what use would a private patron have for so many of the things produced by our leading *avant-garde* artists? It is not that they are necessarily worthless, merely that they are unwieldy. The most passionate admirer of Mr. Robert Rauschenberg's stuffed goat would probably concede that it might prove a thoroughly awkward object to live with. Certainly, it lies at the farthest possible extreme from the charming trifles produced by a sculptor like Clodion. But Rauschenberg in a museum occupies an entirely different category.

It has always amused me to watch the behaviour of visitors to such exhibitions as the one now on at the Tate. The hushed voices, the quiet footsteps, the long contemplative glances cast at this object or that, so frequently remind me of worshippers in a church. Does it seem outrageous to assert that, in a thoroughly secular society, what much *avant-garde* art seems to want to do is to restore the notion of the holy, of the sacred, of the numinous: to turn our museums into cathedrals?

The recent sculpture of Paolozzi, for example, is something which cries out to be enshrined. Those looming, awkward shapes work, if they work at all, not as a series of formal relationships, rationally conceived, but as the bodying forth of something irrational. They are images to gods whose names the sculptor does not as yet know. Other artists try to take the process a step farther—to banish from our minds all notion of the aesthetic. What they want to create is something as unseizable as a moment out of context. Mr. Rauschenberg's stuffed goat is really to be regarded as being evocative, like the *madeleine* in Proust. The artist hopes that the object, presented as he presents it, will arouse a certain nexus of emotion in the spectator, will impinge upon him in a particular way. Therefore an "assemblage" of this sort is something which one visits with due ceremony. One goes deliberately to see it, hoping for some kind of transformation in oneself. Needless to say, this transformation does not usually occur. But it is not always and altogether wrong for an artist to gamble for high stakes.

That the gamble can occasionally come off is perhaps proved by another exhibition—one which most people acknowledge to be an enormous success. Mr. Richard Buckle's celebration of Shakespeare at Stratford-on-Avon is not really an exhibition in the conventional sense at all but what is sometimes called an "environment". It is an assemblage really very much of the Rauschenberg variety, but so large that one does not merely visit it, one is swallowed up by it; it surrounds the visitor on all sides and attempts to control all his sensations as he wanders through it. Paint, canvas, lights, music, recorded voices, and scent are all brought into play. Its relationship to the spectator is, in fact, very much that of the cuckoo pint to the fly. One is in some danger not only of being embraced but also of being eaten.

Attempts have been made to create this kind of total experience before. The "happenings" which were staged by members of the New York *avant-garde* (and rather dismally repeated last year at Edinburgh) were, it must be admitted, of a recognizably similar intent. And the Institute of Contemporary Art in London has occasionally staged exhibitions where the show *was* the painting, which the visitor was invited to enter and explore at his leisure. Mr. Buckle acknowledges these influences even in some details of the style he has adopted—this, I suppose, is why he invited a number of "Pop" artists to take part, and also why they accepted.

But, of course, there is a reason for the success of the "environment" at Stratford, besides the imaginative brilliance which has led Mr. Buckle to seize on advanced ideas and use them to reach a great public. Shakespeare himself lingers—as he should—in every corner. "Imaginary gardens with real toads in them", wrote Marianne Moore, when describing what the modern poet should try to achieve. In an odd way the phrase explains very aptly what both Rauschenberg and Buckle are up to.

9. TOWARDS ARTISTS FOR ARTISTS' SAKES

In last month's issue of *Studio International* there is a long letter from Dr. T. Elder Dickson, the vice-principal of the Edinburgh College of Art. Dr. Elder Dickson is a worried man. What worries him is this: "the paradoxical situation of the 'fine arts' being judiciously freed from academic discipline and 'industrial art' being cautiously geared to the techniques and procedures of science". He finds that "complete freedom in the domain of the 'fine arts' and strict scientific discipline in the 'industrial arts' are each at variance with the basic principles of art and art education by which art colleges must stand".

The question of art education is important enough, but it seems to me that the problem strikes a good deal deeper than this. When we start to think about the condition of painting and sculpture today, we immediately run into a whole series of paradoxes, the first of which is the whole question of categories. How can we say that this object here is a painting, and that a sculpture? What we now see in front of us is a vast and unclassifiable mass of art-objects, capriciously labelled. The new works by Takis, now on show at the Indica gallery—are these, with their flashing lights and carefully orchestrated electronic noises, painting, sculpture, or simply machines? Machines for what? For producing aesthetic sensations, presumably. It is not that artists have abandoned technique, nor even that they have cut themselves off from science—Dr. Elder Dickson makes far too rigid a distinction here. Many artists long to lay their hands on the new inventions of the scientists; they are eager to make the most both of new materials and of newly discovered principles of physics.

The trouble is that it is impossible to predict in advance just what techniques our artists are going to need. Teach all the students at a given art-school electro-magnetism, and five years hence, when they have embarked on their careers, the knowledge will be perfectly useless to them. One solution, according to many art-educators—Richard Hamilton at the Newcastle College of Art, for instance—is to teach the students to think; to think rather than feel. What this leaves out of account is the fact that all artists tend to think in a very particular way, not academically, but physically; with the body as well as the mind.

The old academic methods of teaching art worked because there was a consensus about the nature of art itself, and even the most rebellious students never altogether abandoned this common area of agreement. But now art no longer has this monolithic quality. Its development becomes more and more sporadic; its growth is like that of a fire in gorse, breaking out now in one area and now in another, and leaving the ground desolate behind it. The knowledge that the modern artist needs so often turns out to be disconnected and empirical; a little bit about the properties of a particular kind of plastic; a little bit more about direct welding techniques when using steel. Technical knowledge cannot supply a framework for the growth of intellect, as it did under the old academic system.

Naturally, this makes life very difficult for the art-educators. But it is symptomatic of something else. In my last article I talked about the way in which artists seemed to have abandoned the bourgeoisie, to have become performers and gypsies instead. In fact, all the new techniques that modern artists use can be regarded (unkindly, to be sure) as so many actors' tricks. When the artist becomes, not a maker but a performer, there is a natural shift of emphasis—from the object to the man who created it. The object ceases to have a truly separate existence, just as an actor's performance cannot be truly separated from himself, from his physical being.

Thus we also find a new and very characteristic kind of audience-reaction—what interests us is the fact of being, the fact that someone "is an artist", and not the thing made. But this is a thing that discomfits the modern and scientific state. Nations become more and more geared to the technological idea, and it is therefore not surprising that technology should supply a kind of model for other kinds of national activity, including the patronage which is officially given to art.

From the bureaucratic (and from the democratic) point of view it is much easier to give support to organizations rather than to people, to create museums, and to fill them with objects. But this tends to lead to certain oddities. For, as the artist becomes his own work of art, so he more and more expects support for what he is, rather than for what he does. And this introduces a wholly new and difficult principle.

Let us think about the matter for a moment. A work of art is "something produced by someone who believes that he is making one". This is, by now, a fairly familiar definition. Indeed, it's the only one that seems to be sufficiently elastic. And what about the artist?—The artist is a man "who believes himself to be so". Oh dear, how very difficult! "And what about standards?" cry the jealous, the envious, and those not in line for a government hand-out this year or next. But I think I have already said enough to show that standards are now in the eye of the beholder.

I seem to be moving inexorably towards a single conclusion—and it is, for most of us, a very unpalatable one. The conclusion is this: that a particular class of people exists, who must be supported not for what they do but for what they are. They embody, and often in the most unlikely corporeal forms, some principle of refinement or civilization without which the rest of us are benighted.

In a religious society it would be perfectly possible to imagine a body of people of just this kind, existing peacefully among the rest, and uncomplaining supported by them. One thinks of Zen monks in Japan. But it is scarcely possible to imagine such an arrangement at work in a thoroughly materialist Western democracy, such as our own.

But there is a sufficiently strong unconscious tendency towards it to make the whole logical, technological system of education and state patronage heave and shudder. Will there ever be a shock strong enough to lay these in ruins?

10. AVANT-GARDE, OR ACADEMIC?

One of the saddest works of art I have ever seen is a drawing by Benjamin Robert Haydon. In Haydon's usual, rather scratchy style of pen-and-ink draughtsmanship it shows us the artist (very small) standing at his easel, with (very large) two figures embracing—evidently his models. An inscription, in Haydon's hand, reads: "The immortal B. R. H., painting his 'Solomon'." Haydon, of course, is immortal, but it is a very curious sort of immortality. He is the best documented case of the failed genius—of the man who apparently feels genius stirring within him, who toils and suffers like a genius, and yet who never establishes himself in the pantheon towards which he aspires. Haydon's autobiographical writings are both humbling and frightening—I often think that every painter, and every poet too, should be forced to read them.

When Haydon's painting, as opposed to his writing, gets itself discussed nowadays, it is usually in connection with the vexed topic of the Grand Manner. The Grand Manner is that part of English eighteenth and early nineteenth century painting which has lost its glamour. It never was, as Haydon's outcries remind us, particularly profitable in its own day. Romney's sketchbooks, for example, are full of drawings for ambitious projects which he was never allowed to complete. What his patrons wanted was portraits, and they got what they wanted. People have been found to deplore the way in which Romney was kept to the commercial grindstone. A study of his sketchbooks, however, does not suggest that posterity has much to regret. Romney's visions are interesting, when we see them still in the process of coming to birth. The swirling ink lines on the paper build up forms which are like cloud-caps. We read into them what we wish to see. On the monumental scale for which they were conceived, it is probable that we would find these ideas jejune and boring. One of the few completed Romneys of this kind, "Serena in the Boat of Apathy", which turned up at Christie's some time ago, did not tempt one to wish for more.

Yet, in its day, the Grand Manner seemed very important—even if it sometimes found it difficult to pay its way. The highest authorities gave it their blessing, as the only kind of art that really mattered. The whole tendency of Reynolds's *Discourses* is towards exalting it, even though, as a painter, Reynolds did not always practise what he preached. It was Haydon's misfortune that he believed passionately in what the theorists told him. But there is no doubt that he was acting on the best advice. It was not the conservatives of the period who advocated "high art". They were quite contented to have their own portraits painted by Gainsborough, and their horses painted by Stubbs. It was what would now be thought of as the *avant-garde*, people who took a serious interest in painting. Fuseli, for example, had a very *avant-garde* group of patrons indeed.

I bring up this particular piece of art-history because it seems to me very relevant to what is happening now in the arts. The Modern Movement has achieved just about the degree of success which was granted to the Grand Manner in its palmiest days. Its milder and more acceptable exponents enjoy the rather galling eminence which came to Benjamin West—the official recognition, the big commissions when something "serious" is needed, the failure really to excite the intellectuals. The new Coventry Cathedral is a monument to this sort of modernism. On the other hand, some of the bolder spirits enjoy a covenanted notoriety. Bacon, perhaps, might be thought of as having taken the place of Fuseli. In general, Modern Art completely dominates the minds of the critics and the theorists. Yet the resistance of the public has not been wholly conquered. There is often a dismaying feeling of rootlessness about the whole thing—instead of critical theory hurrying to catch up with the new inventions of the artists, we have once more the spectacle of artists eagerly proclaiming their own originality—always with one ear cocked for what the latest authority is going to say. The trouble is that there is now no opposing conservative tradition. An annual visit to the Royal Academy shows no sign that the corpse is going to stir.

Or, perhaps, "conservative" is the wrong word—born of the preconceptions which Modernism itself has done its best to implant. "Vernacular" would be better. There is a sense in which Modern Art is an invented, artificial language which is native to nobody—a sort of Esperanto which must be deliberately learnt through hard study. The same thing applied to the Grand Manner itself. This, too, struggled under the disadvantage of being no man's native tongue.

Anything artificial tends to be built up from clichés and

formulae—a process not necessarily wrong in itself. Some great artists have notoriously used it in their painting. Poussin is one of them. But do we always realize that the theory of modern art clings to two very stultifying sets of conventions? That, more and more, we have a formula for originality and a formula for genius? It is one of the far-reaching effects of the Modern Movement to have set up originality as an end in itself. From this springs the whole idea of the *avant-garde*. But, of course, we have often been unable to cope with the idea of total originality, even on the rare occasions on which we have found it. Instead we have tested things against a set of rules. *Avant-garde* has become a category, and what is a little worse, a category which we use as an excuse. No need to decide if a particular work is good or bad, providing that we can classify it as *avant-garde*. Occasionally, of course, we change the rules. Abstract Expressionist rules are replaced by "Pop" Art ones. But anyone who doubts that an *avant-garde* painting can also be thoroughly academic should examine the work of the English imitators of Pollock.

More stultifying is the formula which we use for genius. This is old and almost respectable. Haydon himself did his best to conform to it—and in fact it is a legacy from the earliest years of the *Sturm und Drang*. It was almost perfectly expressed, not by a painter but by a poet, James Kirkup, quoted in *New Society* last week: "A poet is an extraordinary being, a person apart. . . . Poets should be willing to be hounded to death for being different." Substitute the word "painter" and Haydon would no doubt have agreed heartily. But is it either safe or sensible to define talent in this way (I say "talent" because "genius" begs the question)? Is a painter to be accepted as a genius because he is passionately convinced that he is one? It often seems that we give more weight to the painter's convictions about himself, and to the details of his personal life and behaviour, than we do to the work he produces.

11. REYNOLDS, RUBENS, AND THE DOCTRINE OF TODAY

We are often apt to believe that the art-criticism of any other age but our own is hopelessly beside the point. I was, therefore, very interested to re-read, the other day, the verdict upon Rubens which Sir Joshua Reynolds penned in his *Journey to Flanders and Holland.* Rubens has recently been the subject of a great deal of research. New discoveries are constantly being announced; some of them are very beautiful. But I wonder how much has happened to change Sir Joshua's verdict?

It is sometimes forgotten, I think, how eloquent a writer Reynolds could be. He speaks, for instance, of "the striking brilliance of [Rubens's] colours, and their lively opposition to each other, the flowing liberty and freedom of his outline, the animated pencil, with which every subject is touched" and says that these "all contribute to awaken and keep alive the attention of the spectator; awaken in him, in some measure, correspondent sensations, and make him feel a degree of the enthusiasm with which the painter was carried away. To this we may add the complete uniformity in all parts of the work, so that the whole seems to be conducted, and grow out of one mind; everything is of a piece and fits its place." Not only does this provide a very interesting anticipation of what later critics would find to say on the subject of empathy; it also, I think, remains the best verdict on the late phase of Rubens's work.

In the National Gallery, there is the copy which Rubens made, around 1630, of one of the Mantegna cartoons which is now at Hampton Court. Rubens has adapted the original in precisely the ways that Reynolds's description would lead us to expect. Mantegna's stately tread has been replaced by something much more fiery, and Rubens's feeling for the subject expresses itself in a freedom of touch which is dazzling. Above all, Rubens has been concerned to impose a new unity on the composition. Where Mantegna is static, he is sinuous; and we gradually become aware, thinking first of one picture, then of the other, of the devices which Rubens has used to animate every corner of his canvas, and to give it that "overall" quality which Reynolds stresses.

Perhaps it is worthwhile to consider the unfavourable part of Sir Joshua's remarks, if only because he picks so unerringly upon the right thing to praise. Reynolds dislikes many of the types which Rubens used in his pictures; he finds his young women unbeautiful—"they are healthy comely women", he says, "but seldom, if ever, possess any degree of excellence". How curious, one thinks, that a critic should have been so sensitive to the essential message of Rubens, and yet should have been unable to recognize this part of it! The abounding vitality of Rubens comes out above all in his depictions of women—these ripe earth-goddesses are meant as reminders of the bountifulness of nature.

And yet, there is something one ought to think about. Reynolds is making his criticism from the point of view of the Ideal. It is the Ideal which speaks when he writes: "In [Rubens's] representation of the highest characters in the Christian or the fabulous world, instead of something above humanity, which might fill the idea which is conceived of such beings, the spectator finds little more than mere mortals, such as he meets with every day." We, in the twentieth century, are apt to dismiss all this with impatience because the "highest characters in the Christian or the fabulous world" in fact mean very little to us—our education does not tend that way.

But the rather mindless fashion in which we enjoy Rubens's sonorous colour and swinging rhythms would probably have upset the artist himself. We know that he took endless pains with his mythological machinery. The negotiations with the French Court over the allegories to be found in the Marie de Medicis cycle lasted for months. If, as Reynolds alleges, the personages in the pictures do not properly embody the qualities which the artist set out to convey, then there *has* been a failure somewhere.

The one occasion that we know about when Rubens came near to making a considered statement of his artistic aims was in a letter to the Dutch scholar Franciscus Junius, who was then acting as the Earl of Arundel's librarian. The letter is dated August 1, 1637, and it contains one very significant statement. "That which is perceived through the senses", Rubens writes, "produces a greater and more durable impression, demands more profound examination, and provides richer material for study than that which we see only in our imaginations and as if dreaming, or else obscured by words which we try three times to seize (as Orpheus tried to seize Eurydice) and which slip away from us and deceive our hopes." Here is a forthright attack on the Ideal as Reynolds understood it. Rubens does not aspire towards some imagined standard, in spite of his lip service to the Ancients. He worshipped the classical world—he had a large collection of antiquities, but even these he had to make part of himself through the free exercise of the senses.

The doctrine which Rubens preaches is basically the doctrine of sensation, and if he seems a peculiarly sympathetic artist today, it is because this doctrine lies at the roots of modern art. Trust in the senses, in the body's rapture, is precisely the thing which all our prophets—such as D. H. Lawrence—have been busy drumming into us.

Yet Reynolds is not to be dodged so easily. Even he is not immune to the impact which Rubens has on the senses: "The effect of his pictures may be not improperly compared to that of clusters of flowers"—as fine a phrase as any which has been applied to a great artist. But he also sees something else, which we are apt to forget: "Rubens was, perhaps, the greatest master of the mechanical part of the art, and the best workman with his tools, that ever exercised a pencil."

Whenever people condemn virtuosity, I think of Rubens. In picture after picture he supplies the proof that virtuosity transcends itself when it is linked to appetite. Rubens wanted to devour the world, to digest it, to make it his own, and he had the equipment to do so. Even a talent for allegory was part of it.

12. MODERN ARTISTS' USE OF ALLEGORY

Modern artists persistently use allegory, modern criticism persistently dodges the issue which allegory presents—or this, at least, is how the current situation looks to me. Half the contortions of current writing about art are undertaken to avoid using the fatal word. Why do painters feel the need for allegory? And why do critics feel uncomfortable when confronted with it?

It is easier to take the second question first. The reason here is, I think, partly an historical one. Till very recently the whole tradition of modern art (and tradition counts far more to critics than to painters) was hostile to the use of "one for one" symbolism. If the painter wanted to use symbolism, then exact equivalents were frowned upon. What was in favour was symbolism in the Mallarméan sense, where the spectator was confronted with a whole nexus of meanings. But when we visit current exhibitions we find that this sort of symbolism has rather fallen out of favour. We often find symbols used in a way that deliberately limits their meaning, and indeed we find pictures which are collections of symbols, designed to be "read", and read in one way only. This in effect means a return to a very ancient tradition in western art.

The correct deployment of allegory was one of the prime skills required of an artist in the Middle Ages, in the Renaissance, and in the Baroque period. His skill in this department was one of the things which his contemporaries most admired about Rubens, and was certainly the foundation of Rubens's worldly success. Antoine Watteau, for all his admiration of Rubens, marks a significant break from this long established tradition. Watteau was symbolical almost in the Mallarméan way (which is why the late nineteenth century symbolists admired him so much). He aimed to convey a mood, but not a precise meaning. We do not read his pictures, we project ourselves into them. And after the revolution effected by Watteau, the tradition of allegory went gradually out of favour. Tiepolo, for all his success, was an anachronism; with Greuze allegory became sickly, with David it became forced. The final reaction against the whole business came with the Impressionists, and after them the Post-Impressionists.

The critics who fought the original battle on behalf of modern art connected the whole idea of allegory with everything that they most despised—it belonged to the world of Bougereau. And allegory, condemned as "literary" by people who were interested in painting, began to fall out of favour with the literary critics too. In English literature, indeed, the allegorical method is still very much an outcast. Hence the deep disfavour which we find bestowed upon Spenser's *Faerie Queene* (*Piers Plowman*, that other allegorical masterpiece, for some reason remains exempt).

It is natural, therefore, that art critics should be reluctant to face the issue. Oddly enough art criticism, for all the scorn which it pours on literary attitudes, always does find it difficult to deal with those problems when the shibboleths of painting differ from those which are currently to be found in literature. The reason is that art-critical method is still very much the client of literary criticism. We adapt to our own use techniques which were first developed in an entirely different field, and these borrowed forms, to some extent at least, govern the things which we are able to say about painting.

But what force is it that drives painting towards allegory again? Before trying to answer this question we must attempt to define the way in which pictorial allegory operates. When I talk about "allegory" I do not mean that painters have gone back to depicting Temperance, and Abundance, for Fortune, and all those other ample ladies whom we meet with in the paintings of Rubens and his contemporaries. What I mean is that painters (and sculptors) too show us objects, not for their own sake, but for a fairly limited meaning which we are meant to read into them. Sometimes we are confronted with a sequence of objects, which add up to a more complex meaning—just as we may find all those ample ladies I have just mentioned grouped together in a single picture, but each bedecked with her own particular set of attributes.

Allegory first began to raise its head again with the Surrealists, whose ambition it of course was to explode all rational meanings. But reason did not prove easy to uproot, nor did cohesion and logic. Surrealist pictures often retain a sufficiency of these qualities to make us classify them as allegories. One undoubtedly allegorical picture, with strong traces of Surrealist influence, is of course Picasso's "Guernica," and it is to "Guernica" that we must turn when we look for an ancestor to the allegorical pictures of the 'sixties.

"Guernica" fathered "Pop" art, if only because it is designed as a public statement, and "Pop" painting (especially in England) represents a revolt against the hermeticism of modern art. Painters, on becoming fascinated with popular culture, with comic strips, and motor-cycles and pin-tables, could not help using this material allegorically. The reason was twofold—first that their interest in it was not so much for its own sake, but for what it stood for in their minds. Secondly, that popular material of this kind is, in any case, deeply steeped in allegorical method. For allegory, when so rudely chased from the Eden of the fine arts, had set up shop elsewhere, in advertising and in graphic design.

Allegory is often condemned as forced and artificial. The cry is that if we don't see things for themselves, then they lose their identity. The answer seems to be that if they aren't thinned out or flattened for us in this way, then we sometimes find it very difficult to know how to take them. Naive painting is heavily allegorical just because of this, and so, when we look at it, is nearly all popular art of whatever period. It is only the African and the South Sea islander who can cope with symbolism undiluted in all its dangerous and uncontrollable power. And it requires great sophistication to see objects without attaching symbolical meanings to them.

Current painting represents a recognition that totality of experience is something which it is very hard for either artist or audience to achieve. It is trying to find a *modus vivendi* with the modern world, and the facts of history. Some recent exhibitions have provided very striking and on the whole very successful examples of the new allegorical method and its advantages. There is a recognition that allegory is one of the ways in which we instinctively try to cope with modern society and its complexities.

13. STILLNESS AND MOTION

David Hockney once painted a picture called, quite simply, "Picture Emphasizing Stillness". It showed two men being attacked by a wild beast—between the assailant and the potential victims, however, was a line of type, which read: "They are quite safe—this is a still." It was a good point, and wittily made. It returned to my mind at the exhibition of seventeenth- and eighteenth-century Italian painting which inaugurates the London branch of the Galerie Heim. Two of the paintings—one by Rosa and the other by Luca Giordano—show a rather uncommon mythological subject, "Perseus and Phineas". The moment chosen is the one when Perseus is turning his assailant to stone, with the help of the Gorgon's head.

The Giordano is an especially splendid baroque composition—a great crowd eddies around the central figure of the hero. The artist imagines them at the moment when they are both attacking and retreating—two impulses hold them fast with equal force. Through and over and under this there runs the lightning flicker of the artist's brushwork, for here is Giordano at his most spontaneous and painterly. Seldom can something still have been so much filled with apparent motion.

What my observations bring me to is this—the idea that solid and void, or the successful balance of elements on a flat surface, are not really the essential things about painting. What impresses us most in pictorial art is simply the dynamism which the artist has managed to give to the surface he is painting on. We often talk of an abstract painter "animating" the space available—it is one of the critical clichés of our time. What we are really saying is that he has given apparent motion to what was formerly blank and void. We reach for exactly the same idea when we talk of "pictorial rhythms", and trace the lines of force from one element in a picture to another.

Motion, or at least, the concept of motion, also enters into the discussion when we talk about the work of painters who are indeed very still, such as Vermeer and Piero della Francesca. What makes us wonder is the fact that these forms, apparently immutable, yet contain within themselves a suggestion of dynamic force. Were it not there, the picture would seem flat and dead.

Rhythm, and the consciousness of rhythm, are of course the things which enable us to bring apparently disparate kinds of art together in our minds. It is possible to link the Luca Giordano I have just been talking about to the thrown ink paintings of the Japanese Zen masters, and these, in turn, can be compared with the paintings in the caves at Lascaux. Everywhere we look, we find that art has at least one constant function—it represents the triumph of motion over stasis.

There is a reason why this is important to modern art. On the whole, the modern artist is very much committed to the introverted view of things. He has abandoned the world of representation in order to try and explore the mysterious inner landscape of the psyche, and some of the reports he has sent back have been pretty curious. We often wonder what standards we can apply; how we can discover whether a given picture is valid or not, now that all objective standards have been swept away. Many artists have denied that their work can be criticized or analysed at all. Yet it seems to me that the principle of rhythm of dynamism is one of the few sure aids we have. When, for example, we begin to try and separate the Abstract Expressionist sheep from the far more numerous Abstract Expressionist goats, we find that we automatically fall back upon this one criterion—that a given painting seems to have a living rhythm, a pulse, almost a melodic line, while this other, outwardly similar work is inherently static.

The quasi-scientific, quasi-poetic world of Op art represents a recent effort to put rhythm on a rational basis—to discover what the "right" pictorial dynamic is, to systematize it, and then to raise it to its highest power. And, by working in this way, the Op painters are only following in the footsteps of the Italian Futurists of the period before the First World War, who made pictorial dynamism into a sacred principle, and were willing to sacrifice almost everything else to it.

There is, however, a further point to be made. I have suggested that rhythm is a kind of governing principle in all art. So far as modern art is concerned, I should like to take matters a little further, and suggest that a great deal of modern painting is, in fact, committed to the idea of giving rhythmic form to sensations, and even to emotions. We must remember, I think, that emotion, in the abstract and in isolation—an emotion such as "happiness" or "sadness"—was really an invention of the Romantic Era. This was what the cult of sensibility was all about. And that cult was a first step on the road to the much greater introversion of today. One qualification must be made—to discover something is not always to know how to handle it. The Romantics often discovered this to their cost. When we consider some of the great Romantic painters, and the great Romantic writers and musicians also, we become a bit impatient with the unseemly chaos which seems to have existed in their souls.

A good deal of modern art is, I think, concerned with the need to set man's house in order, but the concern expresses itself in a new way. Essentially, what the artist does is to provide a physical armature, an object in the world of objects, around which something quite impalpable can form. The rhythm is there in the object, but it enlarges itself and becomes more potent not only in the spectator's mind but in his whole nervous system, his entire sensibility.

This makes the abstract sculpture or the abstract painting seem a little like the totems which savages use—lightning conductors for spiritual electricity, containers where psychic force can be stored, where raw emotional energy can have the poison bleached out of it. And I think that this is a reasonable comparison—with one proviso. The kind of differentiation which the modern artist asks us to make requires a great deal of the spectator. The cry that "modern art is easy", or even that "art is easy", has always alarmed me. However powerful the rhythm on the canvas, the spectator needs practice if he is to receive it, control it, and benefit from it. The grammar of sight is a subject which still remains to be treated and discussed, and uncommonly difficult it is likely to prove. We only have to look at the new office-blocks and the "improving" beds of municipal begonias in order to realize this.

14. STYLE AND THE ARTIST'S DUTY

The Institute of Contemporary Arts is showing an exhibition of work done by students in the Fine Art Department of the City of Coventry College of Art. The exhibition is selected to show the teaching policy of the school. The preface to the catalogue contains the following statement: "Erecting arbitrary hierarchies of value is one of the more obvious pitfalls to try to avoid. In general we have attempted, pragmatically and empirically, to create an environment wherein the student can be, and is, creative, an environment free from over-bearing and doctrinaire attitudes. In short, an open situation." It adds: "What matters here is the student's own experience, there is no question of the staff setting formal exercises or providing facile answers." Obviously, academies of art have ceased to be academic.

The problem of art education is, however, an immensely complex and difficult one, as a discussion arranged in connection with the exhibition went to prove. As it happens, I was one of the participants in this discussion, together with Mr. Bryan Robertson, of the Whitechapel Gallery, and Dr. Anton Ehrensweig. It is not my purpose to recapitulate all our arguments here. But some of the points which emerged have continued to occupy me. There is, for example, the question of whether this kind of non-interference is not in fact still more interfering than the old style of academic art teaching; whether, in fact, it does not border on do-it-yourself psycho-analysis. Is this a good thing?

Obviously one cannot give an immediate answer without examining the whole context. The intellectual assumption, for example, is that the real duty of the artist is to explore himself, his own psyche. The business of the art school is therefore to inculcate good and honest methods of self-examination. The student is persuaded not to trust his own answers, always to push them a little farther. The habit of introversion is, of course, at the very roots of modern abstract art. An artist trained by such method emerges, in one sense, well equipped to deal with the problems of contemporary creativity.

There are, nevertheless, two stumbling blocks—the notion of

"society", and the notion of "style". Both these concepts turned up in the I.C.A. discussion, but I cannot say that we reached any very satisfactory conclusion about them. For once, social ideas caused less uproar than stylistic ones. It seemed to be generally assumed, and indeed I may have fallen into making such an assumption myself, that adjustment to the social context was simply part of the larger business of exploring one's own individuality. In a narrow sense this is true. But where, I wonder, does the idea of self-discovery connect with the idea of making a communication of some kind? If we assume—as indeed I do assume—that a man is not quite a complete entity in himself, but a being who is completed and fulfilled only when he forms part of a larger whole, then we are immediately faced with the problem of how one man links himself to another; of how a reasonably unambiguous meaning is conveyed from one near-entity to the next.

The abstract art of the postwar period will, I think, turn out to be notable for at least one thing—not its difficulty, but its ambiguity, which is something rather different. The range of meanings open to the spectator who confronts certain Abstract Expressionist pictures (a late Pollock, for example, or a Rothko) turns out to be almost infinite. We are not so sharply aware of this as we ought to be because, in fact, the job of defining the context—which in turn tends to govern the meaning—has been taken over by the critics. The more single-minded the artist becomes in his quest for inner truth, the more elaborate the literary underpinnings have to be. Or this, at any rate, is one way of looking at it.

My notion here is, I think, something which cuts directly across a lot of modern art theory. It is that communication in art is, in its essentials, a matter of the recognition of certain fixed symbols or conventions, rather than the direct transfer of emotions. The paradox is that a highly adventurous art can still (and sometimes without knowing it) depend on the use of a stylistic code of some kind, however brokenly or intermittently this is employed. And here the difficulties begin. Style is, in essence, a matter of limitations; we recognize a style because it refuses to cross certain boundaries and we define it in terms of these boundaries. Recognition of this has led many modern artists to a blank hostility to the idea of style, even when they themselves are still visibly entangled. There results a kind of wishful thinking on the subject. The argument is put forward that art history has somehow come to a stop—that there remains only art, freed from the old limitations, ready for the venture into the interior, the only venture worth making.

But we have, in fact, become more and not less involved with the concept of "styles" as the modern movement has continued its course. There are two reasons for this. One—the more basic—is simply the advance of knowledge. For the first time, we have become fully aware of a whole range of civilizations alien to our own, irrevocably divided from it, but still there and visible to us. The artist is no longer imprisoned within his own tradition, but is free to find stimulus where he chooses. Stretched out before us all is a great bazaar—the *musée imaginaire*—wherein we can pick and choose. But how do we choose? By making comparisons. And what do these comparisons establish in our minds? Not the integrity of a given object, but its classifiable differences from other objects. In short, we think in terms of style, a notion which is itself as abstract and general as a great deal of modern art.

This is the larger issue. The smaller one is the question of the dialogue of styles within the modern movement itself. Anyone who makes a work of art is involved in making a series of choices. He makes this mark and not that. Whether these choices are "unconsciously" motivated or not hardly seems to matter. For choice and style are related functions—you might say that one definition of style is this: a style is a sum total of choices. And certainly it is curious how immediately and accurately the subjective motions of the spirit can be classified—how recognizable an Abstract Expressionist picture is, for what it is, simply in terms of style. I am also interested in the way that modern art has again become obsessed with the idea of perception. Op artists explore, coolly, the mechanism of sight; how the retina can be made to lie to us. Meanwhile Jasper Johns, with his targets and flags, questions us about the nature of reality. He asks: "When is a thing so, and in what way is it so when it becomes a painting?"

The two examples I have just cited link up with my main theme in another way also. They seem to provide us with two quite different cases where the subjective exploration has surfaced, has become visible to the rest of us, slap in the middle of a convention—like a seal popping up for air through a hole in the ice. Why should the hole turn out to be just there, in that spot and no other?

But one thing it would be churlish not to admit. The show at the I.C.A., much as one questions some of the assumptions that lie behind it, is of a high standard. The methods adopted at Coventry do seem to work—at least, they work for these particular students.

15. WHEN ART IS UNDERTAKEN IN ORDER TO PROVE A POINT

The other day, when I was looking through a catalogue introduction written by a young American art critic, my eye fell on the following: "By far the most important single characteristic of the new *modus vivendi* between the arts and bourgeois society gradually arrived at during the first decades of the present century has been the tendency of ambitious art to become more and more concerned with problems and issues intrinsic to itself." Though the way of saying it is not mine, I would be the last person to deny the truth of the statement itself. What I want to ask is this: granted that such a situation exists, is it a good thing or a bad one?

Exhibition after exhibition makes us conscious of the "internal dynamic or dialectic" of styles. The Op Art and the coloured sculpture we have been looking at recently—a great deal of it embodies a debate about such topics as roundness and flatness, weight and volume, recession and projection. It often seems that the first question a young artist now asks himself is: "How do I see?" Or, rather, does he ask himself: "How does X see, and how can I prove him wrong?"

Thus it is that it becomes important for the audience to know about style—to react to the concept of style which a given object embodies, rather than to the physical presence of the thing itself. The focus on style which we have noticed over the past two decades has not been entirely the fault of the journalists. The artists themselves are obsessed with the notion of categories.

The result of this situation, so far as criticism is concerned, has been a curious mixture of doctrinaire rigidity and permissive chaos. Another document which recently came into my hands was a compilation called "A Composite Model of the Critical Process". During the last academic year, first-year students at the Royal College of Art were asked to write down their ideas on the subject of criticism in the visual arts, and this document is a summary of the most interesting formulations. Naturally, it is those which flatly contradict one another which are the most interesting. For instance: "Only the artist can criticize his own work", but "The artist probably writes worse nonsense than the critic, since he lacks the critic's comparative detachment". Or, again, "Criticism gives direction to artistic effort, and can act as a stimulus to new creation"—and yet, "Criticism should not influence an artist". It is evident, of course, that there is some confusion over what precisely criticism is. Perhaps it would be better to say that the real difficulty lies in knowing which definition to choose—first one is made to serve, and then another.

The most interesting conflict to be found in the document I have just quoted seems to me to be summed up in the following pair of statements. First of all, there is the declaration that "The factors to which judgment is related should be constant and not transitory ideas". And then the comment, "Criticism always reflects changing ideas about art. It advances as history advances, creating new terminology and concepts. Critical values change in accordance with the art that is available."

And this, I think, brings me back to my American colleague. The Hegelian idea of the dialectic of styles seems to me an effort to reconcile the conflict which I have just touched upon. The idea of the critical absolute is, in effect, a moral idea—it is a moral imperative (so it seems) which drives critics to criticism. On the other hand, when he has arrived—that is, when he has become a critic—the moralist finds himself in a world where all values are demonstrably in a state of flux. The dynamism of modern art, its changeableness—these things have been great underminers of fixed positions. The men who denounced the Impressionists and the Fauves were, in their own way, true prophets.

But why, even though the critic stands perplexed, should the artist himself become involved? There are, I think, a number of reasons. One is the tendency, fostered by the Romantic Movement, and in evidence during the nineteenth century, for the artist to fall out of step with the rest of society—to abandon his accepted place and function in order to pursue the personal individuality which formed such an important part of romantic doctrine. The next stage was to set art up as a rival to society itself. The framework, or absolute, becomes the debate about style, which conveniently excludes all other debates—such as, for instance, the larger one about the nature and function of man himself. The idea of "style", in fact, is both fixed and dynamic—the pressing problem is solved if we discuss art only in terms which are morally two-dimensional.

And thus it is that we now have a new relationship between creation and criticism—no longer a conflict, but an amalgamation. It is possible to feel that all the painters and sculptors have turned critic, and that the galleries are filled with their theses.

But can one look at theses for ever? I mean, without yawning? We often wonder, today, at the fascination which theology exercised over the minds of our ancestors. Will posterity be fascinated by sermons in plastic, philosophy in polystyrene? Am I enough of an absolutist to cry "no"?

16. THE PRICE OF FREEDOM IN ART

The British art world has a—perhaps mercifully—short memory. Twenty years have gone by since the end of the war. During that period British painting and sculpture have been honoured at home and abroad. It is commonly said that London is now, at long last, one of the important centres for the visual arts. What we tend to forget is the price that has been paid. Galleries and critics have always been fickle, perhaps never more so than during the twentieth century. More fickle still is the great public. One highly successful art dealer said to me, only the other day, that he thought that "anyone could make a success of a first exhibition". He added, cynically, "the public loves artistic virgins".

But fickleness aside, cynicism aside, isn't there something rather disturbing about the pattern which we see fulfilling itself in the careers of so many British artists? A striking initial success is followed by an equally striking failure to develop. One thinks of such groups as the "Beaux Arts Realists", or the sculptors who exhibited their work at that memorable Venice Biennale in the early fifties. One wonders if the "New Generation" painters, who exhibited at the Whitechapel Gallery in 1965, and the "New Generation" sculptors of the following year, are going to follow the same course.

Over the perspective of 20 years, British art looks like a (rather lively) layer-cake. By which I mean that we see a series of easily definable styles, each succeeding another with very little overlap. And each stylistic revolution has meant a very considerable turnover of artists. Very few have managed to consolidate an initial success, to go on growing, and to retain unimpaired the interest of critics and public.

It is worth while, I think, to try and discover the reasons for this high mortality of talent. It is almost as if the blatantly commercial reason, which is, to put it bluntly, the public hunger for fresh meat,has now been reinforced by some mysterious weakness in the artists themselves. I believe this weakness can probably be summed up in one word: freedom.

Total freedom of choice tends to paralyse the artist. It leads to a dissipation of psychic energy which can make him unproductive. True enough, I am using the vital word in a fairly radical sense. Artists have been free since the end of the Middle Ages. Free to choose what they would paint, what kind of people they would be. But this choice was, till recently, somewhat illusory. The painter or sculptor still lived within the bounds of a reasonably fixed social framework, and only on rare occasions dreamt of looking outside it. The pet canary regards his cage as home, and hops back into it the moment the cat approaches. The contemporary artist is a little like a canary surrounded by cats, but with nary a cage in sight.

All kinds of things have vanished. The genres, for example. No longer may the artist "choose" whether he will paint landscapes, or portraits, or history-pieces, or still life. The canvas is a baleful blank, waiting to be filled. There isn't even an honest choice to be made between abstraction and figuration. In addition, the artist finds himself uncomfortably placed in regard to the society in which he lives. Not only is it fluid and uncertain, but so many of its aspirations are focused upon him. In his own person, he is taken to represent the existential free-will towards which the rest of us aspire.

Most painters and sculptors feel, I suspect, a real difficulty in becoming engaged with the life which surrounds them. The alternative is to commit oneself to the *métier*, to become engaged with the fact of one's own talent. The result is that all the psychic energy which the artist possesses is concentrated upon the search for a style, and once this is found, the discoverer clings to it with stubborn desperation. The trouble with so many second, and third, and fourth, and fifth one-man exhibitions by moderately talented artists is the self-parody which becomes more and more apparent, the tendency to repeat and exaggerate former successes, to squeeze the lemon till not a drop of juice is left.

But consider, for a moment, the difficulty of pursuing any other course than the disastrous one which I have just outlined. The artist who truly develops, who creates an *oeuvre*, is a man engaged in the infinitely painful and laborious business of pulling himself up by his own bootstraps. There is very little outside himself which he can use as a handhold. No need to concentrate on refining his methods of representation, for example. When the critic admonishes the artist, and adjures him to pursue a steady course of development, the artist is entitled to ask the simple questions: "How? By what means can I test my own progress? What standards apply?"

Something which helps is a variety of stylistic means. But this is apt to conflict with the basic urge I have already mentioned—the need felt by the young artist to establish a well-defined personal identity. Commercial considerations and psychological ones unite in pressing him towards this. A successful first show is usually successful because it offers critics and public something which can be defined, something unified. Is it a paradox to say that the "unity" achieved by an artist in his twenties is usually far too simple? The painter or sculptor in order to achieve it, is forced to suppress some characteristics, some preoccupations, which are very personal to himself, and to exaggerate others. The result may be a permanent distortion of talent.

Indeed, I'm led to wonder if the real villain isn't that well-established institution, the one-man show itself. A work shown in a mixed exhibition makes its own impact; we view it for its own sake, not for the sake of the artist. The one-man show, on the other hand, puts the artist in the tightest of tight corners. He must spread his tail, do his little dance, utter a shrill cry. Will we look, or won't we? The issue remains in doubt. But we all know well enough that it is a personality which is on trial, not a collection of works of art.

17. ART AND THE MASS AUDIENCE

The appearance of the Government White Paper on the future of the arts in Britain sets me speculating about the possible interaction between the modern artist and the new mass-audience—that is if, with official aid, he now succeeds in capturing such an audience. The subject is ticklish—more ticklish, perhaps, than we generally realize. Basically speaking, art has always contained within itself two contradictory trends. One is the creator's desire to speak out to as wide a variety of people as possible—and artists have often preferred to be inclusive rather than exclusive. The other is our unadmitted propensity for using works of art as instruments of social differentiation.

If we examine the long history of the visual arts, we come across few, if any, instances where art has been universal in the modern, democratic sense—where, in fact, the artist has addressed himself to the whole community in which he lived. Even in those cases where the work of art seems most truly accessible, we soon begin to discover that there was an element of exclusion involved in their commissioning and making. The Parthenon frieze, for example, has frequently been cited as public art *par excellence*—the expression of the whole state of Athens at the moment of its greatest glory. But what does this imply? It implies a work of art made for citizens rather than slaves, Athenians rather than Corinthians, Greeks rather than barbarians. The principle of exclusion was already at work. More nearly universal was the religious art of the Middle Ages, designed to instruct all believers. But how far was it made for the believer, and how far for the God whom that believer worshipped—is a cathedral a sermon in stone, or a gratuitous act of faith? What matters more in it—the worshipper or the worshipped?

When we arrive at more modern times, we find many instances of art being used as something which marked off one man from another, which separated the sheep from the goats. We find a good instance of this function in Botticelli's famous picture "The Birth of Spring" in the Uffizi. A whole book has been devoted to its unravelling—Professor Edgar Windt's brilliant study, *The Pagan Mysteries of the Renaissance*. The picture, so Professor Windt informs us, is deliberately esoteric in its references, and was designed to be understood only by the few. And, in a real sense, it continues to withhold itself, despite the thousands who pass before it in homage every year. What they see is not all there is to be seen, and this deprivation was from the very first planned by the artist.

Even today, modern art differentiates—it separates one man from another. As I have said before in these columns, the position it occupies is that of a successful and powerful cult. Those who arrive at its shrines to worship, by that very act cut themselves off from their fellows. Indeed, in a society which is increasingly egalitarian, a commitment to modern art has become one of the ways of asserting a difference which separates the man who has given his allegiance from the rest. To go, for example, to see the Peggy Guggenheim Collection at the Tate, was to assert that one belonged to a minority—even if a considerable minority. And to want to belong to a minority is, I believe, a very human impulse. In this connection, it is perhaps worth pointing to the difference between the response to the Mellon Collection and that to the Guggenheim Collection. The secretary of the Royal Academy has protested at the neglect of the show at Burlington House, and in particular about such things as poor television coverage. Yet I think there is a deeper reason for this sudden turnabout in taste. The Royal Academy exhibitions of before the war—things like the great Chinese exhibition—may have been better attended because (even so recently) the great dividing line was between people who looked at works of art, and those who did not. Now that modern art has established itself, the whole idea of "modernity" has arrived to upset previous criteria. To go to the Mellon Collection was, from the sociological point of view, to assert nothing. There was nothing, any more, which gave the viewer a feeling of his own specialness. At the Tate things were quite otherwise.

It is this analysis which makes me wonder what will happen when modern art becomes even more universally available than it is now. At first, one feels certain, there will be a great response. The newspapers, television, government support itself—these have already broken down many barriers. There is hunger and there is curiosity. More important, the new developments in painting and sculpture have something exotic about them where this potential audience is concerned—and exoticism has, throughout the ages, been one of the highroads to popular success. Since I run, at this point, some danger of being misunderstood, I must point out that "exotic", in the sense that I am using it, is a purely relative term. If we take the pictures of peasants and peasant pastimes which were painted in northern Europe from the sixteenth century until the end of the seventeenth, we discover two important things about them. One is that these pictures were painted in such large numbers because there was a steady demand for them. The other is that this demand certainly did not come from the peasantry, for whom such things were, economically speaking, far out of reach. The truth is that they were made precisely for those who were *not* peasants, who found in these pictures a window which showed a fascinatingly different world.

In a democaracy of the kind we now live in, the issue becomes complicated. First of all there is the feeling that works of art belong of right to everyone, and that everyone ought to be offered the opportunity to enjoy them. The whole idea of using works of art as instruments of social differentiation is therefore repugnant to us, or ought to be. But what will become of art without the kind of emotional engagement which sectarianism and snobbery undoubtedly produce? The *avant-garde* artists are a little like the early Christians coming out of the cellars and catacombs after the conversion of Constantine. What was organized to be clandestine, what was designed to resist persecution, now has to face the perils of daylight and official approbation. The transition will surely not be an easy one.

One danger which opens before the artist is the pressure which may be put upon him to reciprocate the kindnesses of the state—if official patronage is showered upon those whose work, while outwardly "modern", is in fact diluted with an academic element which makes it easy to absorb, then even the naturally rebellious may be tempted. The degree of compromise required, can, on these occasions, seem so very small. But there is another and more pressing danger—which is that the artist's nerve may crack when he realizes the magnitude of the opportunity now offered to him. The hermetic side of modern art protects its practitioners from many things—including the danger of being caught out.

18. THE SOCIOLOGY OF ART

No sooner had I finished writing my last article on this page than a fascinating book came into my hands—a book which seemed to elaborate and explain the points I had just been making. The title is *Canvases and Careers*, and the authors are Harrison C. White and Cynthia A. White—a Professor of Social Relations married to an art historian. The publishers are John Wiley and Sons. What the authors set out to do was to make an analysis of the structure of the French art world during the nineteenth century. They are especially interested in the change of institutions which took place—the way in which a centralized system based on the Academy, the Ecole des Beaux Arts, and the Salons, gradually changed into something much looser, a confederation of dealers, promoters and critics, of group exhibitions and one-man shows.

In fact, what they are talking about is the growth of the system which we have today. The Whites point to quite a number of reasons for change in the French art world. Some of their headings have an alarmingly familiar ring. One section is called: "A Glut in Search of a Market", another: "The Critic as Publicist and Ideologue". But the book has an interest and and applicability which goes well beyond superficial resemblances.

I suggested a fortnight ago that the one-man show, that principal weapon of the dealer-critic system, seemed to have had a distorting effect on the development of painting, and in many cases had persuaded painters to think in terms of painting "an exhibition" rather than a single and intensely experienced work of art. I am still convinced that this is a valid complaint—and a number of readers, to judge from their letters, seem to have agreed. What I would like to do now is to push the inquiry a little farther.

Suppose we abolished the one-man show? Suppose, even, that it began to die a natural death? What could we replace it with? Most of the answers so far given to these questions (which I am not the first to ask) have suggested a return, however modified, to the old academy system. For the French Academy, and even our own Royal Academy, really had their origin in the desire felt by the state to control and regularize artistic institutions, to provide not only a channel for state patronage, but a kind of "career framework" for artists which would bring them into line with other solid citizens.

One thing which greatly interests the Whites is the kind of class-image that French painters had of themselves. They quote Pissaro's complaint: "It's a wonderful business being a bourgeois—without a cent!" Their view, indeed, is that the troubles suffered by the Impressionists were in part due to their firm refusal to admit that middle-class ways and standards were in conflict with the life which the painter had to live.

Since the end of the nineteenth century there has been a certain tendency to question the impeccably middle-class credentials of the artist. Gauguin rebelled against the idea. Picasso, rebelling in another way, has seized for himself the status of a mortal god. But our basic institution, even our methods of state patronage, are all still based on the idea that artists are middle-class people—"professional men", as the polite phrase has it. And our painters, for all their deliberate crowd-pleasing unconventionalities, have themselves been slow to surrender the idea.

But the middle class, in the sense that I have been using the term, seems to be a doomed institution. The solid citizen will soon be rarer than the okapi. The artist, in his role as a bourgeois, finds himself cut off from the more vital currents of the life of his times, and torn between two sets of assumptions, one set imposed on him by the logic of art, and the other by the no less pressing logic of status.

What role will the arts play in the future? This is a problem we ought to try and settle, and settle soon, before we condemn the art world to yet another set of unsuitable or defective institutions. What is wanted is something less rigid, less centralized than the old autocratic institutions of state patronage, and less chaotic, cruel, and corrupt than the dealer-critic at its worst.

One complication is the fact that we now feel a good deal of confusion on the subject of whether we ought to support painters or painting—that is, whether we should focus our attention on the creator or on the work of art he produces. One school of thought, quite a powerful one, seems to feel that the painting is now only a kind of certificate, a validation of an all-important abstract process, which is called "being a painter".

Yet there is a clue, even in this. At the moment, there is plenty of evidence that the arts are drawing closer together, especially the so-called "performing arts" and the plastic ones. If anyone doubts this, I would ask them to take a look at recent issues of *The Melody Maker*, that weekly oracle of "pop". You cannot read *The Melody Maker* these days without coming across a news item about a Happening staged by a beat group, or a discussion of the "psychedelic scene" in New York.

The answer seems to be that painting, in its next incarnation, is going to rank as a branch of show business, and that we had better think up a new and flexible framework to fit. The gypsy and the strolling player are in the process of ousting the bourgeois from his studio. Perhaps the prospect is something to look forward to, after all.

19. MODERN ART AT THE GRASS-ROOTS

An American friend writes to me in a mood of anger and depression induced by a recent Festival of Contemporary Art held in the provincial city where he lives. "Worst of all", he says, "was the interest—fabulous! And, after the Festival is over, the dormant provinces again. Hard crust over a swamp. When cities die they need Festivals: parodies of what has died." Some people will find these words unnecessarily bitter. Many more will fail to see how relevant they are to the situation in Britain. If they apply at all, they apply here as well as in America. As I have already hinted, in my article of a fortnight ago, the brave new world in the arts which we are now officially promised is likely to bring a number of difficulties in its train. One of the greatest of these difficulties is that of finding a rich and nourishing soil for modern art, not only in London but throughout Britain.

Everyone agrees, I think, that our provincial cities are still underprivileged so far as modern painting is concerned. How is this deprivation to be dealt with? The simplest and most obvious solution would seem to be more and better travelling exhibitions. Work of this kind is already undertaken by the Arts Council, and, within the limits of the council's resources, it is done very well. In addition, some of the larger provincial museums, for example Liverpool, play host to such things as the John Moores Exhibition. What is perhaps a little disturbing is the extent to which these exhibitions are still locally regarded as metropolitan phenomena—visitations from on high, which are not strictly relevant to the daily life which surrounds them. True, the public is briefly galvanized by a successful and imaginative exhibition. The audience comes; it looks—and it drifts away.

What one ought to ask, I think, of contemporary art which truly belongs to the people, is that it should in some way enter into the life of the community. In London, with its many galleries, public and private, this does happen. The numerous exhibitions of contemporary art are now part of the fabric of London life. Of course, the situation undoubtedly has its paradoxical side. The Whitechapel Art Gallery, for instance, certainly has a local public of a kind. But it is the faithful from Chelsea and Hampstead who crowd it out on Sunday afternoons. Still, those who go there are probably for the most part Londoners, and that is what counts. As Londoners they identify themselves, however unconsciously and remotely, with the new experiments now being carried forward in such forcing houses as the Royal College of Art and St. Martin's. The new aesthetic attitudes which emerge from these centres are gradually diffused and affect life as it is lived. Paintings influence advertisements, advertisements influence clothes, clothes influence fashions in living. The process is an organic one, and, outrageous though it may seem to assert it, London is the one remaining organic community in Britain; the one place where culture, for better or worse, is all of a piece.

I must, of course, qualify here, and say that I am not forgetful of the fact that such things as television and national newspapers bring the new fashions, the new ways of thinking, as swiftly to the provinces as they do to London itself. But there is still, I think, this nagging sense of irrelevance, of inferiority. Not even the fact that the provinces can boast both brilliant individuals and brilliant art schools can altogether take away this feeling. Indeed (and here I may be quite wrong) it seems to me that a provincial city blessed with such a school of art, or such individuals, tends to remain unaware of the fact until they have been consecrated by London.

This centralization is often regarded as an inevitable evil of modern industrial nations. The reason why London remains "organic" is, in any case, quite simple. The city is more fully representative of the life we live in Britain than any other—urban, industrial, yet in many ways delicately sensitive, introverted, and neurotic. I have already mentioned the Whitechapel Art Gallery, so let me also mention the exhibition of sculpture which is currently on view there. The new work by the younger generation of British sculptors has already been exhaustively discussed—let me point only to one aspect of it. The materials these artists use—fibreglass, aluminium, polystyrene—these seem to be the very colour and texture of modern cities. And London is, above all, the landscape where these colours and textures surround us. And hence these sculptures seem urban in a new way, without nostalgia for the materials or the forms of nature.

Yet ought not this to apply to the other great cities of Britain? We may not admire these places, or think them beautiful, but should not they too give birth to a new art, derived from the very fabric and texture of the townscape? These questions may seem chimerical, but they are, in essence, very important. For the only kind of art that counts is the art that invites some kind of participation or identification from the community at large. It is this which exists in London, and, it seems to me, only spasmodically elsewhere. And a wilderness of travelling exhibitions will not serve to put matters right.

The problem of art for the provinces is, after all, very closely linked to the problems of leisure and the use of leisure. The great challenge and opportunity of contemporary art in Britain is twofold. First of all there is the question of the *avant-garde* itself—of how what is often designed to be exclusive, to mark off one section of the community from another, can become inclusive. The other is even simpler and more brutal. It is that we can now foresee the moment when every individual will have more time at his disposal. The most fruitful use of this time would be for self-enrichment and, of all the roads to self-enrichment, the visual arts offer one of the most attractive. By this I do not mean that more than a tiny minority will want to become even amateur artists. But it does mean a different relationship to the work of art than that which is implied by the caravan of culture, which halts at one spot for a moment, then packs up all its glittering goods and journeys onward. It implies, instead, the constant presence, not only of works of art, but of the idea of art. As my American friend asserts, living communities tend to need festivals of art a good deal less than dead ones.

The essential is to implant the idea of modern art, not as a special event but as a matter of everyday occurrence, and of the modern artist in a provincial city as an integral part of the community. What is needed is not only more chances for people living outside London to see the best in modern art but a more violent diaspora of artists than has yet taken place, and, as far as possible, a decentralization of the metropolitan art world. Otherwise our provincial towns and cities will remain aesthetically under-privileged, however many exhibitions we send out or well-meaning committees we set up.

20. EPOCH OF DISPOSABLE ART?

It has been quite usual to reproach modern art with being out of touch with the way that people "really live". By which is meant, I suppose, that we feel the want of some kind of continuity. In the seventeenth century, for example, there was still no hard and fast line of division between the fine arts and the applied arts. The rhythms, the kind of visual sensibility, to be seen in seventeenth-century painting are also to be found in furniture, in pottery, even in clothes. But, even as early as the eighteenth century, there were growing signs of a divorce. Our own century, for the most part, has been marked by the kind of eclecticism in decoration which the modern painter has rigorously striven to avoid. Of course, the division has not been total. There have been two moments at least, in this century, when a precarious unity was achieved.

One came with the rapid spread of Art Nouveau throughout Europe. The decorative ideas of Art Nouveau also affected the painting of the period. True enough, those painters whom we now think of as characteristically Art Nouveau are valued more for their eccentricity than for their transcendent genius. But, when we look at the work of Bonnard and Vuillard, and even of the young Picasso, we can't help being aware that a part of their work, at least, has its roots in the very same rose-garden which produced the intertwining stems, the stylized blooms, of Art Nouveau fabrics and metalwork. Hot on the heels of Art Nouveau, there followed the age of Jazz Modern, and here we must admit that the style had some very distinguished progenitors among modern artists—Mondrian and also those artists associated with the Bauhaus. Indeed, the Bauhaus stood for a real, not just a theoretical, unity of style, and we now look upon the designs for modern furniture produced by the Bauhaus architects—Breuer and Mies van der Rohe—as being as much classics in their way as those of Chippendale or Hepplewhite.

But both these styles exercised their sway within definite limits. Art Nouveau remained the property of a cult. Jazz Modern is not the pure milk of the Bauhaus gospel. Instead, it shows us how that gospel became debased and vulgarized.

This topic interests me because we have again reached a moment where the fine arts and the applied arts feel an attraction for one another. The explosion of Op art on to the scene is a very recent cultural phenomenon, but already we see its effect in fashion, in furnishing fabrics, and even in such things as clocks and china. At the moment a London department store is holding an exhibition where the Op art trend can be seen at work in all these, and still other, forms of applied art. Let me be the first to say that a fashion of this kind is commercially very convenient. It accelerates the process of planned obsolescence, and it is obsolescence which helps to sustain a manufacturing society such as our own. Crazes, such as that for Op art patterns, are merely economic dynamism bursting to the surface—an insolent proclamation of the values by which we live.

Anyone who expects me to follow this with a root and branch denunciation of industrial, urban civilization, is however, due for a disappointment. I think the question which we ought to examine, when confronted with a craze like the one for Op art, is how much the fashion is to be regarded as something lying entirely on the surface of things, and how far it is rooted in the conditions of modern life.

At one time, for example, there was a passion for the pseudo-Spanish—over-wrought iron and parchment lampshades; a style which a friend of mine has aptly christened "Curzon Street Baroque". A fashion of this kind is entirely rootless and wilful. Somebody has an idea, and manufacturers are encouraged to supply the new needs which the idea brings with it. But let us consider in conjunction with this one of the most "radical" objects in the department-store exhibition which I have just been talking about. This is a chair made of cardboard. Brilliantly patterned with Op art polka-dots, it is designed to be supplied to the customer in kit form. The buyer bends the sections of cardboard and fits them together for himself. It is also—and you are told so frankly—not designed to last. Its estimated life is three to six months, according to the amount of use it gets. Then you throw it away and buy another one, probably with a different pattern.

This chair seems to me to have something in common with Op art painting—something which goes much deeper than a mere similarity of pattern and colour. And that is the idea of impermanence. We don't expect a characteristic Op art picture to last any more than we do the cardboard chair. Such a picture is a mechanism which produces a certain sensation—

often quite a subtle sensation. But, like all mechanisms, it will one day cease to work. The eye will domesticate it in the wrong sense; by which I mean that the picture will lose the power to stimulate the retina and thus to produce the physical sensations which it is meant to bestow on us.

Yet neither the Op art picture nor the Op art chair is as wholly irrelevant to the modern situation as a room expensively, and alas how permanently, decorated in Curzon Street Baroque. Let us look at things a different way. When it comes to works of art, we are a little apt to contradict ourselves. On the one hand, we denounce the products of modern industrialism as unsympathetic and even inhuman. The manufactured object, so we declare, is cold. The picture which apes industrial finishes is a blasphemy. Yet, on the other hand, we have an increasing distaste for possession, which is why we tend to equip ourselves with things which will wear out as rapidly as possible; which won't stay around to cumber our lives when we have finished with them.

The new Op art designs belong to a concept which we may think of as "service" rather than possession. The new attitude is to provide oneself with services rather than goods—to hire a television set or a car in preference to buying one; and, even when we buy things, we expect only a limited life from them. We buy clothes which are immensely smart for a single season, and worn out at the end of it. Art, too, has been affected by this. Many artists, for example, seem to find that museums are their most important patrons; not private clients. A picture in a museum acts in a different way to a picture one lives with. The work of art in a museum is an "event" which some public body provides for the service of citizens. Once the concept of ownership departs, the idea of impermanence enters.

What I'm trying to say is, I think, that we may be moving into the epoch of disposable art as well as of disposable furniture. Op art pictures and cardboard chairs have indeed got more than their spots in common.

21. POP CULTURE AND THE WORLD OF FASHION

With the recent revival of the *Batman* saga at a London cinema, it seems a good moment to talk about that mysterious subject, Pop Culture. *Life International* had a recent brave shot at a definition. Pop Culture, it declared, is "an umbrella term covering nearly anything which is currently in style". Surely one can do a little better than that? The entire phenomenon of Pop Culture has begun to loom so large in our appreciation of the visual arts that I'd like to devote a little time to exploring the subject.

What, for instance, are the things which divide Pop Culture from Mass Culture, or even from culture in general? Pop, we must admit, is a word which now carries with it certain special connotations—the revolt of the young against the old, for example, and the fact that the age-gap is now beginning to count for more than the class-gap. Mass Culture makes itself available to everyone, Pop Culture does no such thing—it has a fierce clannishness which is not the least of its fascinations. In fact, one of the most interesting things about Pop is that it is basically anti-art. One might even argue that the real reason why it fascinates artists is that they have now become anti-art also.

Pop, for example, is hostile to the idea of permanence. Art is, among other things, a form of human activity which protests at the cruel destructiveness of time. Shakespeare tells the young hero of the *Sonnets*:—

> So long as men can breathe, or eyes can see,
> So long lives this, and this gives life to thee.

Such things as advertisements, posters, pop songs, Carnaby Street clothes (all of them part of the Pop ethos) invite us to an avid enjoyment by parading the fact that their creators don't expect them to last. And this, in turn, relates to the kind of society we live in. This is the first age, I think, which has erected the enjoyment of the moment into a moral imperative (or at least, the first age in which the imperative has been so devotedly obeyed).

It is interesting to examine Pop Culture to see what it borrows and what it invents. The involvement of "high culture" with Pop in the postwar era is a thing which has been much discussed. What has been less thoroughly examined is the tendency of Pop to take what it needed from the *avant-garde*. Ever since the beginnings of modernism, *avant-garde* ideas have been infiltrating the commercial sphere. The typography of the Dadaists was not slow to make its impact on the glossy magazines of the twenties. In the same way, the shapes and colours used by Delaunay soon began to turn up in the fabric designs of the "jazz age". Surrealism had a tremendous impact on the shop windows of New York, London, and Paris, and of course the influence of the movement is clearly to be seen in the clothes designed by Schiaparelli.

It is evident that all the examples I've been listing are closely connected with the world of fashion. The object of all fashion is to keep a certain distance between what is "fashionable" and what is not. Fashion, in fact, is something which runs away from acceptance—even if not too rapidly. The fox may not enjoy being chased, but the fashionable do. This perpetual replacement of one fashion by another uses up ideas at a great rate, and it was inevitable that designers should turn to modern art as a source of inspiration. There was also the fact that modern art enjoyed a wide notoriety, without having achieved total acceptance—this helped to preserve the "distance" which makes fashionable things fashionable.

But there was something else which affected fashion: mass production methods brought with them an increasing democratization of design. What I mean by this is that a newly created fashion—in dress, in fabrics, in furniture—could be put on the market more cheaply and in far greater quantity than had ever been possible before. At the same time, more people had the financial resources to try to be fashionable. The result was the gradual transformation of fashion into Pop. Pop is, basically speaking, fashion without class-distinctions, and with an accelerated time-scale. The fashion which would first have been created for the pleasure of a few, and which would have found its way to the mass-audience by means of infinite dilutions and gradations, was now available to almost everyone, at the very moment of its launching.

These new mass-fashions have created the thing we call Pop Culture. Pop Culture, like its sedater predecessor, looks to contemporary art as a reservoir of ideas. Op Art, for example, is no sooner conceived than it is turned into dresses, furnishing fabrics, and table china. But the demands of mass production have taught the designers to look at modern art in a particular way. It is no longer the superficial aspects which attract them, but the idea, the essence, whatever can be translated for the benefit of the machine and made in materials which the machine knows how to handle. The result is something which we often notice in the artifacts of Pop—for all their immediate impact, they are without depth, without real associations. And this fits them for the world in which they exist: because they are in two dimensions (at least intellectually) the consumers soon tire of them, and move on to another fashion. It is this movement which keeps the machines turning.

What is truly fascinating about Pop Culture, however, is that it should have reached so sophisticated a recognition of the terms of its own survival. The hostility to permanence, which I've already mentioned, is due to the instinct for self-preservation. The product itself must be sacrificed to preserving the apparatus which produces products. Obsolescence is a necessity. It is for this reason that all those attempts to teach people to distinguish between good Pop and bad Pop strike me as rather forlorn. Standards are being imported into a situation where they do not apply. Pop Culture has only two measures of judgment—the new and the old-fashioned; the charged and the flat. And often, when we examine them, these two standards turn out to be one. It is the new which is *ipso facto* charged, and last year's notion which is flat. There is something rather Nietzschean about the addicts of Pop; they admire energy itself, and do not question the purposes for which energy is being expended. Creativity becomes a flux of ideas; rather than one idea, worked out in all its terms.

I think it is this aspect of things which has given Pop Culture its present respectability among the artists themselves. For "high art" too, for various reasons, has become fascinated with the concept of energy spent for its own sake. The dynamic of experiment in modern art seems linked to the dynamic of change in Pop. Is this in fact the case? If it is, we shall have to provide ourselves with entirely new standards of judgment in the fine arts.

22. THE FUTURE OF ART IN A CROWDED LAND

The constructivist revival which now seems to be upon us raises quite a few fascinating questions. One is that of the relationship between the "idea"—that is, the concept—and the way in which it is carried out. A few critics have begun to use the phrase "idea art" as a kind of label for a complex and as yet not clearly definable development. What does its use imply? First of all, I think, that the material used is merely the servant of some abstract notion, which can be detached from it and examined on its own. After all, we can think about a chess problem without having to set up the pieces on a chessboard. Secondly, that the true "original" is the concept and not the object itself. Indeed, "idea art" is an art without originals—what is available to our physical senses is merely a pale shadow or reminder, and stands in much the same relationship to the artist's intention as a good colour reproduction does to a masterpiece by Titian. What the artist makes is a diagram, something which serves as a tool, but not, in the strict sense, a work of art. It seems to me that many Op paintings are of exactly this kind.

This may sound like the final dehumanization of the visual arts which the prophets of doom have foreseen for so many years. It certainly represents an extreme reaction from the work of an artist like Pollock, who has only just been accepted into the pantheon. Pollock is a painter who distrusts the mind, who feels that all truth can exist only as gesture, and that every gesture is unique, being governed by the physical structure—the flesh, the nerves, the bones and the blood—of the man who makes it. The flux of paint which we see in Pollock's drip-paintings can be thought of as an effort on the part of the artist to integrate himself with the physical universe.

To understand the precise significance of "idea art", and indeed the precise significance of Pollock, one must, I think, consider the social context within which they exist and operate. In my last article, on Pop culture, I pointed out that Pop is really the result of the forced marriage between fashion and the machine. The vagaries of fashion, and the increasing role played by mechanization, are both things which have been liberally denounced during the past quarter of a century. Pollock might be thought of as one of the protestors. Pollock is against integration into the urban, mechanistic universe; he asserts the right of the individual to *be* an individual. In this he resembles the American beat poets who are more or less his contemporaries. When Allen Ginsberg cried, in the course of that now too-celebrated Albert Hall recital last year:

> Be kind to the heroes that have lost their names in the newspaper
> and hear only their own supplication
> for the peaceful kiss of sex in the giant auditoriums of the planets—
> hear only the nameless voices crying for
> kindness in the orchestra, crying for hope in their own joy . . .

he was making the kind of assertion that Pollock would fully have sympathized with, and acting into a tradition which goes back beyond D. H. Lawrence to William Blake.

Despite the ridicule which Ginsberg usually meets with in England, this is something very much in our own national tradition. The tendency in England has been to resist the machine, to assert that increasing urbanization and industrialization are things which are wholly bad, that they cut men off from the true basis of the good and rich life. Lawrence has become our national symbol of resistance to the "unnatural", or at least artificial, way of life which our century has forced upon us.

"Idea art" interests me because it makes me wonder about this whole problem. Of course, I begin with certain assumptions, but these are not assumptions peculiar to myself. For instance, I assume that the population of Britain will continue to rise—there are already 52 million of us. Great efforts will have to be made to feed, clothe and house this teeming mass of people—and these efforts will lead to a use of machinery which we as yet hardly envisage: machines tending machines, the setting up of an enivronment more remote from the natural than any which we now inhabit. I assume, too, that the egalitarian trend in our society will continue (I deliberately use the word "egalitarian" rather than "democratic"). Even art will become subject to the rule of fair shares for all. We already feel uncomfortable if it is suggested to us that many people are cut off by circumstances rather than temperament from the aesthetic experience.

Do we really suppose that a programme of back to the land, back to a full experience of the physical, can be sustained under these conditions? The "healthy society" advocated by Lawrence's disciples is an economic absurdity unless we first machine-gun three-quarters of the population and sterilize at least half of the remainer. We have not either the room or the resources to create the kind of world which they envisage.

It may, perhaps, be argued that art should at all costs preserve a fiction which everything else conspires to undermine. What this ignores is a problem which has so far received little thought—that of the distribution of art, the way in which it is to be made accessible to the vast quantities of people whom we now encourage to feel a need for the qualities which it has to offer. Already we hear complaints that the provinces are neglected. Already we see the Government making tentative efforts to make art available to everybody. But these efforts are made within a framework which survives from the time when art had no aspirations towards the democratic. The work of art as a unique object is, to say the least of it, an anomaly in a society where nothing else is unique, where objects are no longer made one at a time.

This isn't a plea to abolish all the masterpieces of the past, to take them out of the museums and burn them. Nor is it a demand that artists should be prevented from working with their hands; that they should be shut up in blank little cells and told to get on with the meditation. What I mean is this—that it's surely a good thing that a part of our artistic efforts should be put into trying to solve a problem which seems to me a very pressing one. It isn't works of art which count, so much as what we get from them. The artist is the servant of the spectator. "Idea art" or "art without originals" already exists to a limited extent in such things as lithographs by modern painters. So long as the idea is capable of moving us in the way that we expect of a work of art, why should we care that it is capable of 2,000, or even 2,000,000, identical embodiments?

23. MAGICIANS AND SERVANTS OF THE PUBLIC

Now that art is returning to the public domain—by which I mean that we more and more have the notion that art should be freely available to everyone, like bread; and that it should, furthermore, be an experience rather than a possession—the idea seems to be getting about that there is no difference in the way that art goes to work in the private and the public sphere. This is, for example, one of the assumptions that seem to underlie the present Government's policy towards the visual arts. As a way of thinking, it is not entirely new. The Russian experimentalists who flourished in the years immediately after the Revolution believed quite passionately that art ought to come out into the streets. For them, the easel-painting was a chattel, and reeked of the old system which they had worked to pull down. In England, we are not so radical. But an increased interest in the public role of art is bringing with it not only a return to the kind of constructivism which owes so much to the Russian artists of that period, but a new tendency to play down the role of the artist, and to exalt that of the work of art.

In theory, this is a highly defensible position—and an attractive one. The real relationship, as we all know, is between the spectator and what he sees, not between the spectator and the artist. And this relationship is more likely to be fruitful if the spectator is not feeling self-conscious about the act of looking. Works of art should exist in our environment naturally, and in neighbourly fashion. The whole business of artists publicizing themselves, or being publicized, has grown increasingly dubious, and an artist in the hands of the mass media is not usually an encouraging spectacle. And yet, and yet . . .

The question is, in part, whether painting and sculpture operate precisely like architecture, or whether architecture is something on its own, a special case. This is a position which most architects would be reluctant to accept. In their view, architecture is simply the one form of modern art which the public cannot ignore, which we all have to live with, willy-nilly. It is also naturally more assertive, since buildings tend to be larger than other works of art, and since we explore interior and exterior alike. From the point of view of our aesthetic response to it, a building is an environment which we inhabit, which guides us physically, which makes us behave in certain ways, and which even (as in the case of religious buildings) gives a colour to our feelings. And a painting or a piece of sculpture is a "governor" placed within an environment, something which—it may be—heightens our response to the space in which we find ourselves. The architect, painter or sculptor becomes, under this dispensation, a kind of highly skilled public servant; exceptionally gifted, it may be, but making no claim to be radically different from the rest of society. The artist is highly conscious of his own role and of the contribution which it can make to the whole social complex. His emotions are kept well in leash—he reserves them for his work.

I can imagine that some readers will already be beginning to raise the sort of objections which I have in mind. Even among modern architects, we find certain individuals who possess a kind of magic for their contemporaries. Le Corbusier, who has just died, was one of them. The extent of Le Corbusier's influence went even beyond what might have been expected from his writings and the brilliance of his buildings.

Painters and sculptors also possess this magic. This is an undoubted fact which tends to upset people like myself, who believe so passionately in the social role of art. I believe I found traces of a similar discomfiture in John Berger's recent book about Picasso. And it has been plain to see in some of the recent reviews given to the work of Andy Warhol.

In varying degrees, Picasso and Warhol play the same role—that of the shaman. Picasso's merest scribble on the rim of a bull-fighter's hat confers a mysterious energy to an object otherwise unremarkable. The thing does not become a work of art—the scribble is too slight, too banal, for that. But the master has touched it, and left evidence of his touch. We meet this phenomenon in even purer form when we look at those piles of soup-cans which Andy Warhol has signed, thereby removing them from one reality to another.

The reaction of many people is simply to wax indignant when they are confronted with this kind of thing. They think it is all a ramp, a racket, a plot of the art-dealers. But can we afford this easy condemnation? The fact is that Picasso and Warhol remain ineluctably there. What they do—and still more, what they are—exercises a grip on men's imaginations which is not to be easily broken.

We live in what is, in many ways, a remarkably unmysterious age. The mysteries of the scientists, it is true, tend to grow ever larger—so large that the mind cannot grasp them, and falls back defeated. Arthur Symons said of Browning that "as a thinker he conceives of humanity not as an aggregate but as a collection of units". This is, I think, true of most of us. Defeated by science, we fall back not on human beings in the mass, but on individuals. Artists are particularly apt to focus our attention in this way, because we already think of art as something which escapes the boundaries of the rational, and also as something which is closely connected with the whole idea of human individuality.

And here, I think, we reach the real objection to directly equating the private function of art and the public one. Art in the twentieth century has been, for all kinds of reasons, an exploration of irrationality. Painting, sculpture, and to a lesser extent music and literature, have provided the last refuge of metaphysics. Is this a bad thing? More, is the irrational really something which can be made social and public to the extent that the planners foresee? Alan Moorehead's account of Captain Cook's visit to Tahiti describes how the islanders coupled without shame in public, and were amused when the English seamen wanted to take to the privacy of the woods for their love-making. In England, we are the descendants of those seamen, and even in the South Seas the Puritan ethic has to some extent conquered. An art which is the same in public as it is in private must give up meddling with dangerous things, with the dark parts of the mind.

The myth of the artist—the recognition of the artist's role as, among other things, a professional wonderworker—these are not things which can be killed off by a couple of manifestos and a Government White Paper. Society and modern art both have a long road to travel before they are completely reconciled.

24. PRIVATE FACES IN PUBLIC PLACES

Some days ago a public commission given to a leading contemporary artist caused a stir in the newspapers—and for the usual reasons. Some members of the L.C.C. are apparently disappointed in the statue which was commissioned from Mr. Reg Butler for the new Crystal Palace Recreational Centre. It would be easy enough, I suppose, to dismiss this as being yet another fuss about Modern Art. Heaven knows there have been enough of them already, and some pretty silly things have been said. In this case, however, it seems to have been a slightly different sort of fuss from an Epstein fuss, or even from a Henry Moore fuss, and a different point seems to have been at issue.

Mr. Butler is not, as one can see quite clearly from his current exhibition at the Hanover Gallery, a really *avant-garde* artist. The human figure is in the very forefront of his preoccupations. What is more, he distorts it very little. Mr. Butler's girls—and girls are one of his main themes—are fleshy, sexy creatures: recognizably the daughters of Eve.

What, then, is the cause of the row? Politicians, as we know, are apt to express themselves a little unhappily on the subject of works of art. Mr. A. T. R. Fletcher (Con., Lewisham, N.) described the bronze as a female figure "with no arms and no clothes, standing on a plinth, but not otherwise engaged in any obvious activity". It is, perhaps, not wholly impertinent to suggest that it is only the last part of this observation which is interesting. The bronze, even from a photograph, is very obviously in Mr. Butler's usual idiom. Butler, as a romantic, tends to skimp those parts of the figure which strike him as irrelevant to what he wants to express. He has, in fact, created many figures far more wilful than this. One might indeed venture to murmur to Mr. Fletcher that the lady's arms are not fully worked out because in the sculptor's view they would detract from the rest of her.

Where Mr. Fletcher—in my view, at any rate—is upon somewhat stronger ground is in saying that the figure is "not engaged in any obvious activity". For it is pretty evident that what Mr. Butler has presented to the L.C.C. is a chip off the current block. Any other Butler statue, one feels, would have been just as suitable to the commission as this one. There is no particular reason for setting it up in a recreational centre, apart from the fact that it looks quite nice. It has very little to do with what the place is for; it makes no comment.

As certain recent exhibitions have shown, distinguished modern artists are strangely willing to sail under banners which might be thought to have nothing to do with them. An abstract artist, asked for "something religious", merely sends in something from his current production, equipped with a suitable title. The critic wonders—but does not usually ask—why the painting is called "Gethsemane" instead of "Portofino".

The truth is that an enormous gap seems to be widening between the artist and the rest of us. Artists are not so much unwilling as unable to adapt themselves to the special problems of the "public" work of art. Their whole aesthetic forbids them even to consider it. Where the great Renaissance artists—at least up to the time of Gionvanni da Bologna—seem to have thought very carefully about the exact relevance of the work, not only as to the spot where it was to be placed, but as to the preoccupations of the patron, our contemporaries are apt to fall back on the famous lines of Auden:

> Private faces in public places
> Are wiser and nicer
> Than public faces in private places.

I am not wholly sure that these provide a defence.

If we think of the great public monuments of the past, we find, I think, that the greatest of them move us because of the way in which they respond to a given situation, a given set of circumstances. Though Michelangelo's struggles with his patrons are notorious, it is possible to see how his work in both the Sistine and the Medici Chapels happened in response to a challenge put before him. For example, it would be ridiculous to transpose them. The Vatican frescoes would lose more than half their meaning in Florence; the Florentine statues would seem ill at ease in Rome. But I'm afraid that Mr. Butler's statue, whatever its other merits, would have just as much significance in Tooting or in Timbuctoo.

My difficulty—and I think it is shared by many others, even including Mr. Fletcher—is that I am not as pure in my responses as I would like to be. A good description of the way we respond to works of art was provided by an Elizabethan poet, some hundreds of years ago. In *The Baron's Wars* Drayton describes how Queen Isabella and her lover Mortimer examine the pictures in the Queen's Chamber in Nottingham Castle:—

When on those sundry pictures they devise
And from one piece they to another run,
Commend that face, that arm, that hand, those eyes,
Show how that bird, how well that flower was done,
How this part shadowed, and how that did rise,
This top was clouded, and that trail was spun,
The land-skip, mixture and delineatings,
And in that art a thousand curious things.

"A thousand curious things"—we look for them, but now we seldom find them.

25. THE MODERN ARTIST AND THE MODERN PATRON

Anyone who visits the Wallace Collection or the eighteenth-century rooms at the Victoria and Albert, anyone who leafs through the illustrated catalogues of the René Fribourg Collection (now being dispersed by Sotheby's), is at once conscious of the harmony between the arts of the period, and the way of life they adorned. Painting a sculpture conformed to an ideal of decorative prettiness. Not only were works of art right in scale and material for the rooms which housed them; they echoed in subject and treatment the ideal of civilized behaviour towards which the century aspired.

Some people find the results claustrophobic. While they admit the merits of eighteenth-century furniture, silver and porcelain, they find something relentlessly trivial about its major arts. Yet these still have a huge popularity with the modern collector. The prices of fine eighteenth-century pictures go up steadily year by year. Last season, a very pretty picture by the minor Venetian Pietro Longhi brought the staggering sum of £41,000 when it was sold at auction. It must also be admitted that in some ways eighteenth-century objects fit our way of life very well. They suit, for example, our small rooms. They pander to our need for recreation: they soothe, they comfort, they entertain. In fact, they work hard to please us.

Meanwhile, the modern artist seems to pursue a course which is faroucheley independent. A visitor to some of the exhibitions which have opened the new season may find the works on view enormously interesting and impressive in themselves, but might also wonder what the potential market is. Eduardo Paolozzi, at the Waddington Gallery, is showing a group of sculptures which are of undeniable power. These assemblages of metal bits are at once architectural and magical. They stand about the gallery like the idols of an unknown tribe. One can well imagine the richly suggestive "Diana as an Engine" set up for worship in some secret temple. But it is not a piece for the drawing-room, still less one for the study or the bedroom. In a word, it is impossible to imagine *living* with it. And there is another side to the coin. Too often, when one visits an exhibition, one is conscious that the smaller pictures are mere duty pieces, tossed off by the artist to pacify his dealer.

Yet serious patrons remain for modern art, and these have, to some extent, been brought to accept a new view. The work of art once took its place tactfully, it fitted into the context of daily living, and was admired for its polish and for its completeness. Now we do not like the truly complete work. The patron has become a *voyeur*—"the prying housemaid of the soul"—who watches the creative process with a somewhat illicit excitement. What we ask of the work of art is that it should allow us, too, in our impotence, to take part in the art which made it. But, of course, we are never there on time. The act is over. The picture is just a record of what happened. This is what I find unsatisfactory about most Abstract Expressionist painting. I suspect that the sight of the painter at work was probably more than the finished result.

It is a commonplace that, as art has grown more and more autonomous, more and more an end in itself, more and more an assertion of unique powers on the part of the artist, so the patron has fallen more and more into contempt. Very often, artists think it dishonest to give the patron any consideration at all. Let him take what he gets, and be grateful. Yet the private patron is not to be denied. People may talk glibly of the way public patronage is replacing that offered by the individual, but the process is not complete. In a free society, it never will be. Throw the private patron out through the front door, and he will come in through the back. And as he re-enters, he brings dishonesty with him.

Artists of the eighteenth century and earlier often complained of difficulties with patrons. And it is true that the patron often tried to impose himself, to make the artist merely the servant of an imperious will. But at least the difficulties were out in the open, and the battle raged over a particular picture to be painted, a particular sculpture to be made. Now, the battleground is dangerously ill-defined. The artist, in his egotism, constantly asserts his own uniqueness. The patron assents, but is determined to capture a little of that uniqueness for himself. He has no ambition to spoil a picture, but a very real one to spoil a soul. Artists have this much of the actor in them, that they are very conscious of what the audience expects. And what the audience now expects is that they should "be artists".

This sounds easy enough, agreeable enough. Too easy, and

too agreeable. For "being an artist" is a concept which we have insensibly coarsened and debased. Laying such stress on creativity, and so little on craftsmanship, we, as patrons, look to artists for creative gestures, gestures which we can recognize and classify. We force the painter and sculptor into a constant search for novelty, novelty at all costs—anything to avoid the damning verdict that "it has been done before". Worse still, we encourage artists to treat their paintings and sculptures not as something done and final, but as credentials. The artist looks upon his works as proof of how "artistic" he is; while claiming to exalt them, he despises them. It is the artist's life which becomes the carefully pondered work of art.

People who find these words a trifle harsh should think about the great stress which certain critics and collectors now lay on the quality of an artist's "suffering". To have suffered—and then to sell it for money. Wouldn't skill be an honester commodity?

26. ART AND INDUSTRY—THE NEED FOR A NEW RELATIONSHIP

It often seems to me that the possible relationships between the modern artist and modern technology have never been properly explored. In recent years, for instance, there has been a lot of talk about painters and sculptors finding new patrons among industrial concerns—the Peter Stuyvesant Foundation is, I suppose, the best known example of this in England. But even if the fashion for this kind of patronage spread throughout British industry, it would not strike at the heart of the problem.

Basically, this problem is part of a much larger one—the dislocation of modern social relationships. In the Middle Ages, for example, the distinction between "fine art" and 'applied art" barely existed. The man engaged in creating painting or a piece of sculpture used techniques and processes which, in their essence, would have been understood by any craftsman. And so long as most objects of use—domestic objects, farm implements, vehicles—continued to be made by hand, the artist was still "in context". But with the Industrial Revolution there came a change. Craft was replaced by technology, though for a while what had happened was disguised by nineteenth-century antiquarianism. The one manufacturer whose processes were not industrialized was the artist.

It may be objected that there was every reason for the painter and the sculptor to refuse to join the Gadarene rush towards mass-production. The case for and against this is one which I prefer to argue another time. But in one sense, the artist suffered a real deprivation. Industry generates its own inventiveness; the machines can actually suggest new paths to the alert imagination. Because technology is challenging, because it throws up new materials, new ways of doing things, design itself alters. The artist, left to go his own way with the old, traditional craft techniques, was deprived of a most important stimulus. This was, at least arguably, the reason why the fine arts fell out of step, and lost their predominant role in our culture.

In recent years there have been signs that the artists, and particularly the sculptors, have begun to think very seriously indeed about this problem. The distinguished British sculptor Bryan Kneale, who recently held a successful retrospective exhibition at the Whitechapel Gallery, uses a direct-welding technique which is borrowed from industry. Younger sculptors have become fascinated with the possibilities offered them by vacuum-formed plastics. What I detect in all this is a feeling that art is more likely to be relevant and valid when it adopts the techniques and methods which are characteristic of the times. Technique itself is often the principal crutch of creativity (and here, I think, is a view which Cellini would certainly have shared).

The trouble, of course, is the lack of facilities, and still more, the lack of a real relationship between the creative artist and modern industry. However, the problem is not necessarily an insoluble one. A most imaginative study of the subject has just come into my hands, written by Barbara Latham and Joan Hills. Mrs. Latham and Miss Hills have a clear idea of what they want to achieve. The feeling they have is that patronage as it now exists is gratuitous, and therefore in a way insulting to the artist. What the modern painter or sculptor needs, in their view, is a recognition of his potential usefulness to the world of technology.

For example, they want to get rid of the notion that the only service which the creative artist can do for industry is at those moments when he yokes his talent to the problems of the applied arts—abstract painters designing prettily abstract carpets, and so forth. I do not suppose they have any radical objection to the artist turning his hand to this kind of work if it interests him, but they feel that this is not the point. I agree with them.

Their idea is that the creative artist, given the use of industrial facilities, could actually stimulate technology to fresh growth. The gift of the artist for "creative play", still more, his gift for doing things the wrong way round, just to see what will happen—these, they feel, could supply a valuable point of growth.

This may sound a somewhat terrifying way of setting about things—a blanket recommendation that bulls should always be let loose in china shops. I wonder if such is the case? One of the chief defects of applied technology is that it tends to exist within certain intellectual barriers. The root invention, the root discovery—these create their own terms. Those who exploit such discoveries after the breakthrough has been made, tinker with small things, alter the settings on the dials, but seldom tackle any problem *ab initio*. It is well known, for example, that the real practical usefulness of the "pure" mathematician is his ability to think in radical if unspecific terms, to take a problem from the very beginning. And, to descend to a somewhat humbler level—in fact to the level of puzzles and old-fashioned detective-stories—we see that what the creators of these conundrums have in mind is to set up a convincing, but completely false set of terms, within which the puzzle cannot under any circumstances be solved. We can only find the solution by leaping the barriers they have made for us.

The intellectual leap forward of the sort I am talking about is something which much resembles, just because it is capricious, the creative gift of the painter or sculptor. Any industrialist who undertook to shelter and encourage a rogue elephant of this kind would, of course, be taking a gamble. But then industry has already gambled on the mathematicians, the logicians, and the philosophers (these last have found their *métier* in preparing programmes for computers). And often it has won. So why not take a chance on the *avant-garde* artist?

27. PLAIN-MAN-ISM IN ART

Learned men—historians and scientists, for example—have long been familiar with *la haute vulgarisation*: a phrase which means, very roughly, the unveiling of academic mysteries to those who are not academically inclined. A glance at an assortment of learned journals concerned with very different disciplines shows that on the whole familiarity has bred contempt. Over and over again one finds the same accusations being hurled at popularizing works. It seems that shoddy half-truths are constantly being rooted out by these dedicated reviewers, only to spring up again in time for a fresh assault in the next issue.

I find it hard not to feel a twinge of sympathy for the numerous authors who try to present the latest scientific or historical research in terms which the layman can understand. There is, after all, a real case for writing books of this kind. Often, they make available fascinating material which is otherwise almost inaccessible except to the specialist. And I think that, in recent years, the standard of popularization has gone up very much. Yet the experts will always (and in a way rightly) be dissatisfied, will always find that some important shade or subtlety of meaning has been missed.

If it is proper to remain on one's guard against *la haute vulgarisation* in the academic sphere, perhaps it isn't too priggish or too silly to feel uneasy about its recent manifestations in the field of modern art. More and more I wonder if the cultural programmes on television, the articles in shiny magazines, and all the rest of the mechanism whereby the so-called *avant-garde* is brought to the wider public, are functioning as they should.

One might well begin by asking oneself whether they need to function at all. On the whole, modern art is now surprisingly accessible even outside London. The machinery by which it is "explained"—or so one might argue—acts as a barrier and not as a bridge. It prevents the spectator from confronting the work of art squarely and honestly. Modern artists submit—though somewhat sheepishly—to this process of exegesis. After all, it is an accolade, a mark of celebrity and success. But I doubt if many of them feel at all happy about it. I'd feel sorry for any painter who painted merely so that the explainer could take over—and also extremely doubtful of the worth of his talent. Creators like to feel that they communicate directly.

Nevertheless, a wide public remains hungry for explanations. It is a mixture of curiosity and nervousness which creates this hunger. Somehow, after all the revolutions of the past 60 years, many people have lost the courage to approach contemporary art directly. They feel in need of guidance, and the guidance they want is not so much that of the critic as that of the professional vulgarizer. The critic, I think, assumes that he is talking on level terms to an audience which is quite likely to talk back. His weapons are the weapons of argument. He is probably more interested in the work, the individual object, than in the surrounding *ambiance*, or in the personality behind it. The vulgarizer, on the other hand, is the priest of a mystery, the interpreter of an oracle. He is not, basically speaking, talking on level terms, though he may pretend to be doing so. He is the man who knows, spoon-feeding the man who doesn't know. Willingly or unwillingly, he is talking down to the audience.

This is obviously a difficult situation to occupy, and also not a very healthy one. The diseases of vulgarization are perhaps best studied on television. One of the commonest might be described as "plain-man-ism". The cicerone becomes curiously reluctant to commit himself to the work he is explaining. "*Some* people", he says blandly, "think Mr. X is the most talented sculptor under 40 now working in Britain." The inflection is so ironical you think that some fairly sharp critical comment is to follow. But no, nothing of the sort. Mr. X and his work are trundled on to the screen, and smoothly and noncommittally displayed. The usual explanation is that both sculptor and sculptures are here being treated as "news", and it therefore behoves the commentator to keep his distance. But can art be treated in this way, and remain undimmed? In effect, the audience enters into a kind of conspiracy with the commentator—an agreement that this, though momentarily amusing, is not to be taken at all seriously, that it is something which deserves to occupy the mind only for a moment, and which can then be replaced on the same level of triviality by some other item of "news"—a fat-stock show, or the result of a yacht-race.

More dismal, perhaps, are some of the more elaborate attempts to explain. Here the condescension is inherent in the method of presentation. As I understand it, the assumption is that the audience for a programme of this sort, though "interested" is not informed. "Interested" means, roughly speaking, prepared to switch on in the first place. Two roads of assault are used—the "human touch" and the "gimmick". The first consists in the attempt to persuade the audience that, however odd the objects on the screen, the man who made them is actually "one of us". Hence those familiar cosinesses, those wasted moments where we see (for example) a well-known painter drifting aimlessly round his studio like a goldfish in a bowl, making a cup of tea, smoking a cigarette, fiddling with a piece of string. I invent the occasion, but the pattern is familiar. The second stage is quite the opposite. It lies in the tendency to seize on whatever is tricky, odd, *out* in*ré* the work under discussion, and to play it for all it is worth, irrespective of the artist's intention. "Is it *really* made entirely of beer-cans?" says the interviewer in his best mock-innocent voice. "Is this bit *really* meant to go round and round? Does this built-in geiger-counter *really* work?" Infuriatingly enough, intermixed with this there are usually moments of real power, where we get a glimpse of the sort of job which a medium like television can do. The imaginative juxtaposition of images—a sculpture compared with a plant form, an abstract painting suddenly replaced on the screen by the everyday image from which it derives—these can light up a difficult work of art, and plunge even an uninformed viewer rewardingly and excitingly *in medias res*.

Despite the evident dangers and difficulties, modern art has urgent need of its apostles—whether on the small screen, in the cinema, in the glossy magazines, or in the colour supplements. But—with certain admitted and honourable exceptions—it seems to me a great pity that these apostles do not rate the capacities of the audience a little higher. At the moment, we need more emphasis on the adjective in *la haute vulgarisation*, and less on the noun.

28. ON PICTURES TO LIVE WITH

"Oh, I wouldn't want to live with that!"—this is a cry I seem to hear (or overhear) fairly often at exhibitions of modern art. And sometimes—especially when I visit certain New York collections, or look at photographs of them—I myself wonder how anyone *could* live with such things. But at this point let me pause for a second to make it clear that whether or not one can "live with it" is not really the true criterion of a work of art. No one, after all, proposes to take up residence with the Michelangelo frescos in the Sistine Chapel.

Nevertheless, the fact that "livability" has become a point of praise or dispraise is really something to do with social and economic history, as much as with the history of the visual arts. From the seventeenth century onwards, the prosperous bourgeoisie began to play a leading role as patrons of art. First in Holland, later in France and in England, pictures began to be judged by new criteria—for the contribution they made to the bourgeois interior. At the same time, the whole system of art-patronage began to alter. Art, too, became a commodity, and was dealt with by the new class of merchants in the same way that they dealt with other articles of trade. When works of art began to be valued as private possessions, rather than as public statements, the profession of art-dealer became established.

Though we know that things were once otherwise, we find it hard to accept the knowledge. All around us, we find the remains of the old economic system which (as we now begin to realize) is slowly passing away. One particularly conspicuous piece of lumber is the art trade, which, in its essentials, has hardly changed since the seventeenth century. Indeed, art-dealing as a profession has altered a great deal less than other forms of trade. The great art-dealers are still, for the most part, the unregulated individualists of our present form of society. There is something rather splendid about this—the risks taken, the coups made, the free exercise of taste, knowledge, and judgment, and (above all) the intimate relationship which still exists between the great art-dealer and his client.

Nevertheless, the art trade has something anachronistic about it, and the fact that it is slowly falling out of step with the times leads in the end to a certain falsity—something which affects our own relationship to the work of art. Let us look for a moment at what seems to be the art dealer's greatest strength: the intimate relationship with his clients which I've just mentioned. How can this be maintained under modern conditions? Too often, the whole thing has about it an air of play-acting. The client is no longer a man indulging his own free choice, giving rein to his caprices, and putting his hand in his pocket to pay for them. The remaining private clients, with rare exceptions, buy works of art as they would stocks and shares; guidance as to values is all they require. Even more important are the others—the emissaries of the museums. A museum employee must necessarily buy in quite a different way from a private collector. Caprice is the one thing he can't afford—and for him, the traditional courtesies of the art world are an agreeable pretence, but no more. I have, it is true, known curators who bought more like nabobs than like scholars and servants of the public. I cannot feel they were doing their jobs properly.

But there is another and more important point, one which applies to modern art in its newest and most extreme manifestations. For the dealer in modern art, there is a twofold relationship—not only must he look after his clients: he must cope with the artists whose work he exhibits. Dealers in modern art are frequently blamed for their promotional antics. These often seem to me the product of desperation. Because he is what he is, the dealer still tends to think of the work of art in bourgeois and mercantile terms, as a thing whose *raison d'être* is to be sold to somebody. A Watteau is a "product", and a Terborch is a "product". and a Hogarth is a "product" in just this sense (and I mean no disparagement in saying so). But many works by modern artists hardly fill the bill—instead, we must think of them as events, as things which happen, as activators.

For this reason, they often have greatest validity in a museum context, or as part of an exhibition. They demand our whole selves in a way which is foreign to domesticity. Indeed, the modern works which I most admire are, often, I suspect, those which I would be least prepared to share a living-room with. The kind of response which they draw from me is one which I know I can't produce all the time. Indeed, it's possible to go further than this. I have one friend who roundly declares that he couldn't bear to live with a masterpiece of any kind, and that all he now covets is the purely superficial and decorative. Masterpieces, he feels, are not to be sullied with too great a familiarity. Either they make us feel uncomfortable, or else we become so accustomed to them that we commit the sacrilege of forgetting their greatness.

This attitude perhaps foreshadows things to come. Masterpieces of all kinds are, in any case, slowly but surely removing themselves from the sphere of commercial competition. And we feel, I think, a greater and greater repugnance to the idea that a work of art which is important to all mankind should be detained for the private pleasure of a single individual—ownership, in this sense, is a thing we can no longer stomach. This reflects the growing democratization of the society we live in. As I've said in an earlier article, no one wants to abolish the private ownership of works of art—at least, no one in their right senses. And no one, I think, wants to persucute the art-dealer, or to denigrate the services which a middleman of sensibility can still perform.

But the dislocations which we see in the art market, and its all too evident absurdities, reflect the fact that we ourselves haven't yet succeeded in establishing the true role of the work of art in modern society. It's clear enough, for instance, that a Dutch genre painter and Miss Bridget Riley are doing two entirely different jobs, and from this it follows that we shouldn't try to use their work in exactly the same way. Art, so it seems, doesn't always occupy the same area in our lives, or perform the same services for us. As society develops, the artist shifts his ground. We must be prepared to shift with him.

29. CHANGING ATTITUDE TOWARDS TASTE

A well-known English collector, now dead, often threatened to write a book which was to be called *Le Mauvais Goût à travers les Ages*. In it, he meant to discuss and illustrate all those works of art that, after a lifetime of reflection, struck him as uniquely hideous. I wonder what kind of reception the volume would have received? For the whole subject of good taste and bad is one which makes a modern audience very nervous. True, there is a large and eager market for glossy picture books about interior decoration. But I often think that their appeal is basically a pornographic one. At any rate, they have a flavour of forbidden fruit. And one of the most interesting things about them is the way in which they treat good taste as simply a branch of snobbery—on a level with snobbery about birth or money.

This degradation of an idea which was originally noble is, of course, highly symptomatic of the attitudes which we currently adopt towards the visual arts. The issue is really a twofold one. It concerns both a change in taste and a change in our attitude towards the idea of taste. We sometimes forget, I think, the very radical way in which our preferences have altered during the past 60 or so years, and the complexity of the factors which have led to this revolution. One interesting way of proving this is to look at the commemorative catalogues of the three great exhibitions of Greek art which have been held in this century—the Burlington House exhibitions of 1904 and 1946, and the exhibition held in Basle in 1960. I choose this example because, after all, our ideas about taste are so inextricably bound up with our experience of classical art, and because, in what one might call the "Age of Taste", classical art was the standard which pundits referred to.

The catalogue of the 1904 exhibition shows us a world in which conventional ideas of "classicism" still ruled supreme. The archaic period is entirely neglected. Little distinction is made between Greek objects and Etruscan ones, originals and copies. The next exhibition shows us a transformation which has progressed far, but which is not yet quite complete. Of the three shows, this was by far the most eclectic. The objects shown ranged in date from the earliest times to Greek peasant embroideries of the eighteenth century. The exhibition committee seem to have wavered between a taste for blandness, and a taste for the stylized, the hieratic, the expressive. In the exhibition of four years ago, we find that this latter taste is almost wholly triumphant. The vast bulk of the objects exhibited were of the archaic period or earlier. The whole picture of Greek civilization which the show gave was unrecognizably different from the impressions which would have been received by a visitor to the one of fifty-six years before.

It would be easy to jump to conclusions—to say that this change merely represents an alteration of standards, a veering of fashion from one thing to another. And, in a sense, this is true. It is fascinating, for example, to see what fakes each of these exhibitions contained—or would it be more tactful to say what suspect objects the organizers included? In 1904, there are certain bronzes of an exaggeratedly feminine grace, certain marbles (even) of a rather insensitive blankness. In 1960—without having examined the objects but only the photographs—one would incline to query a handful of things which are too easily, too conveniently assimilable to our ideas about "modern art".

The presence of these few doubtful objects makes an interesting point—which is that of the vitality of taste itself, if by taste we mean simply the necessity to *choose*. Even without meaning it, these exhibitions each present a view, an idea about Greece which is also a commentary on the twentieth century. Forgeries are always interesting because they present taste in its most concentrated form—they are the index of prejudice and expectation.

But this is not the only issue at stake. The difference between the first exhibition and the third is as much a difference of knowledge as a difference of choice or liking. At Basle in 1960 were shown many Greek objects of types which were unknown even to scholars in 1904. If our view of Greek art has changed it is a change which has been forced upon us by circumstances. The implications are far-reaching. For it is the expansion of knowledge, the accumulation of facts, which as much as anything else, has corrupted "good taste" in the narrow sense. What has taken place is a kind of cultural explosion. Instead of one set of absolutes, we have many.

What I am trying to say is that taste in the old sense failed because its "absolute" standards were really only another sort of pragmatism. It was the examples which suggested the rules, and not the rules the examples. But now there is an embarrassment of examples.

30. ON OBJECTS OF UTILITY

I often wonder at what point the utilitarian object sheds its more mundane connotations and becomes a work of art. Many people, hearing me say this, would reply that certain objects can be both useful and beautiful, and that there's no need to stop using them simply because they appeal to us aesthetically. Agreed. But when does the balance of our appreciation tip from one side to the other? Let me give some examples. The collector of Sèvres who eats off it every day must be a rarity (granted that collectors of Sèvres are a rare enough species anyway). Some collectors of porcelain do, however, like to put their treasures to use on special occasions. Yet they—and we, if we are their guests—remain conscious that works of art are here doing a service from which they have, for the most part, long since retired.

Yet in choosing Sèvres—or Chelsea or Meissen, for that matter—I'm not really going straight to the heart of the problem which I wanted to raise. These luxurious porcelains are really not works of art in the strict sense, but decorative objects; that is, if we leave aside such things as the figurines modelled by Kaendler. What I'm thinking of are those much simpler and severer objects which strike us as having all the authority of abstract sculpture, and often something more besides. Sung porcelains, as connoisseurs of Chinese art never tire of reminding us, were regarded as "major" rather than "minor" from the very beginning. And indeed, the pleasure we get from a masterpiece by one of the Sung potters has almost everything to offer us that we expect from a major work of art. Subtlety is there as well as fine proportion. The combination of shape and glaze which meets in a celadon bowl satisfies us both emotionally and intellectually.

This is still more the case with certain objects from the ancient world. The art of the Cyclades, for example, is currently enjoying a great vogue among collectors. These objects—figurines, beakers, lamps, bowls—are made from the creamy marble of the islands. When we look at them, we feel, I think, that no special line of division can be drawn between the figurines and the rest. All the objects have the same care for proportion, the same astonishing formal inventiveness. They appeal to us, it is true, because they seem to anticipate modern art. At the same time, they appeal to us because the time when they were made is so unimaginably remote. But even when we've stripped away everything in our response which seems literary or sentimental, we are left with something which can only be a tribute to the artistic qualities of the objects themselves.

The same response can also be aroused by objects from ages less remote—but not all of them. This piece of kitchenware suddenly stands forth as a masterpiece, but not that; this fragment of armour, but not another. We owe this fresher, subtler response to our surroundings very largely to the modern movement in the arts. When modern artists rejected figuration, they brought about a revolution more drastic than even they had anticipated. What they did, in fact, was to devalue the content of a work of art while calling our attention to its formal qualities. Utilitarian objects seldom have much need of "content" in this sense, and when they do have it, they become pretentious. The anecdotal sideboards, the allegorical china vases, which the Victorians created are enough to prove that. But quite simple utilitarian objects can often compete with painting and sculpture when it comes to sheer beauty of line and subtlety of proportion.

A great Mondrian, for example, finds its true affinities among Sung porcelains and Cycladic marbles. It has far more in common with these than it has with the majority of other paintings—with a Rubens, or a Courbet, or a Watteau. Perhaps the temptation is to rush in and condemn abstract art for this reason; to say that since it can teach us no more than the so-called "minor arts", there is something missing; that art has here been deprived of half its power.

But let me shake the kaleidoscope of argument, and arrange the pattern in a different way. We may assert, and I believe very justly, that it is abstract art which has taught us to look at certain objects in this way. Paintings do not always respond to existing standards, existing ways of perception—instead, they create their own. It is abstract art which has accustomed us to thinking abstractly. And what a lot we have learnt from it! It has stripped the scales from our eyes where many objects of common use are concerned; and it has taught us to see things in nature itself which were previously invisible.

If we make good use of what the great abstract painters have to teach us, it is possible to find an order in the world which we never knew existed. Not only do we see the aesthetic qualities or order and pattern and colour, we are aware of a great reservoir of aesthetic experience, waiting to be tapped. Our response to the arts is one of the ways in which we integrate ourselves with our surroundings, and make them part of ourselves. The added range and subtlety which modern art brings to our perceptions—if we allow it to do so—is one of the great justifications of the revolution in painting and sculpture which has happened during the twentieth century.

Those household gods, those bits of jetsam from the past, which we sometimes too idolatrously worship—these are the outward signs of a new power to see things clearly, to appreciate them for what they are without too much reference to what status the reference books accord them. And yet, there is a kind of *caveat* which must be made. Why is it that the shape which is fittest for use is often (though not always) the one which strikes us as being the most beautiful? Is the aesthetic sense itself linked, however deviously and atavistically, to our sense of the useful?

31. OBJECTS AND THE PRIVATE MEANING

I have always enjoyed reading manifestos—at any rate, those which concern themselves with the arts. No one expects total good sense or total objectivity from these documents—they are hasty reports from the battlefront. The latest manifesto I have read is one which arrived from America last week—a pamphlet published in connection with the "Hard Centre" exhibition, which is now being held at the Thibaut Gallery in New York. The exhibition is an attempt to push yet further the explorations of those artists who experiment with "real" objects. It includes such things as a real non-functioning flashlight, real fuse boxes, and an "all-black construction in which a shovel is hung by a rope from a board which is posed over a heap of charcoal". The genre is not unfamiliar, but the pamphlet (which is by Nicolas and Elena Calas) sets out to give it a new urgency. It begins with the words: "*it is not art. it is not painting. it is not sculpture. IT IS.*" The moderately experienced reader of manifestos will, of course, recognize that this is more a ry to be heard than a piece of solid information.

Yet the joint authors do have something to say for themselves once the preliminary trumpeting is over. Their contention is that "a new generation of artists is shifting the emphasis from the subject to the object". I don't think that I falsify their argument by summing it up in a series of extracts: "Man can no more create than can serpents and beasts, he can only appraise objects in their context. Let us assume, however, that we neither know the nature of things nor understand the order in which they are set. . . . Work-in-progress and the end-in-view have become one. It is fitting that the workman's tools—viewed as implementing action—should be included in a work, though now dissociated from labour. . . . Non-function can be as much a part of aesthetic pleasure as the lifelessness of stone. . . . When we do not strike a match to light a cigarette or to see in the dark, but strike it 'just so'—without rhyme or reason—reflection on the phenomenon may be enlightening."

Yet the new art (or anti-art) has failed to convince some of the most impassioned supporters of modernism. You don't have to be a fogey to dismiss it as so much moonshine. Nor, it must be admitted, does the kind of thing which the Calases are talking about always live up to its own publicity. Two dangers always threaten it. One is habit—the habit of making "fine art". Two of the artists in the Thibaut Gallery exhibition—Jasper Johns and Jim Dine—were recently included in an exhibition at the I.C.A. It was their so-called "painterliness" which came under fire from their British colleagues. The other danger is the danger of total desiccation. With certain objects, the mere description is enough. The recipe has more flavour than the dish. The new style is not free; it walks a dangerous tightrope.

Indeed, the word "style" is probably the wrong one to use. For it seems to me that the tentative phase of Pop Art is being succeeded by a radical attempt to change the functions of art. Many of the latest "paintings" and "sculpture" in England and America are best thought of as crude and inefficient experimental machines. If we treat them as works of art we are on the wrong track—they do not invite that kind of contemplation. Instead, they are there to act; clumsily they try to make us come to terms again with our environment. It is sometimes said that modern living is far too full of objects, that objects crowd in on us, jostle us, hardly allow us room to breathe. Perhaps in sheer self-defence, we shut one of the most important aspects out of our minds: I mean, we are reluctant to see objects as physical presences, we prefer to treat them as symbols. One good way to illustrate this process is to quote a passage from a youngish contemporary poet, George MacBeth:—

> When the sick wish returns
> For the lost country, the dream-Scotland grief
> Was noble in, I clutch at *things*, plain things
> I've lifted to symbols: compasses, a brooch,
> Photographs, draughtsman's T-squares, opal-rings.
> My faith's planted where prayers can't encroach.

The trouble here is that the things listed don't remain "plain" at all. Before we or the poet can look at them, they've slid over the border of subjectivity into being symbolic.

And MacBeth's poem hints at another point—one on which I suppose most people would agree. Not only do we make objects more manageable by turning them into symbols, but the symbolism itself is private. There is little common ground. The artists of the past could use symbols and know that they had more or less the same meaning for every spectator. The most obvious example would be the fixed symbolism in medieval religious painting. Now the artist can take nothing for granted. He cannot even be sure that we will accept the object he uses simply as and for itself. He has to make sure that we look at it as an object, without imposing private meanings. It often seems that the *avant-garde* artist is toiling away at something very simple. All he wants to do is to reach the point where Chardin began.

The defiant, hysterical desperation which colours the latest developments in art suggests that the return to the figurative is not going to be nearly so easy as people once imagined. The thing itself, the uncaring lump of brute matter, tends to hover tantalizingly just out of reach.

32. THE CULT OF THE SIMPLE IN MODERN ART

"Less is more"—the famous dictum of the architect Mies van der Rohe enjoys an enormous, unquestioned authority. But who really thinks that the Seagram Building is simple? Or take the following—a set of statements by the American painter Ad Reinhardt: "There is just one art, one artlessness, one painting, one painterless, one effortlessness. There is one difference, one sameness, one consciousness, one nothingness, one rightness, one indivisibility, one diversity, one essence, one fineness. There is just one thing to be said, just one thing that cannot be said. . . ." It seems to me that modern simplicity needs to be looked into.

The interesting thing about the cult of the simple in modern art is the fact that, on the whole, it is divorced from the European tradition. It is here, indeed, that one might locate the break with the past. The duty of the work of art, right up to comparatively recent times, was to be elaborate. Think, for example, of a medieval manuscript—the *Trés Riches Heures* of the Duc de Berry. In this we are aware of the fact that craft and art are hardly to be separated—the artist *must* be elaborate, in order to demonstrate his skill (which is also his merit). I chose the *Trés Riches Heures* because here, in every sense, is a work of art which presents us with a complete world. The miniatures reflect the real world, but are divided from it; they invite us to move from one cosmos into another.

In the Far East, however, the work of art is traditionally something which offers, not a different world, but a heightening of sensibility within the one we already occupy, so that the vision which we already have becomes clearer. I am thinking, in particular, of the Chinese and Japanese cult of ceramics. I am also thinking of what is called "tea taste" in Japan—the objects, the buildings, the gardens even, which are connected with the cult of the tea-ceremony. It is only recently that we in the west have even begun to try to understand the true nature of Japanese taste.

What the Japanese seem to have been the first to explore is the notion that the aesthetic sensation can be enjoyed and analysed for its own sake, and not in connection with some other idea—religion, for instance, or kingship. I have just come across a beautiful book called *Forms in Japan*, published in Honolulu. In it some characteristic Japanese objects are analysed by Yuichiro Kojiro, who is a well-known Japanese architectural critic. The translator reminds the reader in a foreword that "since Japanese thinking is essentially aesthetic, the Japanese language has evolved non-logically". Kojiro, in fact, proceeds by an elaborate but arbitrary system of classifications—under the main heading "Forms of Unity" there are to be found various sub-heads—forms of continuation, forms of union, forms of collection, forms of arrangement, forms of enclosure. And each of these sub-categories is referred to specific objects—forms of union, for instance, include objects which are tied (an ornamental knot); or bound (a rush blind); or woven (like a basket); or braced (like a ladder). The result is strange—we are precipitated into a world where nothing is special, and everything is special; where the humblest things can provide the subtlest pleasures.

It is natural that we in the west should suddenly begin to find notions of this kind exceedingly attractive. There are two reasons for it. One is that works of art have gradually been deprived of just those extraneous functions which I have been talking about: I mean that they no longer serve a symbolic or didactic purpose. For the very first time in the history of western civilization, the work of art is truly gratuitous, and it has now to find a new justification which is based upon that very gratuitousness. The other reason is that in a sense the artificiality of the modern environment, its abstract, inhuman quality, leads to a defensive concentration on the idea of sensibility.

As a result, a new and self-conscious relationship between the spectator and the work of art is created. Anyone who wants to test this assertion might like to go and look at the pictures by John Plumb which are currently on view at the Axiom Gallery. Plumb is a very distinguished abstract artist, and this show is, I think, his best so far. The pictures, however, are of a kind which deliberately shuts out any response by the aesthetic one. They are fields of colour. The central area—a rich, velvety, but unvarying expanse of one tone—is given dynamism by the intrusion of other, contrasting and complementary colours at the extreme edges of the canvas. These look as if they are trying to force their way to the centre, but they have not got very far. Nevertheless the main colour strains against them, seems to be trying to crush them finally against the edges of the picture.

I find the effect of these pictures to be as complex as they themselves are apparently simple. The colour produces a certain sort of sensation—impossible fully to describe, like all colour perceptions. But there is also a part of me which responds at one remove; which responds to the response; which is interested, so to speak, by the capacity of appreciation which has been aroused, rather than by the picture itself. I am trying to think of a comparison which will explain what I mean. Perhaps the following (symbolic rather than logical) will do: what the pictures remind me of in those moments when, speaking in public, one becomes aware of the self that is speaking as a being divided from one's usual personality, a being who is almost a stranger.

I am not altogether sure that I like this feeling of estrangement, of alienation, which the "purely aesthetic" work of art tends to give men. It sends a chill to the heart. The Japanese—the inventors, as I have said, of this sort of response—escape from the difficulty because their particular kind of sensibility, and even the majority of the opportunities they have for exercising it, lead them back to nature and to natural things. We, with our newer cult of simplicity, seem to have taken over the mechanics of the thing, but we apply them differently. Our simplicities are more abstract, just as our civilization is more mechanized. There may be occasions when less turns out to be less.

33. FOLK ART AND HIGH ART IN COMPARISON

A colleague, reviewing the *Arts of the Commonwealth* exhibition at the Festival Hall, condemns the contemporary Indian paintings, shown upstairs in a room of their own, and praises the Indian folk-art which is part of the main display. Who am I to disagree with him? The Indian paintings do seem to me, for all their sweet romantic charm, weak echoes of things with which we are already familiar in Europe—wavering reflections in a tarnished mirror. The folk-art—toys and basket-work in particular—is enormously itself, and could have come from no other place but India. Here is the innocent intricacy of India; here, too, is the Indian gaudiness. These objects are the modern representatives of a great artistic tradition. We catch in them echoes of the much more magnificent objects which were once made for the rulers and princes of India.

But already I have begun to hint at my objections to what my colleague had to say. If I understood him rightly, he was praising these specimens of folk-art as being not only more exciting to look at than the "high art" of Indian contemporary artists but as being in some way morally superior. This I am unwilling to concede. It seems to me that we tend to sentimentalize the folk-artist. To return to the example which I have already chosen—that of the folk-art of India—I feel that what we see in it is not a new beginning but a ghost-like lingering—the half-life or twilight of a culture.

The study of folk-art, as opposed to primitive art, seems to prove that to a large extent it depends for its vitality upon the "high art" to which it is related. I have referred before in these columns to the inexorable logic shown by certain archaeological series—first, the fully-elaborated type-specimen; then the gradual degeneration of form. Folk-art, too, shows a logic of this kind; a simplification or reinterpretation to suit cruder purposes and less cultivated minds. If a not particularly exotic example is needed, we have only to look at the evolution of French provincial furniture. This, for the most part, is dependent on the great Parisian cabinet-makers. But the full elaboration of the Louis XV style is interpreted in "folk" terms—

which means, chiefly, that French provincial furniture is made by methods which are much simpler and much less refined. There is no veneering; carving takes the place of inlay, and so forth. What is, perhaps, a little astonishing is the way that metropolitan fashions become fossilized in the furniture of the French provinces. Dated specimens show that furniture in Louis XV style was being made as late as the outbreak of the First World War by country craftsmen. And this was due to a living tradition; not to a dead revivalism.

It cannot be claimed, however, that provincial furniture of this kind had any hope of providing a new basis for design after the excesses of the nineteenth century. The reasons for this are not too hard to see. In the remote provinces of France, there still existed cabinet-makers who had remained at some distance from the techniques of industrialism. Furniture of the kind I am thinking of was made by methods which had not altered since the early eighteenth century, when the Louis XV style first came into fashion. But this, by the opening of the twentieth century, was exceptional. Furniture had already, for many years, been turned out by industrial techniques. A great deal of it remained ugly and shoddy enough, even when it, too, paid tribute to the golden days of Louis XV. But amid the shoddiness lay the seeds of the future—a future when design would at long last come to terms with the industrialism.

This case is not so far from the Indian one. India is a country at the very beginning of her industrial revolution, and not at the end of it. We need to remind ourselves how little life has changed for the vast mass of her people. The folk-culture which produces the delightful objects we see at the Festival Hall remains a rural rather than an urban one. Even if the objects which we see are actually produced in cities, the context and customs to which we can refer them are not citified. But we must necessarily suspect that this culture has been deprived of its main source of nourishment. The princely patrons have gone. The traditional "high art" of India had already begun to sicken when the British established their domination in the eighteenth century. By the middle of the nineteenth century it was, to all intents and purposes, dead. We cannot expect new aesthetic inventions which spring directly from the folk-context. This is not the way that things have happened before.

In fact, Indian civilization has now to start the task of remaking itself in a changed context. The paintings we see in the Festival Hall may strike Europeans as unexciting, but we should not be too hard on them. They are the product of a struggle which is cruel enough—a struggle to find a way by which the Indian artist can reintegrate himself with an India which industrialism must slowly but surely transform. Instead of the prince, he finds the bourgeois; in place of the despotic patron, the bureaucratic one. And, in place of submission in the artist, we discover a disturbing self-consciousness. Consciousness of the self is one of the European gifts to India. If we are to try to localize what seems unsatisfactory about contemporary Indian painting as we now see it—unsatisfactory, that is, apart from sheer imitativeness—it is the lack of a sense of personal identity. Even where a particular painting nearly succeeds, we fail to find in it the urgent egotistical statement which we have taught ourselves to look for.

How is the difficulty to be overcome? Certainly, folk-art is not to be despised as a possible source of inspiration. Central European musicians learned that lesson long ago—it was thus that Smetana, Janacek, and Dvorak learned to forge a new and valid kind or artistic creation. But the culture of the folk is heady stuff, as both the world of music and the world of art have learnt in our epoch. An artist like Jamini Roy—one of the best of contemporary Indian painters—lies only just this side of fancy dress.

The truth is that art has to rise out of the existing circumstances; it cannot be imposed on them. Folk-art, by its very limitations, can rise only a little way. India waits for artists who will speak directly; it also, I suspect, waits for patrons who will accept what is said without flinching from it.

34. ARTISTS AND THE VISION OF NATURE

Looking at Edward Calvert's famous little wood-engraving, "The Ploughman", at Colnaghi's recent exhibition of prints by Old Masters I began to think about the whole question of "nature" and the artist. Calvert's print is a celebration of nature; everything in it seems to blossom and burgeon; the tiny piece of paper is bursting with energy and life. Yet, when one looks at it carefully, one realizes that nearly everything shown in it is governed by a convention of some kind, rather than by what is rather tendentiously called "direct observation".

These conventions all have a single aim—an intensification of the spectator's feelings. The ploughman is built like a hero, the leaves on the trees are huge and sharply distinct, even the tendril which springs from the tree on the left is imbued with a ferocious, knotted energy. The inscription which Calvert placed on the print confirms these observations. It reads: "Seen in the Kingdom of Heaven by Vision through Iesvs Christ our Saviour." In fact "The Ploughman" is a symbolical work, and directness of observation was certainly not the artist's aim. Why then is the print so moving? Why is it impossible to look at certain aspects of the English landscape without remembering it? The answer is that Calvert has achieved a truth to nature which is not representational, which corresponds (perhaps) to some ideal image which we carry with us in our minds.

If we start looking for parallels and contrasts the matter begins both to explain and to complicate itself. Calvert's colleague and friend at the time when "The Ploughman" was created was Samuel Palmer. Palmer knew very well what Calvert was seeking, and wrote to him about another engraving, "The Cider-Press", "I don't set up for a judge, but, like a blind baby feeling for the breast, know the taste of milk, with a somewhat precocious appetite for cream. I find the cream in your *Cider Press*, which, in poetic richness, beats anything I know, ancient and modern." We, in our turn, have an appetite for cream, and find satisfaction for it in Palmer's wonderful visions of Shoreham.

When we try to define the effect which Palmer's drawings of

the Shoreham period have on us, we turn instinctively to Marvell's poem:—

> What wond'rous Life is this I lead!
> Ripe Apples drop about my head;
> The Luscious Clusters of the Vine
> Upon my Mouth do crush their Wine;
> The Nectaren, and curious Peach,
> Into my hands themselves do reach;
> Stumbling on Melons, as I pass,
> Insnar'd with Flow'rs, I fall on Grass.

In this verse, as in Palmer's drawing of "The Magic Apple-Tree" in the Victoria and Albert Museum, we get a feeling that all objects are not only distinct but over-distinct. The landscape seems to hurl itself towards us, clamouring to be experienced, to be known and drained to the uttermost dregs.

Nor are Palmer's pictures and drawings, and Calvert's wood-engravings the only works of art through which we can know this vertiginous sensation. We find it again, for example, in certain Indian miniatures, and more especially in those of the Kangra School. Here the lovers clasp each other as the lightning flashes; here the love-sick lady waits in the midst of a dark wood; here Krishna and his favourite gopi shelter from the rain beneath a single shawl. And again everything is seen with a vision preternaturally distinct, and yet not naturalistic.

The miniatures triumph, just as Palmer does, by twining together two strands. First of all, by showing us every detail with elaborate clarity. The monkeys playing among the branches of the distant trees are as minutely drawn and characterized as the lovers who are the ostensible subject of the picture. Since we do not normally see with such distinctness ourselves, and wish we could, this detail gives us the sensation of heightened awareness. Marvell does something of the same kind when he makes us take his images one by one, as he deliberately enumerates them for us. But there is also the principle of selection and stylization which I have already mentioned—the fact that these shapes, the monkeys on their branch for example, are still only stereotypes cunningly deployed. The minuteness of vision which we think we find is often only a cheat. Our own preconceptions of lushness, richness, beauty, poetry, have been cunningly imposed upon a natural world which is not like that at all.

I realize that the point may not yet be altogether clear.

Perhaps I can enlarge upon it by turning from "vision" pure and simple to the visionary naturalism of science. The most extreme form of this can be found in the drawings which used to be made to illustrate works on natural history. Before the days of photography the artist had to be employed. What was asked of him was at once simple and very difficult—he was required to show *precisely* what was in front of him, no more and no less. Yet these shells, these flowers, these insects—so painstakingly delineated—they carry with them an air not so much of reality but of super-reality (the distinction was to be recognized when someone invented the term "magic realism"). When we hold the real, the identical shell next to the shell in the drawing, the product of nature pales before the product of man. In order to make his drawing the artist has had to comprehend the shell fully. His whole intellect has been engaged. And inevitably such effort leaves its traces. When we look at the drawing, however dull we are, we grasp the structure, the colour, the pattern, more firmly than ever we could from the shell which we hold in our hands. It glitters before us in the cold light of intellectual analysis.

Then, as we look, the reality begins to diminish. It is the shell which we hold that is real, after all. The totality of intellectual commitment is as betraying, and as seductive, as the total commitment of the emotions which Palmer asks of us. The artificiality of this so-called "scientific" approach can be seen if we turn from a seventeenth-century drawing of shells to a bouquet of flowers as painted by Monet. Here the veil of the atmosphere shimmers between us and the intricate forms of petal and stamen. We are now on the brink of being convinced that all we apprehend, or need to apprehend, are the effects of atmosphere and light.

"On the brink of being convinced"—this brinkmanship is indeed the essence of all our attitudes to nature. Is it there at all? We cannot be fully certain, even when we touch the petal, taste the peach, hold up the shell before our own eyes. Even amidst the anti-naturalistic gestures of modern art the obsession with nature remains. We listen to the visionaries, who try to persuade us that nature at its most seductive is only a projection of our own thoughts and desires; we listen to the scientific analysts, who try to persuade us that we can penetrate the secrets of a firmly external reality. Since the discoveries of the Impressionists we have also had to lend an ear to those who want to replace one kind of scientific vision with another, more comprehensive one. But the one thing we can never see whole and complete is ourselves as we stand in nature. This is, I suppose, both one of the reasons for art; and the basic psychological dilemma that plagues the artist.

35. THE GREEKS RECONSIDERED

Today, one is usually thought sentimental if one equates the work of art with the *genius loci*. We have had enough of such fiddle. Canaletto paints Venice itself, and it is therefore permissible to speak of the influence which the city had upon his work. But one meets with faint smiles of disdain if one begins to talk about the "light of the lagoons" and its influence upon Titian. It therefore seems peculiarly dangerous to embark on the theme of ancient Greek art as seen in the context of the landscape, the physical aspect, of the country which produced it. Yet, having just returned from Greece, I find the temptation irresistible.

One must be wary, I think, of assuming that the link between object and landscape is a simple one, even if one assumes that it exists. Part of the fascination of Crete is the weird dissonance between Minoan art and the island as one sees it today. Almost more than any other place I have seen, Crete administers visual shocks—the rhythm of the landscape is subtly wrong, the outline of the mountains boldly simple, yet tense with a slightly sinister energy. To abandon this for the delights of the Iraklion Museum is to change moods almost too abruptly. For however much one may mistrust the authenticity of those "restored" frescos, there remains the honest gaiety of so many of the smaller objects, and especially of the pottery, with its lively designs of sea-creatures and growing plants. The imagination strives and shudders, but something is out of gear.

Yet in other parts of Greece the marriage of object and landscape still seems almost perfect. To visit Amorgos, and then to look at the various prehistoric objects which have been found in the island, and especially at the so-called "Cycladic idols" is to experience a pleasure which is almost mathematical. One term of the equation fits so exactly with the other. The white town on the hill in present-day Amorgos, typically Cycladic with its blindingly bright walls, neat cubical houses, whitewashed pavements, is merely another outcropping of the same force as the one which is embodied in those mysterious marble figures. In both of them there is the same drive towards simplicity. The repetition of form in the statuettes is like the satisfying monotony of Cycladic architecture. The context here was so demanding—the light so pitiless, the rock so hard—that only one response has been possible. As one passes from one Cycladic island to another, one small village or town to another, one develops a kind or architectural hyperaesthesia. Where everything is the same, even a small difference, a small discord, strikes one like a blow. On the island of Siphnos there is an aristocratic little fortified town dating from the Venetian occupation of the fifteenth and sixteenth century, a town which is in many respects astonishingly well preserved, with Venetian details radically simplified by the native spirit of the Cyclades. But the intrusion of tasteless modern concrete jars one severely. I still remember the shock effect of two elegant Ionic columns encased up to the capitals in brown pebble-dash.

But the Cyclades make things a little too easy for the romantic eye and the romantic spirit. For some reason I am reminded of an anecdote which was, I believe, fathered by Maurice Baring. Not having the book to hand, I cannot quote exactly, but, as I recall it, Baring says that one day he was sitting on the Acropolis reading Sappho in the original when he suddenly became aware that someone was reading the book over his shoulder—a modern Athenian, who remarked "It's Greek—but it's in dialect". This story occurred to me more than once, wandering through the National Museum in Athens. Standing before this sculpture or that, I was tempted to murmur "It's Greek—but it's in dialect".

This reaction may perhaps seem the odder because, as everyone knows, modern Greek art is a good deal less distinguished than modern Greek literature. And modern Athens, fascinating as I find it, is not a city which suggests that its inhabitants are greatly gifted aesthetically. Yet the more one looks at ancient sculpture in Greece—or, should I say, the more I look at it—the more one becomes conscious of a national identity which closely resembles the Greeks and the Greece of today. Against this no logical or historical arguments prevail. The link is there.

But it is a strange link. On the whole, it is archaic art which benefits most from being seen on the soil of Greece—perhaps a fortunate circumstance, as it exists in far greater quantity there than elsewhere. It is useful, for example, to be able to pass from the archaic maidens in the Acropolis Museum to the elaborate folk-costumes on display in the Benaki Museum. Somehow their adornment, their slightly naive elaboration of attire, chimes with these later dresses. But there are subtler, more elusive links as well. If one looks at an early kouros, for example, one is conscious that this is sculpture to be "read"—not only that the whole thing is a symbol, but that each separate part is a symbol rather than a literal representation. Thus the muscles of the stomach are signs engraved in the marble, not muscles literally (or even freely) copied. One detects this attitude still even in the commonplaces of Greek life—the formal greetings punctiliously exchanged as part of the concern to establish identity, even with the stranger.

Is it for this reason, too, that the "classical style" itself be comes more, and not less mysterious on its native ground. Greece is the country where people are connoisseurs of water—where every villager prefers his own well or spring to the water in the next village. The distilled style should be as unthinkable as water distilled—and as flat.

36. THE TRUE FUNCTION OF ICONS

Just off the Brompton Road, at the Temple Gallery in Yeoman's Row, is something very unusual in London—a first-class show of Greek and Russian icons, ranging from the twelfth century to the eighteenth. Indeed, this is a country where it is impossible to find any such display in a public gallery, as Tamara Talbot-Rice points out in her introduction to the catalogue. Icons are things which we find it difficult to categorize. An icon is a picture—but at Sotheby's and Christie's you will most frequently find them catalogued for sale among the *objets de vertu*. Many picture-collectors profess to find icons unintelligible or boring. "Poor men's primitives", some people call them.

Yet there are signs that icons are becoming very much sought after, and this exhibition is one of them. The mystique which surrounds the subject is perhaps a little off-putting to the layman. For example, in the catalogue of the exhibition at the Temple Gallery (a very scholarly affair) we are told that "Russian iconography divides the Annunciation into three separate phases. First: The Perturbation and Fear of the Holy Virgin, where the Madonna is shown surprised at the apparition of the Archangel. . . . Secondly, the Perplexity and Prudence of the Mother of God. Thirdly . . . the Consent of the Mother of God, where she is shown making the gesture of acceptance." It doesn't sound very much like any world we know.

But these little pictures, painted to a rigorous formula, carry an immense emotional charge. The Archangel of the Annunciation becomes both impeccably aristocratic and impeccably supernatural as the painter follows the rules laid down for him. The slender Virgin is marvellously touching. The architecture in the background glitters with improbable colours and contradictory perspectives. As we look at this—the scenery for the event—we suddenly realize that it is all descended from the old pagan world, that another place where we see architecture like this is in some of the frescos at Pompeii. It brings home to us the weight of tradition in all icons, even the humblest and most countrified.

Perhaps it leads us to reflect about other things as well—for one thing, about the nature of "originality" in art. We must always remember that it was not the aim of the icon-painter to be original or to invent, in the sense that we now understand these words. For him, painting an icon was not an assertion of his own individuality, but a magical act. He was setting up a field within which powerful forces could operate. If he strayed too far from the accepted model, then perhaps the magic would not happen. The holiest icons were copied over and over again throughout the centuries because it was felt that into each copy there passed some of the virtues of the original. Indeed, some of the most reputed icons were said not to be the work of human hands.

Icon-painters were, however, human, and this led to inevitable changes in their art. Taken to Russia from Byzantium, icons adapted themselves to their new environment. A pair of fifteenth-century Russian icons at the Temple Gallery illustrate the nature of the change. Already, though Constantinople has only just fallen to the Turks, we are conscious of a Russification in the designs and in the colouring. The icon showing "The Entry into Jerusalem" is far more sombre than its Byzantine counterpart would have been. The lines are harsher; the drawing less classical; the colours tell us of a bleaker and more northern climate, with their browns, creams, dull greens and yellows.

If, by contrast, we look at a Greek icon of the "Transfiguration" dating from the sixteenth century, and compare it with something genuinely Byzantine, such as the large "Christ Pantocrator" which dates from two centuries earlier, we are made aware of the effects of the disaster on the whole of the Greek world. The lines are tense with neurotic anguish, there is now something hard and dry about both drawing and colouring. The sixteenth-century icon is the product of a religion and a culture which are anxiously on the defensive, and I find it moving for that reason.

The long continuation of icons, the great range in quality, are the clues to their appeal. Icon painting is both high art and folk art. One category shades so insensibly into the other that we are never certain where to draw the line. The humble village icon can still call the masterpiece "cousin". Such a close bond reminds us of the true function of icons—to be vessels of the spirit. Those which are fine in quality may therefore be the more worthy of the truths which they house, the emotions which they carry; but the rough ones, the products of unskilled village painters, are not necessarily unworthy of the task.

But this in turn means that here is a kind of painting towards which we cannot take up a purely detached and aesthetic attitude. Icons are justly famous for their astonishing combinations of colour. At the Temple Gallery, for instance, there is a very early Russian icon of the Madonna, the Virgin pressing her head to the Child. The two faces are shown against a scarlet background—it rings like metal against the warm, soft tones of the flesh. The combination gives one, it is true, an aesthetic *frisson.* But can one stand apart from the meaning of the icon, and from the romantic aura which surrounds it, as a thing to which for centuries men have attributed mysterious powers? The answer is, of course, that it is impossible to do any such thing.

I am not arguing that icons are only for the Orthodox, or even for professing Christians. What I am saying is that to get the most from these mysteriously beautiful objects, one needs to be in a special frame of mind—one which opens to the mystery. And isn't this, after all, rather an immoral way for an art critic to talk? Doesn't it open the door to aesthetic chaos? Perhaps it does. But here is another question—do we adapt ourselves to works of art, or do we demand that they fit in with our own preconceptions? The oftener I look at such special cases as icon-painting, the more convinced I become that a wary pragmatism is the only answer.

37. THE ARCHITECTURAL IMAGINATION

Architecture is a subject which arouses great passions—witness the current fuss about St. Paul's. And architectural controversies seem to interest a far wider audience than arguments about painting. There are, of course, good reasons for this. Of necessity a building is a public statement—exposed to the gaze of all. Yet architecture is, in a way, much more intimately part of the fabric of our lives than painting or sculpture. With a work of art, we converse. A dialogue grows up between the eloquent object and the attentive spectator. But a building we inhabit. We penetrate to its innermost chambers. We issue from its orifices. It swallows us; it spews us out again.

And then, there is the pragmatism which is imposed on the architect. We no longer, I think, hold tightly to the idea that a building is function and nothing but function. But every building is an attempt to solve a problem. Architecture, on the whole, tends to lack the gratuitous element which we find in painting and sculpture. There are, I know, a few exceptions to this rule—Gaudi's work in Barcelona, for example. But architecture straddles the dividing line between art and craft, between that is created to exist for its own sake and what is made to be used.

Perhaps this complexity is the reason for the unsatisfactory state of our attitudes towards architecture. This is not to say that architecture is neglected as a subject of study, even by the mere amateur, as opposed to the professional. Architectural historians flourish as never before. Pilgrimages are made to study Palladio. Pevsner is to be found on every bookshelf. All of this represents one side of our interest in architecture—a field, we think, where every cultivated man may dabble. But we have our solemn moments about the matter, too. I mean those moments which come to all of us, when we worry about the town-planners, the vandals, the enemies of Hawksmoor or of Wren.

It will be noticed that, in giving this somewhat biased account, I have said little which refers directly to modern architecture. It is still customary to deplore the lack of good modern architecture in England. The truth is a little more cheerful than some Jeremiahs might lead one to suppose. England has some good buildings in a thoroughly contemporary idiom. But it is always right to wish for more. And the whole subject of modern architecture is constantly and brilliantly debated by a handful of excellent specialist magazines. My only trouble is, when by chance I pick up one of these publications, that the terms of the discussion strike me as being so intensely narrow —I almost said, so intensely arid. A room full of architects I find very nearly as unrewarding as a room full of mathematicians.

What seems to me to be missing is some sort of bridge—the bridge which can only be supplied by general ideas. This thought strikes one especially forcibly at a new exhibition which has just been staged by the Royal College of Art. This enterprising show is devoted to the work of an Italian architect who is, as yet, very little known in England. Indeed, by all English standards, Gino Valle is an extraordinary figure—the more extraordinary because his practice does not lie at the centre of things. Valle lives in the small North Italian town of Udine, and most of his work is done in the surrounding district. The photographs and drawings at the Royal College make it plain that Valle is an architect of no mean talent. But what is more interesting still is the fact that all his buildings are so evidently linked by a system of ideas about architecture, ideas relevant not only to the job in hand, but to the whole practice of the art. We expect this dialectic in, for example, a Renaissance architectural theorist, but somehow it seems strange in an architect of the twentieth century.

Obviously this is not the place to enter into a detailed discussion of Valle's ideas. One, however, may be briefly touched upon, and that is his vision of buildings as being "microcosms" —that is, things which reproduce in their own form the order of the universe which surrounds them. This is not an altogether original idea. The ancient Chinese knew it, and Valle shares it with some very distinguished modern architects. But he puts it boldly into action—and it makes artistic sense. We see it appearing, for example, in the strange, harsh Monument to the Resistance, now being built in Udine, where the brickwork piers are deliberately used as extensions of the earth from which they rise. It appears in an elegant savings-bank, where the airy roof-structure becomes a metaphor for "sky".

Or are such ideas, after all, merely fanciful? It might be argued that if the architect is pleased to think in such a way it may do him no harm—but ought to remain a purely private matter. For my own part I do not think so. Broad general assumptions about the nature of architecture are always liable to attack as being impractical and "unscientific". An architect who (like Valle) seems to believe in the medieval concept of the four elements—earth, air, fire, water—is in danger, we might assert, of indulging in mumbo-jumbo. Yet I don't think that these apparently "unscientific" hypotheses are to be lightly dismissed. The best architecture seems to spring from a marriage between the immediate task in hand and the long-cherished intuitions of the man who sets out to complete it. In finding the solution metaphor is a useful tool. As in all the arts, "that" is made to stand for "this" as the intractable pieces of the puzzle are shifted around in the architect's mind. And the spectator understands the finished building all the better for knowing what part metaphor has played in its creation.

PART II

38. ART-HISTORIANS AND OUR OWN PERIOD

Such episodes as the Van Meegeren scandal (about which a new book has just been published) brings into question all our attitudes to the visual arts—and particularly our standards of judgment. The same doubts arise, in a form perhaps less sensational, but certainly no less acute, with the publication of every scholarly catalogue.

For example, in the handsome new Catalogue of Italian sculpture in the Victoria and Albert Museum we see several abrupt changes of fortune. The "Narcissus", now attributed to Valerio Cioli, and the "Leda and the Swan", now given to Vicenzo Danti, were in comparatively recent times considered to be the work of Michelangelo himself, and aroused appropriate sensations of admiration and awe—emotions which we can hardly credit when we look at them now.

The catalogue quotes a letter from Lady Millais (wife of the painter, Sir John Everett Millais, who bought the "Leda" in Italy). In it she describes the initial reaction to the statue: "It is put up in the South Kensington Museum and many sculptors and painters have been to see it, and it is thought not only by Michelangelo but one of the finest things in the world."

Art-historians are not abashed by these misjudgments. They are apt, and maybe rightly, to use them as occasions for defending the real utility of their profession. Van Meegeren, they argue, was far more a justification of art-historical research than a criticism of it. The whole affair shows the necessity of ever-higher standards of factual accuracy, because it is fact which gives sensibility the necessary ballast, and without the best connoisseur is liable to go astray. Only scholarship can protect us against ridiculous errors—otherwise we must expect to be deceived and humiliated by our own preconceptions. If we think we are going to see a masterpiece, we *will* see one—at least for a time. Research maps out for us the fixed boundaries of fact, and it is only within these boundaries that we can allow sensibility its head. But fact itself can never make a masterpiece—a point which some scholars would do well to remember.

The argument, taken thus far, seems to me irrefutable. But it does present a difficulty—instinctively we react against it. When it comes to interpreting the art of our own time we are apt to revolt altogether. Are we right to do so? Can we assume that modern art is its own communication? If we cannot, must we appeal to intermediaries? Again, instinct holds us back. Just as surely as it is possible to prove the necessity of art-historical scholarship when we are dealing with the art of the past, so it is possible to make out a case for the intermediary and yet to show that intermediaries constantly distort and cheapen the art of the present. But here again, we must pause and ask ourselves another question: do we see the individual work of art as "a thing in itself", or do we see it as only a fragment of a larger whole, meaningless unless we also consider the society in which it has its roots and the cultural context which surrounds it? The modern artist would plump for the former alternative.

Avant-garde artists—or the majority of them—seem to think of the work they produce as being an affair of individuals. One, or at the most two, individuals the maker, and the spectator. The extreme attitude is to aver that even the spectator is an irrelevance; that the work of art is a by-product, that what matters is the turmoil within the artist himself. This doctrine is less popular than it was, and has now modified itself into the idea that what matters is the direct confrontation between the spectator and the work of art, which is really the direct confrontation between the artist and his audience.

To talk about "the cultural context" is to be very ill-received. Many artists strenuously resist social glosses or interpretations. Yet, if we project *avant-garde* art into the future, to the point where it becomes the concern of some art-historian yet unborn, we may guess that the moment is sure to come when it will be interpreted in purely social terms. Indeed, it seems to be a characteristic of objects of art that, as the individuality, so to speak, dies out of them in the course of centuries we tend to interpret them more and more as social phenomena. When we turn to the art of Ancient Egypt, or Babylonia, for example, there is almost nothing but this kind of interpretation left.

But perhaps we ought to consider again what exactly it is that the art-historian sets out to do. It can be argued that his task is mainly negative—that however brilliant his perceptions, however direct his intuitions about the nature of the work of art in front of him, all he really does is to guard the rest of us from error. By setting out as exactly as possible the conditions under which the work of art was produced, who commissioned it, and in what circumstances, and with what particular aesthetic ideas in mind, he provides us with a basis for judgment. Yet I can hear art-historians of my acquaintance protesting that this sets too narrow a limit on their role. For there is one side of the task where the line between fact and opinion, evidence, and judgment, becomes difficult to draw—I mean, when they have to deal with the idea of sequence.

This idea is, after all, the very essence of historical thought. We see its utility demonstrated, in crude enough fashion, in some of the work of the pre-historian or archaeologist, where pots and other objects are put "in sequence" for dating purposes. But when we apply the idea of sequence to the work of the individual artist we begin to see that there are many subtleties to be found—from the idea of mere chronological sequence, or "one damn thing after another", we step forward to the idea of creative development, of each new work existing in seminal form in the works which have preceded it, and of the interaction between the unique personality, the solitary creative being, and the whole society which surrounds him and which may, and probably does, alter at a pace different from his own. It is here that the intuitive, uncheckable side of art-history comes into play; and it is here, paradoxically enough, that the art-historian can be most illuminating. As well as setting limits, he opens horizons.

When we turn to modern art we see that things are simpler in one way, and more difficult in others. There is no need for a historian to recreate the context of the work of art for us: we live in that context. And time has not yet simplified it; it impinges on us in all its complexity, all its possible irrelevance. When we call in the intermediary we are really following a counsel of despair—we are confessing that we have no knowledge of our own time, that we cannot interpret it even to ourselves. On the other hand, what we see is incomplete—at least in the terms of the art-historian. The sequence has a beginning, but as yet no end. We may guess what an artist is moving towards, but we cannot know for certain, any more than he can himself. We are tempted to impose too rigid a pattern on the basis of the little that we do know; or else we are tempted to reject all pattern, to look merely for the "shock of recognition". And if this is what we are after, we assume that the intellect plays no part, that the shock and the recognition alike occur on a level which is purely emotion. That is, we are either too timid (and consequently demand interpreters for all things in modern art) or too bold (and refuse them for any).

Modern society is admittedly very complex, and so is the art it produces. There is good reason for accepting help when we need it, as we do from the art-historian when we look at the art of the past. But we accept on one condition—that we recognize that the work of art has its own integrity, and bears its own message. Yet this, again, is not to claim that the message must be regarded as absolute. We are entitled to measure what is communicated by the work of art against our own experience—and against common experience. This is how aesthetic judgments ought to be made—indeed, there is no other way of making them. The communication is direct, but it makes sense only when we put it in context.

39. A VIEW OF ROMAN ART IN PARIS

We talk about the "internationalism" of modern art: often, I think, without considering what the word means. The exhibition which is now being held at the Louvre. *L'Art dans l'Occident Romain*, gives one a chance to look at the topic again. For Roman art was truly international. Throughout the whole empire only one standard was acknowledged—the standard set by classical Greece. Yet Roman art is not really part of a continuous development from Greek times. Its ideas and purposes were often ill-adapted to the classical mould. The exhibition in Paris is in many ways unsatisfactory. The extremely sketchy cataloguing and the presence of certain intrusive objects (such as a fine late Archaic Greek bronze of a goat) reflect the current state of confusion among scholars. Yet the show does have the great merit of presenting us with a large and varied panorama of art throughout the western half of the empire. This turns out to be full of tension and conflict, rather like our own.

Basically speaking, the objects in the exhibition fall into two categories. There are those which speak an official language—which are in a manner which was evidently understood and approved everywhere. These are the things which are closely dependent on Greek sculpture—versions of types invented by Polycleitus, and so forth. The leading characteristic of these is their utter uniformity of style, their finicking craftsmanship, and their coldness. It is these two latter qualities which tell us at once that they are not, and never could be, Greek. We are conscious that these are mandarin works; they have nothing relaxed about them, no spontaneity.

More compelling are the things where classical style is in conflict with something else—either with a subject for which Greek art provided no model, or else with local tradition. Into the first group come the extremely interesting bronzes connected with the circus, such as the group of a retiarius in conflict with a secutor which was found at Autun. The circus bronzes impress not only by their feeling of energy and movement, but by the entirely new system of proportions which informs them. Unlike the "official" works, these are short, stocky, with large heads and thick limbs. The stiff angular poses are quite unlike anything which we find in Greek sculpture. And because these bronzes lay such stress on the equipment of the gladiator, they have a markedly expressionist quality—they project ideas of violence and even of sadism which are quite foreign to the classical ideal.

More interesting still are the objects where local style is in direct conflict with classicism, such as the marvellous little statuette from Neuvy-en-Sullias. This piece is particularly interesting for two reasons. One is that it is signed, and the signature is a Roman one—Scuto. The other is that it is so very un-Roman in appearance. All thoughts of regularity and proportion have been forgotten. The legs are spindly, the torso powerful but unduly long; the tilt of the head is alert yet oddly coquettish. More important still, the actual modelling is counter to all classical convention, the musculature twists and slides on the torso in a way which reminds me of some of Picasso's early experiments. Yet the statuette is not something which could have been made without the idea of classicism. Official art has given the artist something to react against. It has also provided him with a grammar of form, which he now distorts and garbles.

The Roman Empire gave art a greater impulse towards internationalism than the modern network of dealers and travelling exhibitions can provide. Yet anyone who visits the great London galleries must be more and more conscious of style which ignores frontiers. Tachism and the new figuration provide artistic languages which are spoken everywhere. Yet within that context how often one feels that they are spoken either too glibly or too awkwardly, that the idea of style has somehow got between the artist and what he really wanted to do. The extreme slickness of certain French action-painters makes us see that this is a method which they have mastered, rather than one in which they are truly at home. Similarly, it is fascinating to trace the differences between British "pop" painting and its American equivalent. British painting of this sort has an indomitable drive towards narrative. American painting such as that by Rauschenberg and Dine does not feel this impulse at all. Instead we have an emblematic art which makes a nihilist attack on modern society.

The differences and the similarities make me more uneasy than the ones I find in Roman art. In theory, just like the Roman official patrons, I believe that what is sauce for the goose is sauce for the gander—that a principle, such as classicism or modernism, should be more powerful than mere race-memory, or whatever it is which equips an artist with national characteristics of a recognizable sort. Yet it must be acknowledged that very many British artists fail for just this reason: that on some deep level they have failed to reconcile what they want to do with what their temperaments prompt them to achieve. In Turner's efforts to rival Claude, we see a brilliant if rather shrill and uneasy attempt to marry impulse and conviction. With many contemporary British artists the whole enterprise seems to have been hopeless from the start. The will to be modern, the desire to cut an impressive and modish figure on the international scene—these win every time.

All this may sound as if I'm advocating a sort of Little Englandism in the visual arts. Far from it. The ease of modern communications (to cite only one factor) means that artists can no longer remain cosily insulated from one another. But the sophistication of modern art also means that painters and sculptors cannot afford to be simple-minded in the way that certain Gallo-Roman artists were. The *faux-naif* is the most disastrous international style of all.

40. THE FUNCTIONAL ART OF TRIBAL AFRICA

Currently, the Musée des Arts Decoratifs in Paris is acting as host to a superb exhibition of African Art, which is called *Afrique, Cent Tribus—Cent Chefs d'Oeuvre.* It seems a good moment to reassess our responses to primitive sculpture. When we think of African art, there are two things which must be taken into account. One is the part which African sculpture played in the birth of what we now know as Modern Art—the spell which it cast over the minds of such artists as Picasso and Dérain. The other is its role in providing a heritage for the emergent nations of Africa.

The way in which African sculpture was caught up into the modernist revolution tends to condition our responses in ways which are not wholly helpful. We cannot help seeing it through Picasso's eyes, or Braque's—we impose on it preconceptions which were never there originally. Collectors of modern painting find that a few Bambara or Benin pieces help to set off their cherished pictures. But one suspects that African sculpture is used by *avant-garde* collectors merely as background material—that it is seldom looked at for its own sake. There are many collections where the modern pictures are superb, but the primitive sculpture only so-so.

The African attitude is a little different. The new African countries, very properly, think of tribal sculpture as a precious heritage, to be preserved at all costs. It provides, so to speak, a kind of cultural *raison d'être* for the emergence of African nationalism. It is regarded as proof of identity; it justifies, though in retrospect, the organs of the state. This is a heavy burden to lay on objects of art. Sometimes we may be forgiven for suspecting that African sculpture cannot entirely support it.

For, as the organizers of the exhibition in Paris are very much aware, African sculpture began to be corrupted very soon after its discovery. We all know about "airport art". Recently collectors have become very frightened of a subtler form of faking—of the tribal object made to the dealer's order. This mistrust has to some extent been reflected in falling prices at auction. Benin bronzes with a known provenance retain their value, and have even increased it, but the market is suspicious of carvings in wood, however venerable and dilapidated they may seem.

In addition to this, the rising vogue for modern sculpture has tended to push African art out of the public favour. We have begun to see that the qualities which the Post-Impressionists read into African sculpture were after all qualities which sprang from a European cast of mind. African art was an excuse for a certain sort of change, rather than actually the cause of it. Now that we have learnt to accept modern sculpture (an acceptance which was far slower in coming than the acceptance of modern painting) tribal art seems otiose. From being familiar and reassuring, it has begun to seem alien again. And the growth of the science of anthropology has tended to exaggerate this divorce. The things which it tells us about African sculpture and its purposes tend to be the things which we least want to learn.

The real difficulty, I believe, lies in the fact that African art, as much as art in medieval Europe, is the client of religious belief and practice. The organizers of the Paris exhibition put forward the idea that African sculpture is concerned with the concept of "force", which may be paralleled by the Christian notion of grace. Obviously such a notion is apt to bear us into the world of Pascal, rather than that of Picasso. At the very least, it means that we can no longer discuss the art of Africa in purely aesthetic terms, as a matter of exciting relationships between abstract forms. Instead, we must begin to think in terms of a whole culture, of a tribe which is driven by instinct and tradition to express itself in a certain way, for a certain kind of ritual purpose.

It takes an exhibition as well selected as the one in Paris to show that the effort of the imagination which this requires can bring its own rewards to the European spectator. The organizers, as the title they have chosen implies, have picked only one sculpture from each of a hundred tribes. They have preferred the masterwork to the "typical" piece. And they have been very careful to choose objects which are untainted by the European enthusiasm for Africa, and which probably played a part in the life of the tribe which made them.

The objects are simply but perfectly displayed—softly lit against a background of dark blue which melts into the dimness of a Paris November. What does one see as one gazes at them? Primarily a kind of poise, a total unselfconsciousness, such as otherwise only exists among some of the civilizations of antiquity. One is often conscious of the way in which these pieces echo the dignity of Ancient Egyptian art (and the Egypt of the Pharaohs was also a civilization of Africa). These are objects so wholly representative of the mode of living which produced them that we are conscious of no divorce. The tribesman remained a tribesman, even when he became an artist. The creation of a work of art was only a small facet of his activity, and fitted perfectly into the context of tribal life. That life may seem to us bitter or brutish, and the objects show sinister traces of it. We may be forgiven for looking a little askance at the carving from the Wabende tribe over which a slave was killed to mark the death of a chief—the story is not a reassuring one, nor, for that matter, is the sculpture.

But at least, for good or ill, all these objects stand forth as representatives of the role which art can play, not only in the life of the individual but the community. They show us art as a communal necessity, even if they are not "civilized". When we ask the meaning of art, they have an answer, and are not ashamed to give it.

41. MAN AND THE MATERIAL OF ART

"All art is 'image-making' and all image-making is rooted in the creation of substitutes"—thus Professor E. H. Gombrich in his new book, *Meditations on a Hobby Horse.* The sentence sticks in my mind. Of course, Professor Gombrich hedges it about with all sorts of qualifications. And, in general, he argues brilliantly the case for art as visual metaphor. Yet, like all explanations in this field, it seems either too simple or not simple enough. For one thing, it leaves out the idea of the uniqueness of the work of art—the fact that most works of art have a material being which cannot satisfactorily be reproduced or duplicated. In this sense nothing will serve as a substitute for anything.

The beautiful exhibition of sculpture from India and Siam, now on at Spinks, supplies a case in point. For the modern westerner, pieces such as these are both easy and difficult. They are remote in time; they are informed by ideas which most of us find alien. Then again, most of them formed part of elaborate decorative ensembles, and we therefore see them out of context. Yet, in the last resort, it is the direct appeal of each individual piece to the senses which conquers us. And in this case, it simply will not do to murmur a Berensonian "tactile values" and then be on our way.

Indian sculpture triumphs not so much by its feeling for structure as by its feeling for substance—in a word, for flesh. There is one elegant figure in the exhibition where one's eye is drawn at once to the navel—not usually the most expressive part of the human anatomy. Yet the delicate modelling makes us experience our own bodies anew. We are conscious not only of stone made flesh, but of *this* stone. The softness which the carving imparts is a kind of pun—a pun that could only happen through some unique conjunction of image and material.

Perhaps one does not have this feeling so strongly with modern European sculpture. If we look, say, at a bronze like the "Ouragan" by the late Germaine Richier, we are far more interested in the image than we are in the material which embodies it. "Ouragan" is a visual metaphor in exactly Professor Gombrich's sense—a figure which is also a storm. It has such a charge of energy that one feels the wind as one stands in front of it. Much other modern sculpture falls into this category—Elisabeth Frink's new work at the Waddington supplies another example. But the two obsessions—with metaphor and with material—sometimes remain in perfect equilibrium. Henry Moore's reclining women are sometimes like this. We see in them figure and landscape, a tract of flesh and a tract of limestone country, image and thing.

All the same, however the balance is tilted, I believe that one of the very basic things which attract us to the visual arts is the physical solidity with which painting, and especially sculpture, is endowed. There is still, in all of us, the childish desire to touch the very stone that Michelangelo attacked with his chisel. This, I would guess, is still a good though unsubtle reason, for our insistence on the original, our rejection of the copy—even when the copy is as faithful as modern reproductions of sculpture can sometimes be.

But there is something more to it than that. We see it more clearly perhaps in certain exotic styles than in modern art. The Indian and Siamese sculptures on view at Spinks are, as the spectator instantly realizes, the work of men who saw themselves not as something separate and divorced from Nature, but as intimately part of it. For them, there was no firm division between the block of stone and the hand which carved it—only infinite gradations of consciousness. Matter acted upon matter; spirit acted upon spirit. The image was something which pre-existed in the stone, and all that was necessary was to set it free. The subsidiary images which the main one suggests—the way, for example, in which the ornaments adorning several of the Indian figures suggest tropical vines looped round a tree—are quite spontaneous. Yet we are right to read into them a hint of how the continuum works.

By the art criticism of the west, a firm division is now drawn. On this side is placed the active principle—man. On that side is the passive one—the material from which the image must be made. What acts is the conscious or unconscious will—or, more frequently, so critics agree, the two in conjunction. Even so, by introducing the doctrine of "spontaneity", we find ourselves opting for the idea that every work of art contains something unique, almost, indeed, for the paradoxical notion of a shell of idea, but a material essence. Hence the fine distinctions we find ourselves making between the "original" lithograph and the reprint; between the original casting of a Rodin bronze and the aftercasts.

But, whatever disputes there may be about borderline cases, in theory we reject all copies outright. The spirit is not in them. If the eye for a moment accepts those clever reproductions of sculpture which are now sold by the British Museum, the hand recoils. And where the hand recoils, the mind also draws back. I would like not so much to dispute Professor Gombrich's proposition, as to extend it. Art is not only image-making, or at least the plastic arts are not. By making works of art, men come to terms with the intractable nature of matter itself. By freeing the unique image within the block of stone (and this concept may or may not be a romantic and illusory one) we somehow both outflank stone's obdurate stoniness, and yet, in the same moment, affirm our kinship with its ability to endure.

42. IMPLICATIONS OF MAGIC REALISM

Looking through Michel Faré's classic book on French still-life painting—*La Nature Morte en France*—I began to think once again of all the implications which lie hidden in the phrase "magic realism". So many of the pictures which M. Faré discusses and illustrates fall within the scope of this useful yet ambiguous term. There is, for example, a painting by the seventeenth-century artist Lubin Baugin which many visitors to the Louvre will remember with special affection. This painting employs a not uncommon allegorical theme, that of the Five Senses. Arranged on a shallow ledge are such things as a mirror, a chess board, a glass of wine, a bottle with three flowers in it, a loaf of bread, a lute and a pack of cards. It is a small picture, and this enumeration may seem long. Yet it impresses the spectator by the extraordinary air of stillness and tranquility which pervades the whole composition.

The easy explanation is the subtle geometry which underlies the arrangement of the objects—a geometry as severe as that in a Cubist masterpiece. Yet, when we look again, the explanation is not sufficient. The painting has qualities which geometry—even geometry of the subtlest and most skilful kind—cannot account for. One is driven into dangerous and unsatisfactory metaphorical explanations; one runs aground on the shoals of the pathetic fallacy. Quite simply, these quotidian objects seem so enormously sure of themselves. They have an existence denser and more actual than the existence they would have if we saw them in real life.

How is this achieved? How can a representation be more powerful, more "living" (if this is not a paradoxical term to use about still-life) than the objects themselves? It is not, after all, that they have been idealized. A figure by Piero della Francesca seems more powerful, grander, than a living man, because some of the attributes of ordinary humanity have been stripped away—the individual has been replaced by the ideal representation of man. But in Baugin's picture everything is emphatically itself—the flowers he paints are individual blooms, minutely realized, and not just the idea of a flower. The loaf is a real loaf, baked that morning.

We can get a clue to what is happening, I think, by searching for the artist's intention as it manifests itself in the picture. And Baugin's intention is neatly summed up in a few lines from William Carlos Williams's epic poem *Paterson*:

> There is no direction. Whither? I
> cannot say. I cannot say
> more than how. . . .

That is, what impresses us about the picture is the feeling that judgment is being deliberately withheld, that the objects depicted are being shown in such a way as to speak for themselves. They seem no more and no less than what they *are*.

Yet does this get us any closer to the heart of the problem? And it is not, after all, an academic problem, something for the art historians to puzzle over. The whole development of twentieth-century painting is really the story of the artists' struggle with the idea of reality, or, rather, with their search for reality itself. The invention of the camera certainly destroyed the painter's self-confidence, but not in the way usually described. It was not that the artist was turned loose, rudderless, now that this quicker and easier and cheaper way of recording and representing things had come to replace him. Rather, photography stripped the painter of his defences—because the camera proved so inept at catching the living essence of the subjects put before it. Formerly, the artist had been able to pretend that he was a mere slave to what he saw. With new testimony at hand, he suddenly made the vertiginous discovery that reality lay within himself.

What I am saying, in effect, is that Baugin *imposes* reality upon the objects he paints, lays it upon their backs like a solemn burden. That bottle is an Atlas, supporting a whole universe. That chessboard reaffirms the human contact, it links the subjective to the objective, the animate to the inanimate. By existing so densely, it reassures us that we ourselves exist.

After a period of revolt, the search for this kind of affirmation resumes its importance. Not that it was ever really given up. Giorgio Morandi died the other day, after having pursued this heightened reality almost throughout his working life as a painter. And the striking thing about his paintings is that they keep abreast of the times—Morandi's contribution to the recent Guggenheim Exhibition at the Tate seemed more, rather than less, advanced than the clamorous throng of pictures surrounding it. When we look at the work of the newest generation of American and British artists we often find that their whole aim is to give us the kind of shock that only confrontation with the *real* can bring. Thus we get Jim Dine's apparently eccentric assemblages: the objects which he fastens to his paintings, the tools, the bathroom fittings—these are treated in such a way as to make them sally out at us; they are more themselves than if we saw them in their proper context. And thus one of the most difficult of all the theories put forward by Marcel Duchamp begins to fall into place. The "found" objects which Duchamp (and others after him) have put on show in exhibitions—these are not necessarily meaningless. Certainly, in Duchamp's case, we might argue that Duchamp himself supplies a context—that he forces us to look at the objects he has chosen in a very particular way, and in thus channelling our gaze he is doing us a real service.

For how do we look at these "found" objects of Duchamp's? Perhaps—I will not say that it will always and everywhere happen—but *perhaps* with increased apprehension, new awareness. And certainly, to revert to the picture with which I started, we look at the Baugin with an increased awareness—an increased awareness of ourselves. The picture has the faculty of making us understand our own capabilities. In its geometry we sense the geometry—or architecture, rather—of the human body. The picture responds to us, it echoes us. And in its very particularity it echoes our power to respond to the particular, draws it forth. It is possible to think of such a picture as being not a thing entirely cut off from the context which surrounds it, but as a tool for exploring that context more thoroughly, more delicately. By forcing us to apprehend a few objects so totally, Baugin gives us more knowledge of all objects. The sensual world moves a fraction closer.

43. EIGHTEENTH-CENTURY ENGLISH PAINTING AND THE POETRY OF FACT

The exhibition of English pictures of the period 1730-1830, now at Agnews in aid of Enterprise Neptune, is entirely drawn from the collections in houses which belong to the National Trust. The show serves as a kind of confirmation, if not canonization, of a change in taste which has been taking place for some time now. We have more respect for English painting, and we look at it in a new way.

This change began in the broad sense with Professor Pevsner's memorable series of Reith lectures on the "Englishness of English Art". In a narrower sense it gathered impetus from the exhibition of the work of George Stubbs which was held some years ago at the Whitechapel Gallery. We can see the results of the change in the astonishing prices which have recently been paid at auction for English pictures of high quality. William Scott costs almost as much as Canaletto, and Brooking more than van de Velde. And it must be said that, though American collectors, and Mr. Paul Mellon in particular, have been pioneers in this field of collecting, the renewal of interest in English eighteenth-century art is not simply a revival of the old Duveen taste for full-length portraits of pretty children and glamorously aristocratic ladies. What holds our interest today are the conversation pieces, the landscapes, the pictures of ships and shipping—all those things, in fact, which bring us closest to the real England of the eighteenth century, to the country and the people as they actually existed.

But though the change has taken place, it has not yet been supplied with a rationale. *Post hoc* justifications are of course suspect, and never more so than when they concern the movement of fashion in the visual arts. Yet it seems to me that there is now a real case for the critical re-examination and re-evaluation of the English painting of the eighteenth century. We have never looked at it in its proper context, and this is what has led to its being neglected for so long. What I shall say here is only a sketch—the details need filling in, and no doubt some of my generalizations will turn out to be risky ones. But I hope, at least, to supply the framework for a new discussion of the subject.

Let me begin, then, by acknowledging that the English art of the period is usually thought of as occupying a marginal place on the European scene. Compared with French or Italian (and particularly Venetian) painting, it appears provincial and unsophisticated. English painters, we are told, had very little in the way of a native tradition behind them—in the seventeenth century, almost all the notable artists in England had been foreigners—and they were much less free than painters on the Continent to create as they pleased. Patrons had a clear idea of what they required, and what they required was the prosaic depiction of themselves, their families, their houses and their domestic animals.

This summary of the condition of English painting is no more than a half-truth. To understand why this is so, we must consider the position which was held by England and Englishmen in the politics and thought of the eighteenth century as a whole. One of the basic facts about the condition of England at the time is that it is almost the only country which was not, potentially at any rate, a breeding ground for revolution. Englishmen were content with the main outlines of the social and political system of their country, and the advanced political theorists of the Continent (and in particular the philosophers of the Enlightenment) held up English institutions as a model to the rest of the world. English political thinkers, such as Locke, had in any case exercised an immense influence over the new doctrines which were being preached in Europe.

English painting reflects this situation in a curious way. It is an art of acceptance, not an art of escape. The Rococo fantasy which we now so much admire in a painter like Watteau represents a retreat from reality which is in complete contrast to what we find in an Englishman like Hogarth. The Hogarth conversation piece from Ickworth, which is now on show at Agnews, provides a good example of this. It is at least as fluently and elegantly painted as any Watteau which I can think of. Especially marvellous is the free and fluid brushwork with which the artist has created the fruit on the table, and the basket of fruit on the ground. But Hogarth is not creating a dream world, an ideal society. He is content to show us what *is*.

Of course, the picture is not completely without artifice. The grouping derives from what Hogarth saw on the stage. Everything is arranged to be more typical, more telling, more concentrated than "real life" would be. Little anecdotal touches are brought in to catch the spectator's interest—a good example can be found on the left of the picture, where the clergyman with the telescope clapped to his eye is just about to be tipped off the chair he is standing on. The picture is not, perhaps, as miraculously resolved and unified as a mature *fête galante* by Watteau. But Hogarth is, in a sense, undertaking a more difficult task. He is not providing a substitute; he is trying to show us the genuine thing, to explain how these particular people conducted themselves, and what their relationships were to each other. The picture has a concentration of meaning in it which is absent from contemporary conversation pieces painted in France or Italy. It is a great deal more intense than any picture by Longhi, for example.

The growing economic power of England during the eighteenth century attracted many painters from abroad—in particular, many of the most distinguished Venetian painters were employed by British patrons, not only Canaletto, but decorators such as Pelligrini and Amigoni. It says something for the integrity of English painting that the influences which these painters brought with them were painlessly absorbed. It is true that a certain snobbery often led the rich Whig magnates of England (the principal source of patronage) to prefer foreigners to native-born artists, with the result that a painter of imaginative landscapes like Richard Wilson tended to have a hard time of it. Towards the end of the century, too, the growing obsession with the idea of History Painting led to an impatience with the conditions imposed by English patrons. Artists like Reynolds and Romney undoubtedly felt that their talents had not been employed to best effect, simply because of the conditions in which they found themselves.

On the other hand, those specimens of History Painting which we have from the brushes of these and other artists do not encourage us to feel that we have suffered any great loss. The cult of History Painting was, in part at least, an expression of the revolt against the inferior social status of the artist which was taking place all over Europe. The theoretical issue was a cover for the more practical and pressing one.

Meanwhile, in the second half of the eighteenth century, English painters were producing masterpieces which cannot be matched elsewhere. I am thinking, in particular of the two country scenes by Stubbs, which are also included in the exhibition at Agnews. These show harvesting and haymaking. They are a strange and beautiful combination of the utterly natural and the mathematically precise. The intervals between the various figures are as calculated as they would be in a great mythological composition by Poussin. Yet the other comparison which we think of is with some of Peter Breughel the Elder's pictures of seasonal occupations. Stubbs has the same reverence for the natural, seasonal rhythm which Breughel displays, and he shares Breughel's ability to recreate reality and to make the spectator experience it at its highest power. What we find in Stubbs' best work is the poetry of fact. It is this poetry which touches us again and again when we look at English eighteenth-century painting.

44. NEO-CLASSICISM—THE FIRST MODERN MOVEMENT

The rich and enterprising Cleveland Museum of Art has just staged an exhibition devoted to the theme of Nec-classicism. This is a significant event for more than one reason. Not only is this the first major exhibition ever devoted to the style, but Neo-classicism itself was one of the major revolutions in the history of European art—indeed, I don't think that it is going too far to call it "the first modern movement", for reasons which I hope to make plain in a moment. Some of those reasons already emerge in the article which Norbert Lynton devoted to Winckelmann in these columns a week ago. Winckelmann is indisputably the great theorist of Neo-classicism, and it was one of the movement's real originalities to be dominated by theory.

Some people may feel inclined to protest that this reliance on theory was also characteristic of the Renaissance. Yet a writer like Alberti does not really have the ambitions, nor, ultimately, the far reaching influence which Winckelmann possessed. When we look at Neo-classicism we are looking at a style which was brought into being by an effort of will. Here, as never before, objects are made to symbolize ideas. Even furniture is moralized. It is this which the Cleveland exhibition provides—not just a context for certain objects, but an intellectual whole. A table by the great Franco-German *ébeniste* Adam Weisweiler, for example, is seen to bear a clear and definite relation to a sculpture by Canova, a picture by Tischbein, an architectural project by George Dance the Younger. The relationship is not just one of congruity, or even simply of mood—it is that all these things are related to a coherent framework of ideas.

In my view, the dominance of theory is precisely what cuts Neo-classicism off from the styles which preceded it. It is also the thing which, among others, brings it into a close relationship with everything which has happened since in the visual arts. Like many another revolution, Neo-classicism disguised the desire for change as a demand for the revival of old standards. But its truly and shockingly revolutionary character may perhaps be gauged by noticing its close link with political events. The style had its genesis in the middle of the eighteenth century. To be precise, we find a new movement in painting growing up in the Rome of the late 1750s and early 1760s, under the influence of Winckelmann himself (who arrived in Rome in 1755), and of the Scotsman Gavin Hamilton, and the German Anton Raphael Mengs. Even at this very early date, both the intellectual nature of the style and its internationalism were apparent. From this beginning its conquest of Europe was very rapid. In 1763, the architect Gabriel began to build the Petit Trianon for Madame de Pompadour. In 1784, David painted the "Oath of the Horatii", perhaps the most significant of all neo-classical pictures.

The course and speed of this development exactly matches the development of those philosophical ideas which were to lead to the French Revolution. It is often said that Winckelmann finds his counterpart in Rousseau. But there is more to it than this. When David's picture was exhibited, it met with an immediate success, not only because the ground was already prepared, but because of the political ideas that worked within it. David's picture owes its quintessential Neo-classicism not merely to its style and subject, but to its didacticism. What we find there, as much as in the pages of the philosophers of the Enlightenment, is a discourse about man's nature, delivered with all the force and impact that the visual arts can give. All of this came naturally to David. It does not seem strange that he, an artist, should have gone on to become a member of the Convention, and should have voted for the death of Louis XVI. Even if crudely, he corresponds to our modern notion of the artist as a man who bears a responsibility to society, and who must be prepared to shoulder the burden. Of course, our ideas as to how this "responsibility" should be defined have changed very much, thanks to many thinkers, including Freud. But the point of importance is that, with David, the artist becomes consciously a spokesman for those among whom he lives.

To a large extent, this remains true. The artist speaks; the critic interprets. The trouble is that no one is quite certain that the critic has not previously given instructions as to what is to be said. Neo-classicism, as I originally pointed out—and as others, including Mr. Lynton, have pointed out before me—began not with an artist but with a critic. It was the critics who invented the idea of the "representative role", and who forced the artist to play it.

As we examine this problem, we begin to see that there are two other things which mark out Neo-classicism as the first of the modern movements. I refer to the cult of feeling (a paradoxical child of the new intellectualism) and to the idea of a philosophy of aesthetics. The two matters are closely linked, as the main business of modern aesthetics seems to be to explain to us the feelings which we get from a work of art, which is (now) another way of saying our relationship to it. This is not to say that men had never considered these matters previously —we find them discussed, in some form, by Plato. But the extremely rapid growth of modern aesthetics has arisen in response to a demand from artist, critic, and spectator alike. Neo-classicism made it necessary to *have* an intellectual attitude, because the work of art demanded it. David's great didactic pictures call for this as no other works of art had ever done before them. However different the pictures in the recent Gulbenkian Exhibition at the Tate may seem from what David set out to do, they have at least this much in common with him—that our engagement with them, as spectators, is, at least in part, an intellectual engagement. They require not only thought, but, more specifically, thought about what we feel.

"Ugliness is not an aesthetic value, not even a negative one", says a well-known modern philosopher who has concerned himself with aesthetics. "There are no negative aesthetic qualities. We call that ugly which resists the influx of our emotions into it, or repels them, or bruises them if they succeed in getting installed therein. The object in the presence of which it is difficult to assume the aesthetic attitude is ugly. And until the aesthetic attitude *is* assumed, there is no aesthetic quality at all." In the historical sense, these words express something which is directly traceable to the "sense of law and reason" which we find in Neo-classicism, and even to the demand for purity, if not of style, as Winckelmann wished, then at least of emotion. It only surprises me that we have had to wait so long for a comprehensive exhibition such as the one in Cleveland.

45. WHEN STYLE DEVELOPS INTO STYLISHNESS

Art Nouveau has made a thorough, rapid, and complete return to public favour. A new exhibition at the Piccadilly Gallery—the more telling because most of the objects in it are on a small scale—leads me to ponder not only the nature of the Art Nouveau style itself, but our current reaction to it. Indeed, it is this very word "style", so all-embracing, and so inseparable from any discussion of Art Nouveau, which gives me pause.

The prophets of the Art Nouveau revival always make such a point of telling us that this was the last moment in history when a "unified style" could be seen affecting all the visual arts: not only furniture design, jewelry and ceramics; but architecture, sculpture, and painting. Certainly, as far as the minor arts are concerned, we are seldom in doubt as to what is an Art Nouveau object. Whether the ruling influence be Celtic, Japanese or Persian, or whether it springs from much nearer home—the press at Kelmscott or the plant-houses at Kew—it is impossible to mistake the leading characteristics of Art Nouveau design. That wilfulness, that slipperiness, that sinuosity: we can tell where we are at once.

Or can we? It often seems to me that the important issues are being dodged: that Art Nouveau is not in fact a style like other styles. There is in it a very strong element, not only of style, but of stylishness—of what one might call the will to style. Though this, perhaps, may sound like mere word-play. Yet we must consider one thing at least—the extent to which Art Nouveau is self-conscious, the extent to which it stands apart from the current of its times. If we consider the development of the great historical styles—not only the sudden revolutions, but the gradual, insidious transformations of one thing into another, Gothic into Renaissance, Renaissance into Baroque, Boroque into Rococo, Rococo into Neo-Classical—we are conscious of the extent to which these changes are linked to other changes, affecting all the departments of living. The whole development is organic, from first to last. I cannot see that Art Nouveau is the logical progression from the High Victorian style, even though ancestors may be found for the

Art Nouveau designers among the Pre-Raphaeilites.

And it is one of the significant things about Art Nouveau that, while hospitable to all sorts of minor talents, it tended to find no room for the major artists of the period. I think, in particular, of the early career of Picasso—who at one stage came very near to reaching an accommodation with Art Nouveau. Yet Picasso's work of the Blue and Rose periods has about it an air of falsity which disturbs (and rightly) some of his greatest admirers. These harlequins, acrobats, beggars, children—there is about them all something which is distinctly *voulu*. Though Picasso's own circumstances were for the most part miserable enough when these pictures were painted, we feel sure that the *misérabilisme* we find in them springs from quite another impulse. They are not meant to harrow, but to reassure. And so skilfully, so sweetly, so fluently is it done that they have gone on offering reassurance ever since: and especially to those who have the money to pay for it.

Picasso, of course, was intelligent enough to revolt after a time—and so violent was the explosion that painting has never been quite the same since. But what about the minor Art Nouveau artists—the predecessors and contemporaries of the young Spaniard? It has often been pointed out, and with some complacency, that their work was feverish and erotic. We lick our lips, and at the same time we permit ourselves to smile at the naïvety of it all. Yet I suspect that it is often their cynicism, rather than their feverishness or their eroticism, which has made these artists popular again.

To understand this, we must go back a little way. At first sight, many Art Nouveau objects seem to offer one thing which High Victorian objects had also offered—a means of escape from the horrors of nineteenth-century industrialism. Throughout the nineteenth century, the retreat towards an imagined Middle Ages had tempted both the wealthy and the intellectual. The Victorians had at least the merit of taking this dream world seriously. Nobody who looks at Butterfield's Keble can doubt that. Art Nouveau represents the betrayal of this seriousness. Dreams were now to be mocked. One of the leading characteristics of Art Nouveau is the element of parody in its make-up. The wit of Beardsley is a wit of totally ungenial burlesque, as his contemporaries well knew. But we get a glimpse of this stylistic clowning even in some of the most ordinary and mundane objects turned out by the Art Nouveau designers. A Liberty jewel-box may seem a casket for an

Isolde, but is a denial, at the same time, that Isoldes are possible.

But why pull such long faces? Doesn't the phenomenon I've been describing have its admirable side? The answer is that the parody and the cynicism of Art Nouveau are only part of its total effect, just as dreaminess is another part. What we see in Art Nouveau —the exception being the work of a few creative architects—is a deliberate choice of shallowness over profundity, of convention over freedom. The wild success of art Nouveau with its first public was based on the fact that Art Nouveau design is so entirely self-regarding. It ignored all problems which it had not itself created, and severed its connections with social ideas. Yet, though unconsciously, it remained the perfect expression of the plutocracy of the period: restless, avid for novelty, and afraid of thought. Art Nouveau set out to be *salient*—the impact was to be immediate, the chosen characteristics were to be few and easy to remember. But the cry of "art for art's sake" takes on distinctly savage and sinister overtones when we consider that it heralded the First World War.

Yet, again, there is a postscript to this. It may seem absurd, having already mentioned Picasso, to introduce the name of that minor Victorian painter William Dyce, who is now being honoured with a retrospective exhibition at Agnew's. But to move from the assertive jungle of objects in the Piccadilly Gallery to look at Dyce's well-known picture "Pegwell Bay" (which is, in fact, normally visible at the Tate) is almost to fall into a trap. Surely there is no style here—and surely we are well enough without it? A glance at the preliminary drawing makes clear the mistake. The scene is subtly ordered, the various figures are placed in their setting with a geometry which, however faintly, echoes Piero della Francesca. Style as a servant—as that which promotes an underlying pictorial harmony—can never be discarded. It is only when style develops into stylishness that it becomes tyrannical.

46. ARTISTS IN THE THROES OF ADJUSTMENT

People who never go to art galleries are apt to assert that modern painters are "illiterate". The accusation is wide of the mark. Seldom, since the Renaissance, can artists have been more anxious to prove that they can read and write. Their pictures are full of letters, of words, of phrases; one even finds a whole sentence now and then. I imagine a prudent foreigner sallying out to do a round of our more advanced exhibitions with a dictionary clasped firmly in his hand.

The fascination which words and letters have for modern artists derives from many sources. In part, it can be traced back to Cubist collages, and to pioneers such as Kurt Schwitters. In part, it has its roots in an interest in the alphabet as a ready-made repertoire of shapes—shapes which are satisfyingly enigmatic yet still familiar. The American artist, Jasper Johns, makes paintings and prints which are simply rows of letters. The interest of these works (which I find very beautiful) lies in the shimmering veil of brushwork which he casts over the rigid design. But usually letters are not used just for themselves; as elements carefully quarantined from verbal meaning; but in sequence to communicate something.

Particularly, words have played a big part in the new narrative painting in England. Pop art, it seems to me, owes its astonishing success as much to the words as to the images. One imagines patrons crying, in the speech of Kipling's *Just So Stories:* "And after thousands and thousands and thousands of years, and after Hieroglyphics, and Demotics, and Nilotics, and Cryptics, and Cufics, and Runics, and Dorics, and Ionics, and all sorts of other ricks and tricks (because the Woons, and the Neguses, and the Akhoonds, and the Repositories of Tradition would never leave a good thing alone when they saw it), the fine old easy, understandable Alphabet—A, B, C, D, E, and the rest of 'em—got back into its proper shape again for all the Best Beloveds to learn when they are old enough." Certainly, buyers have found both charm and reassurance in such pictures as the one by David Hockney which shows a beast about to spring on two men. The label says: "They are quite safe, this is a still", and firmly bars the predator from his intended victims.

It would be easy to take all this docketing and labelling as I think some of the customers do take it—as part of a campaign of delicious, deliberate silliness. Certainly the role of holy fool is one which modern artists find all too congenial, besides the fact that it goes over big with the audience. Yet I think we owe this fashion for words the debt of a slightly closer inspection. There is more to it than infantilism. What we see, in my view, is the artist in the throes of adjusting himself to an entirely new kind of visual experience. Thanks to modern advertising techniques, we have stopped thinking of words and pictures as separate categories. Especially if we live in cities, they come to us indissolubly wedded, in the form of posters and advertisements. The whole aim of commercial graphic design is to get us to absorb word and picture together, without effort, in a single instant. In a good advertisement, as the advertising manuals tell us, neither the headline nor the picture gives the full story. They overlap; but they do not coincide.

The extent of our current sophistication in these matters can perhaps be gauged by taking a look at the posters by the Art Nouveau designer Alphonse Mucha, now on view at the Victoria and Albert Museum and elsewhere. To the eye of the modern advertising man, these posters look almost inconceivably amateur. One sees *la Divine Sarah* in lots of sinuous poses, surrounded by quantities of hair. But what on earth is she acting in? The title of the play takes a bit of finding. Surely designs such as these were amazingly inefficient, even for the horse-and-buggy era?

The strength of this reaction is the measure of the distance which graphic design has travelled. But not only is it now scientific, it is still markedly vital and imaginative. It often seems that our fashion-magazines, our direct-mail advertising, our counter-leaflets, have more zest and visual inventiveness than most contemporary painters can muster. Advertising may plead doubtful causes, but it speaks up and speaks eloquently. But the sheer volume of sound and the genuine eloquence have made their appeal to young artists. The result is painting in which words play an integral part, because it approaches reality sidelong, through a love-hate relationship with commercial art.

Painting such as this may be called pop, but really it is hermetic and learned. We have to be careful that we have seen the right things—not only the advertisements, but the horror comics, the motor-cycling journals, the muscle-magazines—before we approach it. Otherwise it has only a surface meaning for us; and even this we may misunderstand, in fact, are likely to misunderstand. And already there are signs that it is about to be challenged by a new barbarism. Comments scribbled in the margins of the glossy magazines are being followed by more direct and brutal assaults. Anyone interested might care to visit two current London exhibitions. One is at the Kasmin Gallery, where Latham creates strange assemblages of burnt, torn and battered books—a literal rape of the word. The other is at Gallery One, where David Oxtoby creates almost equally savage images, often conjured from the flickerings of the television screen.

47. CATEGORIES OF MODERN ART

It seems to me that, when talking about modern art, one of the basic difficulties which we all have is over the business of categories—"how does this picture fit in?" Already I can hear a voice protesting that works of art ought to be judged for themselves, and not racked on the Procrustean bed of theory. Yet it is undoubtedly true that categories affect our most spontaneous reactions. We find it easier to judge—easier, even, simply to *see*—a picture which fits in with our previous experience. The wider the experience we have of art, the more systematic we are apt to be, otherwise we would find it impossible to control that great throng of memories and sense-impressions which make up our "data" on painting.

There is also the way in which every work of art we meet with modifies, even if ever so little, our attitude towards what we have seen in the past and what we hope to see in the future. Thus, Picasso's strange and ravishing picture of women bathing, which is one of the highlights of the Guggenheim Collection now at the Tate, alters the attitude which we take up towards the Arcadian painting of the past—towards Poussin, for example, or towards Renoir's "Baigneuse Blonde". What Picasso brings out is a quality of removal which is almost sinister. The great head which cranes itself up above the horizon to look at the figures who crouch in the foreground: this is a reminder of the loneliness, even of the potential terror, which the Arcadian landscape implies. It is also a reminder that the spectator is an intruder, who thrusts his way in to this closed, hermetic world.

But already I am beginning to demonstrate a little of what I mean by the word "categories". In bringing our experience of pictures to bear on this one Picasso, we sort out those paintings which seem the most relevant, and we try to work out what the common factors and what the differences are. In discussing modern art, most of the groupings we use are very loose—so loose that they are of little good to us. One of the main divisions, for example, is that between abstract and non-abstract art. Yet it seems to me that this way of dividing the sheep from the goats is bound to produce many more problems than it solves. Thus, we instinctively feel that a Cubist still-life by Braque, and a late abstraction by Mondrian in some way "belong" together—the painters concerned pose similar problems, and that part of us which responds to them is the same in each case. Thus, the Braque still-life will strike us as unspecific. The bowl, the bottle, the grapes, the guitar—these have a minimum of content, and, separated from its companions, each shape would hardly make sense. What matters is the relationship of shape to shape, of one colour to another within the framework of the design.

If we turn our attention to the Mondrian we find very much the same thing going on, only with no reference to the objects which we see about us in our daily existences. The paintings and the painters in fact conduct a sort of dialogue with one another. Braque reminds us that our experiences of colour, shape, and design, our response to pictorial rhythm, is something which springs from our own daily lives. As we move about the streets, or in our houses, we impose shapes, patterns, sequences on things—this, indeed, is how we comprehend them. Mondrian, on the other hand, reminds us that these shapes, patterns, and sequences can be abstracted from nature, and presented as absolutes.

The appeal which he makes, is, however, to very much the same set of reactions. When he thinks of the spectator, the guise in which he sees him is not so very different from the form envisaged by Braque. For both these artists, the spectator is a man whose normal, day-to-day responses—the responses which he uses to pilot himself through the daily round of living—must be extended and heightened. They try to confirm us—Braque and Mondrian—in things which we already know. They also want to tell us that the operations of our senses and of our minds can be enjoyed for their own sake, quite free of overtones, detached from personal emotion.

The situation is very different when we turn to a Surrealist painter like Magritte. Magritte and Braque, though both figurative painters, are radically different from each other. Magritte uses the objects he paints to make a kind of rebus. We "read" the picture, rather than experience it. For Magritte the senses, and particularly the sense of sight, are simply the conveyors of a message to the brain. It does not at all suit his purpose to evoke the reactions which Braque is looking for. Braque tries to show us the essentials, Magritte wants the recognizable surface. The more "illusion" he can pack into a picture, the greater its success (in his terms) is likely to be. He persuades us by disorienting our senses, rather than by trying to heighten our awareness of sensuality. By confusing the signals, he tries to slide some idea about the nature of reality, about the nature of mankind itself, into our consciousness.

There is another word which is sometimes used for Magritte and his colleagues. This word is "literary". The implications of the adjective are threefold. First of all, there is the implication that Magritte is somehow less essentially a painter than Braque, or than painters who resemble Braque. Then there is the idea that what a picture by Magritte has to say could equally well be expressed in words. Thirdly, there is the feeling that a picture by Magritte belongs to a quite different order of experience from "non-literary" painting. Of these three implications it is the third which has most truth in it. So far as the true nature of painting goes we cannot really hope to determine whether its main task should be to extend awareness through the physical senses or through the psyche. The painters of the past—Mantegna or Rembrandt, for example—entwine the two things so closely that the question does not arise. On the other hand, one has only to make the experiment to see that it is difficult to provide a true verbal equivalent to a Surrealist picture, because even the briefest and most cryptic verbal description fails to catch the simultaneity which only a picture can give—and this is true despite what I have just said about a surrealist picture having to be "read" rather than experienced plastically.

Just as Mondrian relates to Braque, so there is a great deal of abstract and semi-abstract painting which is closely related to "figurative" Surrealism. Thus Matta and Arshile Gorky try to find shapes which, without actually representing anything, are full of implications of the kind that Magritte, too, wants to convey. These semi-abstract Surrealists are, in turn, closely related to Abstract Expressionism. Thus it is that Jackson Pollock's aims, are, in the end, closer to Magritte's than to Mondrian's. The increasing tendency we have to find Pollock "pretty" and "decorative" is perhaps the best example I can think of to illustrate the chaotic state of opinion about contemporary art, and the need for new categories and groupings.

48. FACT AS FICTION—HISTORY AS MYTH

One day, somebody will write an essay entitled, in all solemnity, "Mid-twentieth century history painters". The time is not yet—nevertheless I more and more begin to wonder what the learned author will find to say. To remark on the interest which contemporary artists now take in historical themes is now almost a commonplace. But it is not easy to define the way in which that interest operates. Perhaps one can begin to work towards a definition by pointing to the very variable success which modern painters have had when trying to cope with the events of their own time—with history in the making.

During the first 40 years or so of this century, two almost equally powerful forces were at work. One was the prejudice which the modern painter felt, not only towards representation in the old sense, but towards becoming involved, at least in the way that newspaper headlines suggested he should. Newsprint was there to be used as an artist like Schwitters used it—its physical characteristics were of more interest than anything which the journalists had to say. On the other hand, history was being made at such a headlong pace that the artists could not help being affected by it. Sometimes, indeed, they became inextricably enmeshed. Occasionally the result was an outright masterpiece, like Picasso's "Guernica", still perhaps the most concentratedly eloquent and passionate work of art produced in this century. The dangers of becoming involved in this way are, however, illustrated not only by the official artists of Soviet Russia, but even by Picasso himself in a more recent phase of his development—I am thinking, in particular, of the paintings inspired by the events of the Korean War.

Yet against these failures must be set the success of what one might call the reluctant history painters—and here I am thinking in particular of English artists during the two World Wars. It is possible to argue, I think, that some of the most genuinely valid and moving and permanent pictures to have been created by the British school were those painted by "war artists"—official and unofficial. Nevinson found reserves of talent during the First World War which he was never again able to tap.

Paul Nash has a depth in a picture like "Totes Meer" which stands a little apart from the gentle dreaminess of his other work.

All the instances I have so far mentioned do, however, belong to a sort of no-man's land between history and *reportage*. "Guernica" is a masterpiece of history-painting because Picasso has succeeded in raising the subject out of the context of journalism, just as Goya did with his two pictures of the Madrid revolt against the French—"The Second of May" and "The Third of May". And it is easy to be blinded by the originality of Picasso's formal language to the rather traditional nature of his aim. "Guernica" is the last in a long line. It descends from Velasquez's "Surrender at Breda" and from David's "Oath of the Horatii" as well as from Goya. That is—it commemorates, and it admonishes.

It is surprising how much of the history-painting of the nineteenth century and earlier falls into just these two categories. That is, if I can put it another way, history was used by artists as a vehicle for public statements. An artist who tackled a historical subject was speaking not intimately, but to the world at large. If idiosyncrasy and obsession crept in (as they did in such pictures as Gericault's "Raft of the Medusa" and Delacroix's "Death of Sardanapalus", this was not something which the painters concerned had either courted or planned.

On the other hand, when one looks at a series of key works in what one might call the current "revival of the historical mode"—I mean Sidney Nolan's famous Ned Kelly series, now on view at the Qantas Gallery—one is struck by the extent to which they are wilful, personal, capricious; by the cavalier attitude which they take towards the historical material upon which they are based. The Ned Kelly series was painted in 1946 and 1947, and Nolan's impact was first felt in England rather later than this. All the same, 1946 or thereabouts seems a key date—certainly the new attitude was by then established. One can best define it by examining the Ned Kelly pictures themselves, and then by considering the reception which they received and Nolan's subsequent development. On the whole, the pictures seem to have been judged far more solemnly than need be or, I suspect, than the artist intended.

In one way the merits of the Ned Kelly pictures are very much the merits of Chagall—we find in them a highly personal colour-sense, and a sophisticated use of the *faux-naif*. But what is most memorable about them is their insolence—the way in which the artist seizes on a cherished national myth, and turns it to personal, introverted ends. It is exhilarating, at least to me, when an artist like Nolan treats the leaden certainty of historical fact as being something as flexible and as malleable as mythological material once seemed to a painter like Boucher.

But this is not quite how the Ned Kelly series is usually thought of. The Australian hunger for a national identity has overridden Nolan's delicate ironies, and even the English public has discovered large moral statements where none were intended. Or am I in fact too bold in making this assumption? At any rate, some facets of Nolan's later work seem to illustrate the dangers that lie in wait for an artist who loses the whip hand over history.

It is an observation which bears repeating to say that frivolity can sometimes be just as important to art as high seriousness. And recent painting seems to have rediscovered this truth in its treatment of historical material—in its outrageous assumption that what is vouched for by a thousand documents, what is past and immutable, can be overturned in a moment by the iron whim of the artist. In fact, history has become, paradoxically, a good field for the assertion of the artist's personal identity. Meanwhile, certain facts, certain truths, perhaps more important than the facts of history, leer at us just where the fantasy seems most outrageous, the caprice most wilful and childish.

49. SAFETY IN THE SECOND-HAND IMAGE

Roy Lichtenstein's near-miss in Venice, when, amid a great deal of talk, he failed to win the main prize at the Biennale, brought the whole topic of Pop Art back to my mind. Pop has shown a remarkable vitality in some ways, and a disappointing lack of stamina in others. The Pop artists have not proved to be quite the flash in the pan which many critics predicted. Some of them, Lichtenstein included, have shown a continuous and interesting development. But Pop has remained a kind of magic circle; the artists of the second generation have been feebler even than those of the second generation of Abstract Expressionism. What this suggests is that we have all been looking at Pop Art from the wrong angle.

When Pop first put in an appearance, it was hailed as the New Figuration. This label, it now seems to me, was very misleading. True enough, there are images in Pop—comic-strip heroes, Jackie Kennedy, pin ups, pin ball machines, old Uncle Tom Cobley and all. But how did these images *get* there? Not from direct observation. That girl already existed in two dimensions long before the painter got hold of her. She is a pin up from a movie magazine, not a girl that the artist saw on the beach. In fact, Pop images are usually second-hand. And this seems to me to be their most important characteristic, the "popular" or "commercial" side of it is by the way.

What it all begins to remind me of is the story of Perseus and the head of Medusa. It will be remembered that it was fatal to look at Medusa directly, but she could be seen in perfect safety provided one looked in a polished shield. Pop painters seem to think of the world of reality as dangerous, and they tame it in very much the same way. It is worthwhile to look for a reason.

First of all, there is the question of what reality means to the painter. A painter who projects himself into the world of objects is exposing himself, making some kind of surrender. Pop Art, as we all know, is distinguished by its coolness, its refusal of commitment. The artist gives nothing of himself. I remember a painting by Robert Rauschenberg which contained, among other things, a photograph of a nude by Rubens, an image in glaring contrast to all that surrounded it. The only way the Pop painter can deal comfortably with images is when they are being used as examples, and not for their own sake. What I am trying to say is this—the function of the image in Pop painting is very much that of the quotation or image in learned discourse. The speaker pauses for a moment, in the midst of a flow of abstract argument, to say "for example", or "for instance". Or else another comparison springs to mind, and this is that the image, in a Pop painting, serves much the same function as the epic simile does in an epic—it provides a point of rest, an expansive moment.

One objection immediately springs to mind—what about the kind of painting which seems to be *all* image? Lichtenstein's own paintings seem to fall into this category—the girl's head borrowed from a comic-strip fills the whole gigantic canvas: there is no flow of discourse here, only something unified and monumental. Yet what is the effect of the way in which Lichtenstein uses his material? Or of the way in which Andy Warhol uses his repeated silk-screen images? Isn't it that reality drains out of them? As we look, we become increasingly aware of the picture as abstract pattern or rhythm, and less and less aware of what it actually depicts.

The determination to think of Pop as a branch of abstract art does pay a number of immediate dividends—that is, if one has a tidy mind. For instance, it becomes much easier to explain the development of post war painting as a logical progression, with various kinds of abstraction being explored one after the other. Painting in this century seems to become increasingly generalized, and increasingly introverted, and Pop was the exception to this. There are a number of borderline cases which suggest that Pop has a much closer relationship to "conventional" abstract painting than is usually realized. The British painter, Anthony Donaldson, has produced paintings in which the silhouettes of pin up girls were used as abstract elements. Derek Boshier and Richard Smith have both made paintings which, while abstract, were closely related to modern packagings and thus to the whole ethos of Pop.

Arguments about classification are apt, I know, to seem a little arid, but this one carries with it important consequences. The inability to grasp specific reality shows itself quite generally in the sort of society we live in. It seems to mark a change in man himself. Formerly, man's life was intimately concerned with objects, and these objects were specific; each differed from all the others. Now, many of the objects we use are made for us, in series, by machines, and have therefore lost this kind of precise identity. We become more and more ready to define things by their functions, rather than by what they look like; we become more and more adept in handling abstract ideas.

A lot of people find all this rather terrifying, and maybe some Pop painters do so too. There is, after all, a rather different kind of painting from the sort though we still label it Pop. The paintings of Peter Blake, for example, show a nostalgic pleasure in what they depict, they are "engaged" in just the way that Lichtenstein and Warhol are not. But just a moment. Is not there something rather nostalgic about Blake's work, and about all Pop painting of this kind? Indeed there is—this quality of nostalgia has been commented upon again and again. Pop of this sort is a commentary not on the present but the past. The lovely lady is never Julie Christie but always Jean Harlow.

So again, it seems, one encounters the retreat from the specific reality of things. I can only think of one other society where it has happened so universally. We find just such a tendency in the art of Southern Sung China, and just such wistful antiquarianism. It is a nice thought—celadon and Lichtenstein, Peter Blake and "A Thousand Miles of Rivers and Mountains".

50. A CONFUSION OF IMAGES IN 20 YEARS OF POSTWAR PAINTING

Recently I have been looking through a great mass of exhibition catalogues and photographs, as I drew up the list of illustrations for a book. The period which this archive covered was comparatively brief—the past 20 years. What it gave me, as I went through it, was a sweeping and thoroughly unselective view of artistic activity in Europe and the United States during the two decades since the war. Here they all were—the talented and the untalented, the self-promoters and the retiring. Here were those astonishingly inflated prefaces (most of them written by French art critics), those ultraglossy and ultragimmicky catalogues (mostly from Milanese art galleries).

How closely did this archive correspond to my own memories, my own impressions? The files provided the facts—how did *this* truth correspond to *my* truth, as a critic? The experience led me to certain conclusions. The best, so it seemed to me, was precisely as one had always remembered it. The great pictures painted by Braque towards the end of his life are still just as good as I thought they were when I first saw them. Jackson Pollock is still an immensely important artist. De Kooning's "Women" have a tremendous, garish, primitive power. On the other hand, certain reputations have already begun to fade, and I doubt if they will ever completely recover. Those many abstracts by Serge Poliakoff, for instance, are all alike, and the charm of the resonant colour soon begins to pall when one looks at them in quantity. Here is a painter who is peculiarly of the fifties, just as certain Pop artists belong, without a doubt, to the early sixties—the only epoch that could have produced and encouraged them.

Indeed, the two most prolific traditions in postwar painting also seem to me to have been the two poorest in really talented artists. We tend to forget what a great swarm there has been of "informal" abstract painters, just as we tend to forget the sheer numerousness of the Pop fraternity. It is interesting to speculate just why these two particular styles of painting should have been so popular, not only among the artists themselves, but with the people who bought their work.

"Informal" abstract painting is, in a way, easier to place, because its vogue has now so obviously passed. Basically, it was the European child of American Abstract Expressionism, mingled with certain tendencies which already existed among the younger generation of the Ecole de Paris. As Georges Mathieu remarked in a catalogue-note to one of his wildly successful shows in the middle fifties: "It was not until somewhere between 1945 and 1947 that the discovery was really made for the first time that a painting could exist and owe nothing to the exterior aspects of reality. Forty years after the birth of the first non-objective work!" This has the tone of a man who is simultaneously making a discovery and proclaiming a new dawn. And indeed, this is quite probably what was wrong with the kind of painting I am talking about—there was no real resistance to it; it sprang up like one of those rampant annual vines; it sprawled through the art galleries of the world, blossomed in a riot of colour, and then withered.

Help for the new painters came from several different directions at once. There was, first of all, the determination to re-establish Europe, and especially Paris, as the artistic centre of the world. At the same time, the new American painters had already begun to make their impact; it was impossible for European painters to start again from the point reached in 1939, even if they had wanted to. The basic research, the basic development, had been done in America, and this work could not be ignored. But it gave the new painting an oddly rootless air, a rootlessness which many critics explained in terms of the then dominant Existentialist philosophy. At the same time, once economic recovery began, people were anxious to buy modern pictures—more anxious than ever before. The great rise in price of the Impressionist and Post-Impressionist masters had already started, and collectors were determined not to be caught. Despite the lack of "subject matter", they found the new abstract painters easy to like. Colours were bright, textures were lush; the pictures were intellectually undemanding. The mid-fifties brought an art boom which many dealers remember with nostalgia.

"Pop", though superficially very different, had the same quality of marketability. It is interesting to see, for instance, that while British Pop is already much softer than American Pop, the Pop of Paris and Rome and Milan is softer still—the style is turned almost wholly to favour and to prettiness, to a kind of thin eroticism and a slapdash familiarity with the more obvious aspects of modern urban living. Pop did, in fact, bring with it an element which many people had already began to miss in the abstract painting which preceded it—there was an air of social engagement. But it is, I believe, the true failure of so much Pop painting that this air is largely illusory. The artist does not care about the imagery he is manipulating, nor try to understand its significance.

These two styles are not, however, the only ones to have flourished in the two decades since the war. Indeed, one of the difficulties for any historian of the art of the period is going to be to try and find a way of making sense of such a vast confusion of images and styles. For instance, I have not as yet mentioned the survival of quite another tradition of abstract painting—the "hard edge" abstraction which ultimately derives from Mondrian. It has not found nearly so much favour in the market, but it has attracted impassioned allegiance from both painters and critics.

I think the reason for this loyalty is to be found in the situation I have just mentioned. Hard edge abstraction has its own logic; it forms a closed system, and therefore protects the painter from a threatening confusion. The only trouble is, so it seems to me, that the style is too closed; that it is art about art, proceeding away from mankind and the ordinary concerns of mankind by impeccably logical steps.

Indeed, the real lesson of my search through the archives seemed to me to be this: that modern art has not come near to solving, during the past 20 years, the question of its relationship to the society in which it exists.

51. PURITY AND THINNESS IN CONCRETE POETRY

The fascination with the idea of the total aesthetic experience—an experience which fuses the ideas and sensations offered by two or more of the arts—is beginning to acquire a great significance for modern writers and painters and even (I suspect) for musicians. A symptom is provided by the very well-mounted little exhibition called "Between Poetry and Painting", which is now on view at the Institute of Contemporary Arts, in Dover Street. The scope is, perhaps, narrower than the title suggests. Though the exhibition casts a backward glance at such pioneers as Kurt Schwitters and Guillaume Apollinaire, it is, in fact, a celebration of the new "concrete poetry" movement.

Concrete poetry is difficult to describe, but easy to recognize. The aim is to give words a new dynamism for the eye—to make the poem a kind of emblem or ikon of what is being said. This has some immediately striking results. If we choose to regard the products of the movement as belonging to literature, then it is the internationalism which strikes us. The exhibitors at the I.C.A. are French, German, Czech, and Austrian, as well as English and Scottish. The techniques they have in common seem to provide them with a kind of Esperanto. Words one doesn't in fact know signal their meaning thanks to the design in which they are set.

But it is by no means certain that concrete poetry belongs more to literature than it does to the visual arts (one practitioner says frankly that "a more accurate term for this sort of work has still to be invented"). My own inclination is to see concrete poetry as somewhat closer to painting than it is to writing. Yet perhaps this preference is an irrational one, and counts as a comment on the very different atmospheres which now seem to surround poetry and painting in England. The show has none of that characteristic defensiveness which one associates with literary experiment. Nor does it have that excessive regard for the vagaries of the writer's own personality. How can one be satisfactorily "confessional" when one is also being "concrete"?

All the same, whether or not it inclines more to art than to literature, let me try to place the movement among the competing styles of modern painting. Its ancestry is, of course, very distinguished. It includes the Italian Futurists and Dada. In the guise that it now presents itself, however, concrete poetry seems to be the meeting ground of a number of absolutely contemporary ideas. It is, for example, a branch of abstract painting of the severe and geometrical sort. But the image creeps in at the back door, through the word which forms the unit of pattern. And often the meaning the image conveys is basically rather sentimental. If one examines the work of Ian Hamilton Finlay (the most highly regarded British practitioner) one is surprised to find that what he so often hints at is the refined and rather bloodless pastoralism of the Georgians—shut up inside the severe patterns he makes, a lyric from *The Week End Book* is mewing to be let out. But, to do Mr. Hamilton Finlay justice, he has another line of experiment which seems to me more fruitful. In his more recent work, he introduces the idea of sequences in time—a booklet whose pages you turn so that you encounter certain words in isolation, following each other in staccato rhythm. What one sees here is something like the revolt against the completely static image which one finds in Op Art.

Another topic which fascinates the concrete poets, as indeed it does many modern painters, is the relationship to be found between the word and the actual thing it stands for. It was an interest in this problem which seems to have inspired Appollinaire to create the *Calligrammes*—still the most beautiful and lyrical things of their kind. But this, in turn, inspires me to a brief digression—one cannot, I think, discuss the topic of concerte poetry without remarking that, even if it sometimes seems sentimental, it also has a genuinely lyrical strain. There is a purity and innocence about some of these typographical diagrams which can make the processes of conventional literature seem very laboured. Why bother to pile image on image when a diagram can give you the thing itself—the very object you wanted to represent?

But sometimes—and here I return to my main theme—concrete poetry is genuinely abstract. Letters become the basis for experiments in form—a ready made vocabulary of shapes from which interesting patterns and rhythms can be built up, but whose "ready made" quality provides the artist with a kind of necessary recalcitrance, a resistance to what he wants to do.

The work of poets and typographical designers here finds a point of contact with what is being done by one or two of the most highly regarded American painters, notably Jasper Johns. Some of John's most beautiful paintings are based upon sequences of numbers or of letters. These numbers and letters are, it is true, there so that John can "redeem" them with his beautiful brushwork, and in the severe typographical patterns favoured by some of the exhibitors at the I.C.A. one feels, perhaps, the want of just such an act of redemption.

It is here, I think, that one encounters the real weakness of the whole movement, in both its visual and its verbal aspect, as it has so far shown itself to us. The purity I have mentioned is paid for by a certain thinness. Even Apollinaire's *Calligrammes* seem notably less substantial than his other work. The constant fault of whimsicality, which one finds in so much concerte poetry, is perhaps one of the results of this thinness. But to pick upon this alone is not to go to the heart of the matter. The wish to provide a "total" experience of the kind I mentioned in my opening sentence was also a wish which was known at the period of the Baroque. Baroque theatre, with its elaborate stage machinery, its masques and pageants, was the product of just such a desire. On its less ambitious scale, and with a characteristically modern spareness, concrete poetry tries to do the same thing—to occupy all our faculties. It is significant that the exhibition at the I.C.A. appeals to the ear as well as the eye—there are recordings of the poets reading their own work; either specially created "sound poems", or the verbal translation of the images we see before us.

The dividing line between being occupied and being distracted is, one discovers, very narrow. I found myself delighted by the exhibition as a whole, but unable to regard many of the exhibits as independent works of art in their own right. Concrete poetry is, at the moment, a visual-verbal laboratory from which something wholly convincing has yet to emerge.

This piece represents a snap-reaction which I now consider to be ungenerous. Concrete poetry, and especially the work of Ian Hamilton Finlay, becomes richer as one studies it. Concrete poetry now seems to me to be a process of compression, whereby rich ideas are forced into few and simple words, which "tell" by their arrangement as well as through their content of verbal meaning and shades of meaning.

52. WHEN THE PATHS OF PAINTER AND THE WRITER MEET

Art and literature sometimes seem to have pursued oddly different paths in our century. True enough, at certain moments there has been a strong sympathy between painters and poets—one thinks of Picasso and Apollinaire, Picasso and Max Jacob, Picasso and Eluard; one thinks, too, of Mayakovsky and the early futurists in Russia. But the modern prejudice against the "literary" in painting has not, somehow, encouraged artists to read. At least, this is what one thinks at first.

Yet, in fact, the whole course of the Modern Movement is littered with splendid suites of illustrations. The superb books produced by Vollard encouraged Picasso and Matisse to do some of their very finest work. Of course, the modern *edition de luxe* is not really what a true book-collector would call a book. That is, one is not meant to read it—or not very often. Nevertheless, some of the famous French illustrated books have been moving tributes to the power of great literature over the artist's mind.

In England we have, on the whole, been less fortunate—at least until recently. There is a curious lack of information about the work of contemporary English artists in this field, and often the books themselves seem to be valued at less than their true worth. Gascoyne's *Poems 1937-1942*, with romantic illustrations by Graham Sutherland, is a sought-after book and by now a rather scarce one—but not nearly so sought after or so scarce as it would be were author and illustrator French. Nicholas Moore's wartime volume of poetry, *The Glass Tower*, with its strange illustrations by Lucien Freud, is hardly sought after at all, though it deserves to be.

Of course, these two books I've just mentioned were not designed as luxury objects—they are ordinary, commercial publications, produced, furthermore, under wartime conditions. The English competitors of Vollard have been few and far between. English book-collectors, unlike French ones, have tended to prefer the rare, but rather ugly, books of the sixteenth and seventeenth centuries to sumptuous productions by contemporaries. And the difference in taste is almost a matter of tradition—there is no real English equivalent of the fine illustrated editions which were produced in eighteenth-century France. The one moment when England was in the forefront as a producer of illustrated books was towards the end of the nineteenth century, and at the very beginning of our own. The books produced by Morris at the Kelmscott Press were followed by the volumes illustrated by Aubrey Beardsley.

Now, as I've said, the illustrator tends to take charge so firmly that the book almost disappears—one is left with a portfolio of prints, which happen to be connected with a particular text. In a way I regret this. It is pleasant to turn the pages of a fine volume and to absorb text and illustrations with one sweep of the eye. On the other hand, some recent book illustrations have seemed to me very splendid. The Ganymed Press edition of *King Lear*, illustrated by Kokoschka, was a happy marriage of artist and author. Kokoschka's bold Expressionist style did really seem to have something to tell us about the storm on the heath.

The revival of interest in artists' prints seems now to have brought about a renewed activity in the field of illustration. Every day brings news of a fresh project. These projects take very different forms. Some are modest, such as Bridget Riley's recent designs to accompany a text by the American painter and art-theorist, Ad Reinhardt, undertaken for *Poor . Old . Tired . Horse*, an enterprising literary magazine based in Scotland. The format is necessarily cheap—the magazine costs the princely sum of 9d., plus another 3d. for postage, from its publisher, the Wild Hawthorn Press. Surely the bargain of the year.

Much more ambitious, I imagine, will be the book which the American poet Jonathan Williams is currently at work on with his English-domiciled compatriot, R. B. Kitaj. This, by all accounts, is something very rare—a true collaboration between author and artist so that the book is being created from the very beginning as a collaborative project between the two. One looks forward to the result with yet keener anticipation because Williams is the man behind the Jargon Press, and has been responsible for some of the handsomest private-press books ever done in America.

Finally, there is news of another fascinating project—a suite of etchings by the irrepressible David Hockney, to illustrate poems by Cavafy. At first hearing, this sounds an unlikely combination, but I think the marriage of talents is likely to prove an inspired one. I have just seen the first pulls from some of the plates, and thought them not only the best work I had ever seen by the artist, but probably the finest prints produced in England since the war. Hockney uses the medium with staggering virtuosity—the deliberately naive style of his earlier days has become much more varied and flexible, and matches the sophistication of the Alexandrian poet stroke for stroke.

These developments are interesting in themselves—but still more fascinating when seen in a slightly broader context. Hockney's new involvement with literature is doubly significant because it is true to say that the Pop Art movement with which he was once identified marked a sudden break-through for "literariness" in a broader sense. If one thinks of the recent work done by some of the most important English and American artists, one realizes with a shock how near they have come to invading the field which is normally occupied by the writer. Paolozzi's recent series of screen-prints on the Wittgenstein theme, for instance, is a kind of personal commentary on the work of this knotty philosopher. Robert Rauschenberg's series of drawings (shown in his exhibition at the Whitechapel Gallery) based on Dante's *Inferno* were far less a series of illustrations than a kind of metaphor for the artist's own state of mind.

And this gives us a clue to what is happening in the book illustrations done by modern artists. The painter is no longer concerned with bodying forth the incidents and characters in the text. Instead, he is trying to tell us about a personal experience of particular words; or even, simply, about a particular author. What happens when a boy from Bradford meets a world-weary Alexandrian? Hockney will let us know.

PART III

53. ART AND THE PRIVATE SELF

The exhibition currently on view at Cyril Humphris Ltd., in Old Bond Street, is one which gives me a good deal of pleasure. For me, its chief interest is to be found in a small group of Renaissance bronzes from the collection of Prince Nicolas of Rumania. Here are things of a quality now very rarely to be found on the art market; a seated satyr of Riccio, a Pan by Antico, a putto mounted on a fabulous animal by Arendt van Bolten, and a statuette of a pacing horse which is Mantuan, and which dates from the late fifteenth century. Each of these little sculptures is the product of a powerful artistic personality. In the Riccio, for example, we find a reminder of the stony classicism of Mantegna; while the piping Pan is a more refined, a more poetic creation. In turn, both of these make a striking contrast with the wild, late-Mannerist fantasy of the piece by van Bolten. Yet all have one thing in common. These are pre-eminently works made for private contemplation. And this affects them deeply in the matter of style and technique.

The Antico, for instance, does not give up all its secrets at first glance. It is striking, first of all, for the marvellous virtuosity with which the metal is handled. The artist is at pains to emphasize the nature and possibilities of the medium—surfaces are smooth, hard; resistant to the glance as well as to the touch. The mat of hair on Pan's goat-legs is chased in meticulous detail, so is the vine-wreath in his hair. The eyes are inlaid with little spots of silver. The piece looks what it is: expensive, the best that money can buy. For the modern audience, such a piece presents difficulties. The artist seems too much in love with his own skill. However, if one has time and patience to look again, the mood subtly alters. The expression of the face begins to make its impact. Pan is playing his pipe, yet he seems to be sunk in melancholy. The left arm—the one not occupied with the instrument—is stretched out in a gesture which seems curiously searching and tentative.

Indeed, on this further examination, it seems a piece which invites us to Pateresque reverie. It tempts the onlooker to weave a rich and personal web of fantasy. It is only later still—perhaps at a third visit—that one realizes that all of these effects are intended; that here is a work of art which both offers aesthetic satisfaction, and takes it away. What lies at the bottom of the ambiguities? Simply, I think, that the artist is making something which is meant to be looked at by one man alone, or at most by very few people. All that is public is rejected. This does not, like the charming Sienese madonna in wood (also to be found in Mr. Humphris's exhibition), refer to the iconography of a religion many of whose ceremonies are public acts. The patron could afford it; the patron commissioned it. And damn the common good.

Thus it is that we find the reason for a kind of style which Antico adopts. His beautiful craftsmanship is not merely a matter of the artist worshipping his own power over his material. It is meant to armour the statuette against the indifference which comes with total familiarity. When we live with a work of art, carelessnesses and minor imperfections soon assume a wholly disproportionate role. Our response is governed not by the grandeur of the concept but by the meanness of the flaw. Antico intends the glittering polish of his style to act not as a barrier but as a doorway. A work of art which is to be looked at again and again—lived with as a friend—can afford to be a little reticent about living up its message.

I have chosen to talk about this group of bronzes not only because they excite me as works of art but because they seem to me to sum up a modern dilemma. With works of this quality, we are apt to think it a pity when they are not permanently available to the public—or, to be blunt, we disapprove when they are not in a museum. Yet here is a very real sense in which museums are inimical to our appreciation of such things. I remember my disappointment with the recent exhibition of Renaissance bronzes at the Victoria and Albert Museum. Not that the show was lacking in masterpieces. But this throng of bronzes proved to be an indigestible banquet. The treasures of the world's museums were there, four and five to a case, and (in museum terms) decently enough displayed. But one became more and more conscious that this was not the way to see them. The exhibition informed, but it did not satisfy. It was rather like watching a superb production of a play where every actor spoke in a whisper.

If this problem—because of a radical change in society, and in consequence of social attitudes—seems to be an insoluble one, it does at least suggest two quite different trains of thought. One is that we should at least pause and consider before we demand that all works of art of any consequence should pass into public ownership. It may be unfair that not every man can own an original Antico—but is the personal communication which such a work of art can only make in private to be so lightly sacrificed and destroyed? I ask this question with the purpose of asking another, which concerns not the art of the past but the art of our own day. It is this: does the idea of personal communication any longer have a place in contemporary art?

I would suggest that one place to look for an answer is a little farther up Bond Street, where the Kasmin Gallery has an exhibition of pictures by the American artist Kenneth Noland. Mr. Noland's huge diamond-shaped canvases, with their chevrons of colour, have already aroused a good deal of controversy. Reactions from art critics have ranged from the excited to the indifferent. If I now find myself on the side of the excited it is, I think, because Noland strikes me as being an artist who is ambiguous in almost the way that Antico is, but one who has, so to speak, rearranged his ambiguity to fit a different set of circumstances.

The two biggest pictures, for example, are each about 8ft. or more broad. They are something, so the size tells us, for the public gallery rather than for the private collector. Yet they are not, in any obvious sense, "public statements" in the sense in which we usually understand this phrase. The painter is addressing himself to the individual consciousness. This he does however many people may be present to look at his work. In this he reminds us—I do not think this is a new comparison—of the designers of some of the famous temple-gardens in Japan: for instance, the famous raked sand garden of the Ryoanjo temple at Kyoto. These Zen gardens embrace the individual consciousness, just as Noland's pictures do. The Renaissance statuette, on the other hand, seeks to focus consciousness intensely on a point. Yet each is concerned with the notion of private experience. The dog goes off to its corner with a bone; privacy, real or imagined, often seems essential if we are to get the real marrow from a work of art.

54. MASTER DRAUGHTSMEN AND THEIR ART

Under the proud yet modest title "Masterpieces of the Print Room", the British Museum has just mounted an exhibition such as, I believe, no other collection in the world could show. The screens are filled with the fine flower of the museum's collection of drawings—an endless procession of great names passes before the gaze of the enraptured viewer: Pisanello, Mantegna, Botticelli, Leonardo, Raphael, Correggio, Dürer, Holbein, Clouet, Rembrandt, Rubens, Van Dyck, Claude, Watteau, Tiepolo, Piranesi, Turner. In the centre of the room, a number of cases are devoted to the museum's collection of sketchbooks, and here the display includes Claude's "Liber Veritatis" and the only surviving Shoreham-period sketchbook by Samuel Palmer.

The museum claims that the exhibition "has been arranged primarily for those of our visitors—especially those from abroad—who may wish to have a general view of some of the riches of the department but have not sufficient time at their disposal for a more leisurely and detailed study of our collection". Certainly no one within reach should fail to see it—here is one of the essential experiences in the fine arts, a unique opportunity to compare, one with another, the greatest draughtsmen of the western European tradition.

But before I exhaust my rapidly dwindling stock of superlatives, let me turn to a slightly different topic—from the collection on view at the British Museum to the nature of draughtsmanship. What is a drawing? A simple question, but one which requires a complicated answer. Here, as so often with the visual arts, the most fruitful approach is crab-wise—stealthy rather than direct. As it happens, I have just been reading the *Treatise on Images* by the eighth-century Byzantine theologian, St. John Damascene. The images which the author of this work had in mind were of course those of the saints, attacked and destroyed by fanatics during the Iconoclast Controversy. Nevertheless, let me quote one or two definitions from his treatise. "An image", he says, "is a likeness and representation of someone, containing in itself the person who is imagined." And then, again: "Every image is a revelation and representation of something hidden. For instance, man has not a clear knowledge of what is invisible, the spirit being veiled to the body, nor of future things, nor of things apart and distant, because he is circumscribed by place and time." Let me be the first to admit, before shocked Byzantinists arise and denounce me, that I am quoting out of context. But not, I think, frivolously. These passages sprang irresistibly to mind when I visited the exhibition I have just been talking about.

What was the reason? Chiefly that draughtsmanship is that aspect of the visual arts which concentrates most thoroughly upon the image (using the word now in the broad sense) and upon the making of images. The pen or the pencil can be a powerful vehicle for the fantasy of the artist. The whiplash line of Botticelli does indeed produce the "likeness and representation of someone"—we see it clearly in the famous drawing of "Abundance", which is now on show. Nor does it matter that the "someone" is here imaginary. Botticelli's drawing still "contains in itself the person who is imaged". Or, rather, if we prefer, it contains the *quality* which is imaged.

But let me now pass on to my other quotation, that in which St. John Damascene talks about "the revelation and representation of something hidden". There are two ways in which we might choose to apply this. In the first place, one can point—as indeed I have already done—to the place of draughtsmanship as a vehicle for the artist's fantasy. In the second place, one might talk of drawing as the vehicle for sensibility (which, I submit, is something a bit different).

The drawings on show at the British Museum cover a very wide range in time, and the artists use a great variety of media. There is pen and ink, pen and ink and wash, silverpoint on a prepared surface, chalk, watercolour, and gouache. Yet always, compared to painting, we notice the simplicity of the means used. Every artist speaks more intimately in his drawings; he is more relaxed and informal; he is using a medium in which his thoughts are immediately given form, without, for the most part, any intervening, preparatory stage. Some drawings, it is true, are more "finished" than others, but always the sense of immediacy is preserved.

There results, I believe, a kind of collaboration between the inner impulses of the draughtsman and the image which he consciously wants to body forth. At times these inner impulses are imprisoned and almost subdued. I am thinking, here, of Holbein's hard, practical outlines in his designs for goldsmith's work, and also of Dürer's very similar project for a table fountain. At other times, impulse is given free play, and some of the most beautiful drawings on view show evidence of this. There are, for example, the landscapes by Dürer himself, by Claude, and by Rubens. In each of these our interest is focused not so much on the thing represented, or, rather, the place depicted, as on the way in which a unique and powerful sensibility is expressing itself through tree and rock and water. The angle of a branch, the trembling flick of the brush which creates a leaf—these give us an insight into the veiled recesses of the artist's soul.

In figure drawings, the play of sensibility becomes a subtler matter still. Let us compare the drawing of a female nude by Watteau with a figure drawing by Tiepolo. The Watteau, all rounded contours and silken shading, is carried out in three colours of chalk. The Tiepolo, sharp, dynamic, and somewhat sinister, is drawn in the characteristic medium of the Venetian eighteenth-century pen and ink and bistre wash. What very different attitudes to our fleshy envelope are here exposed! And what a totally different rhythm the two artists have! Watteau is reflectively sensuous, melancholy, yet hedonistic. Tiepolo relies on an almost inconceivable rapidity of hand, which argues, at the same time, a slight contempt for the flesh as opposed to the spirit. The figures in his drawings are conjured up with the impatient gestures of a magician.

It is sometimes said that drawings are things which require an intellectual appreciation of their qualities, rather than a direct sensuous reaction. It is certainly true that the study of Old Master drawings is one of the most exacting specialties open to the art-historian. But it is exacting because it requires such a delicate responsiveness—mere learning is not enough. If we want the directest possible access to the springs of artistic creation, it is drawings we must turn to. The scholars know this still better than the rest of us.

55. ON DECADENCE AND VIRTUOSITY

It is sometimes salutary to view the art of a civilization which is in decline. Yet, curiously enough, the medicine is hard to come by. So many cultures formerly regarded as "decadent" have now been rescued from that verdict by the efforts of scholars, or else by the mere alteration of taste. Byzantium, for example, once a by-word for mummification, is now something we have been taught to see in a new light. Only recently the publication of the Reverend Gervase Matthew's brilliant little book, *Byzantine Aesthetics*, carried the rehabilitation a step further, and taught us to respect the secular achievements of Byzantine art, as well as its spirituality. Indeed, by the tenets of true pragmatism—and our approach to the arts has of necessity become almost purely pragmatic—the art of one epoch is seldom either better or worse than that of another, but only different.

The current exhibition at the Arts Council Gallery—"The Arts of the Ch'ing Dynasty"—is a trifle difficult to fit into this comfortable scheme of things, this egg-and-spoon race where prizes are automatically given to all the contestants. There is no way out of it: Ch'ing art is not despicable, but it represents a decline from the art of the Ming, or the Sung, or the T'ang. We are conscious, as we look at this exhibition, that we are looking at the products of a dying culture, of a civilization which has ceased to adapt itself, which has become both stiff and brittle.

Though the time has long gone when the only Chinese art which Occidentals liked, or indeed knew anything about, was that of the late seventeenth and eighteenth century, and though there is even a sense in which Ch'ing art is now "out of fashion", it is possible to see all too clearly why the most sumptuous products of the dynasty still fetch high prices in the saleroom. They have the tact not to ask us to think. This particular piece of jade may imitate an archaic bronze vessel; that porcelain vase may display a technical control, a mastery of material which has seldom been equalled. But their appeal lies chiefly in mere complication and richness.

Even when we look at the self-coloured porcelains—technically, I suppose, amongst the most perfect things which the potter has ever produced—we are conscious of a lack. We appreciate the products of the best Japanese artist-potters, despite their occasional affectation, for a quality which, loosely enough, we name "spontaneity". We appreciate the celadons of Sung for their inwardness. But when we look at even the most restrained and tasteful of the Ch'ing self-colours, even, for example, when we look at the wonderfully elegant, wonderfully restrained *clair de lune* brushspot included in the present exhibition, we are conscious of an element of virtuosity, and with that element comes a coldness in our response.

The word "virtuosity" of course brings me to the nub of my feelings about the exhibition. It always seems a pity to take up a word which has been used so wildly and so unfairly, and set it rolling on its course once again. There is no doubt that "virtuosity" is now amongst the most damning pejoratives in the critic's vocabulary. It is a way of condemning skill, control, conscious enjoyment of the act of creation—all qualities which once counted as artistic virtues. Now we are asked to regard all this with displeasure. What the critic normally means when he uses the word "virtuosity" is that he feels shut out—that the artist has performed a conjuring trick, and brought forth the creation whole before the critic could see which sleeve it came from. We do not, on the whole, object to conjuring when it is slow and clumsy.

Yet the fact that the thing created is not untidy enough, indeed not wounded and bleeding and crippled and imperfect enough, to allow the critic to identify himself with its struggle to be born, is no real condemnation. Works of art have a right to be wounded and crippled and altogether monstrous if the life-force within them is strong enough to overcome what are really defects. But they also, it seems to me, have a right to be spruce and trim, if they wish to be. A picture by Chardin, for example, often has such an air of rightness and being at ease with itself that we never pause to ask by what process it was made—more, we never try to project ourselves into the act of its creation. We are content to enjoy it as it is, without forethought or afterthought.

It is worth saying then, that by virtuosity I do not mean merely that self-contained quality, that air of completeness, which certain works of art possess, and which we wrongly resent because we are blinded by prejudice. What I mean is, quite simply, that in nearly all late Chinese work, there is an element of showing off. Things are not done for their own sake, but to reflect credit on the maker. We are asked to admire, not the perfection of the thing, but the cleverness of the man who has achieved such a complicated yet tidy result, and now wishes to be praised for it. We see this clearly enough, I think, in the painting by Ch'ing artists, which are so often "in the manner of" some admired earlier artist.

It is false, of course, to assume that these are no better than fakes—or even that they are honest copies, striving to get as close to the original as possible. The artist who paints like this is a man assuming a role—the brush is an actor, the paper is a stage. We see this especially clearly in Chinese painting because here gesture is everything: it is a short step from the motions of the actor to those of the painter. And here, I think, is the point at which we find the real definition of the idea of decadence with which we began. Decadence in art depends upon this shift from creation to interpretation. It is when the artist wishes to be thought of as a performer and not as a maker that the trouble begins.

The art of our own day, with its almost frantic emphasis on innovation, might lead us to imagine that the disease has nothing to do with us. I think we should be foolish to think anything of the kind. How often in modern art are we asked to transfer our attention from the object to the man who made it, to interest ourselves in the personality rather than the product? This is the eternal demand that actors make.

56. A GLIMPSE OF GERICAULT

The excellent exhibition, "Géricault to Courbet", which is now to be seen at Roland, Browse and Delbanco, was to me particularly exciting because I found in it no fewer than three works by Géricault himself—an unusual event in a London gallery. For some reason, I have always been fascinated by this artist. Géricault is so various, so forceful, and, above all, so mysterious. The three works on view represent three totally different aspects of a complicated personality. One is a water colour of a leaping tiger which shows all that penetrating sympathy with animals which we often find in the best artists of the Romantic period. Another is a portrait of a boy with flowing hair. Painted in very few colours, the whole picture is of marvellous force—the white paint of the collar sets off the firmly modelled head. The third painting is one of Géricault's studies for his masterpiece, "Le Radeau de la Méduse". Like so many other things in the artist's *oeuvre*, it both horrifies and seduces. The head of a cadaver—wrenched back on to the shoulder, the dead eyes half-open, one a faint gleam in the midst of a pool of shadow—is created with broad, rapid strokes of greenish paint, so cunningly used that it seems phosphorescent. The brush-work, both here and in the portrait, has Géricault's characteristic bluntness of touch. Few artists have so definite and masculine a way of putting paint on canvas.

But of course these three works give us only a glimpse of what Géricault could do. His variousness springs from many sources—temperament being not the least important. But it does help to explain Géricault when we recall that his brief career spanned two entirely different political epochs, the Empire and the Restoration. He exhibited his first important picture, the "Officier de Chasseurs à Cheval, Chargeant", at the Salon of 1812. In this picture are united two themes which haunted the artist's imagination—horseflesh, and the Napoleonic legend. Yet it was Géricault who, as a member of the King's guard, accompanied Louis XVIII on his flight at the beginning of the xundred Days.

Constantly we find the unexpected. Clément—Géricault's earliest and best biographer—describes the artist as being outwardly a typical romantic dandy of the early part of the nineteenth century, athletically built, a superb horseman, handsome and seductive—"*ses yeux surtout, pleins d'éclairs at de caresses, avaient un charme irrésistible.*" Such a man might well delight in some of the subjects which Géricault depicted: the horse-races, the prize-fights, the pretty amazon on her spirited mount. Such a man might even have the cultivation to attempt some of the classical themes we find in Géricault. But what of the rest? For he has yet other images to offer us, and in these his true originality is to be found. It is they which complete the picture of his work, and give meaning to whatever else he chooses to paint.

These images are those of death and suffering, and of ordinary life. War, for Géricault, is more terrible than romantic. What he seeks out is the cart full of wounded men—its slow, jolting, agonized progress haunts his imagination, he makes it haunt ours. The studies for "Le Radeau de la Méduse" are literally a charnel house—severed heads and limbs—the heads wrapped in stained cloth, the limbs piled together like so many joints of meat. No one has ever painted a more terrifying still-life than the one by Géricault which is in the Musée Fabre, Montpellier—a pile of arms and legs. Yet Clément very justly calls it "*un des plus beaux morceaux que Géricault ait peints*". Equally marvellous in their way are the late studies of various types of madness—the series contains some of the most brilliant portraits produced during the nineteenth century. We feel in these pictures a hard, keen, pitiless observation which is unmatchable elsewhere.

More fascinating still are the scenes of ordinary life, many of them done in England. Here we meet not only the old rural crafts, but the new industrialism, and the life of towns. One lithograph, for example, shows us the old paralytic woman being dragged along in her rough wooden chair, while the passers-by look at her with horror and pity. Nothing is exaggerated; there is no touch of sentimentality. The artist tells us what *is*, and we are convinced. In this power over reality Géricault resembles some of his predecessors in French art, and especially Louis Le Nain, who gives us the same feeling of careful respect for the facts, yet who has (as Géricault also has) the power to infuse these facts with feeling.

Most extraordinary of all, in view of Géricault's character and background, are the pictures which lead us into the world of work. Chief among these is "Le Four à Plâtre", now in the

Louvre. This picture was lent to the Romantic Exhibition at the Tate, and I still remember Mr. John Berger's brilliant analysis of it. What matters about his picture is that the scene is painted with such absolute seriousness, yet without any touch of heroic exaggeration, and certainly without the least trace of caricature. It is the impassivity of the presentation which makes its point.

Géricault was not a detached observer by temperament—much the opposite. Throughout his work, from first to last, we are aware of a titanic struggle—a great talent at grips with powerful neurosis. The executions, the corpses, the wounded men—in these there is more than a touch of the sadist. In every death, in every wound, Géricault finds something which both obsesses him and yet makes him deeply afraid. In recreating these images, he is also exorcizing them. It is impressive how the painter continues to grow, right up to the very end of his short life. The struggle with the classic, and with the art of Michelangelo, which we see during Géricault's stay in Rome in 1816 to 1818, is especially instructive. This is the one moment when Géricault is at odds with his own style: when the great boa-constrictor from the Sistine Chapel threatens to swallow him up. Yet, once he has absorbed the lesson of Michelangelo, how marvellously he applies it! This, for example, is the hidden root—one of the hidden roots—of wha_ we see in "Le Four". The massive work-horses in the fore ground are descendants of Michelangelo's Adam.

57. THE IMAGE OF VIOLENCE

"To become a real beast", said Mr. Arthur Koestler at the Institute of Contemporary Arts the other day, "man needs a perfect cause". One was tempted to stretch the words a bit further than he meant them to go. Mr. Koestler was performing the opening ceremony at the I.C.A.'s newly hung "Study for an Exhibition of Violence in Contemporary Art". He spoke extremely cogently. Yet there was one point which he did not make. Walking round the exhibition, I was struck by the huge field which it covered. At first, this seemed to be merely over-enthusiasm on the part of the organizers. Anything, it seemed, was "violent" if you looked at it closely enough—from Boccioni, to Mondrian, to Mathieu. But, after all, wasn't there some guiding thread which linked the whole thing together?

The thread, I think, is the concept of the modern artist as a sort of superman. We have tried to banish Nietzsche from politics, but we still tacitly approve of him in the arts. Peter Porter has a good image for the artist's attitude in a new poem called "The Great Poet Comes Here in Winter". The protagonist speaks:—

> Frau Antonia is a cabbage;
> If I were a grub, I'd eat a hole in her.

Most modern painters don't even offer us the diffidence of the "if".

As Mr. Koestler was careful to point out in his speech, aggression of some kind plays, and always has played, an important part in artistic activity. He also reminded his audience that when we talk of any "revolution" in the arts we imply, by the very use of the word, a certain degree of violence and upset. But our own epoch is the first in which the artist has laid claim to such a sweeping command over existence. It is his act which counts, and not what is acted upon.

Perhaps I can best explain this rather gnomic phrase by taking a small excursion into politics. I have never found Marxist hostility to experimental art at all surprising or illogical. At first, it is true, the Russians worked on the naïve assumption that the political revolution must necessarily be sympathetic to the artistic one. But soon enough they reached the correct conclusion—that the experimental artist must always be a rival to the monolithic state. The reason was simple. Both the artist and the state claimed total hegemony over the world as it exists. And both took it upon themselves to change the world to conform to their own image.

The term "bourgeois individualism" has such a weary familiarity that all the meaning seems to have drained out of it. But, if we put the emphasis on the noun instead of the adjective, it begins to regain a little of its old force. As Hobbes reminds us, an individual—a man alone—is hardly a man at all. What we often see in modern art is the individual attempting to escape from the claims of society—to revert to the god-like or beast-like state. It is the claim to pure, untrammelled liberty which generates the violence which we see in contemporary art, and which is also, in a sense, the justification of that violence.

Included in the exhibition at the I.C.A. is a picture by Richard Hamilton which already enjoys a certain notoriety. It is called "Portrait of Hugh Gaitskell as a Famous Monster of Filmland". The medium is oil and collage used to transform a photographic image—the image of Gaitskell's face. The catalogue of the exhibition classifies it as an example of "Violence as a Weapon". What sort of a weapon, and used against whom? Is it an assault on Gaitskell's memory? Or his political beliefs? On the conventional idea of good taste? It might be any or all of these things. But it is also something else—a particularly sharp assertion of the artist's right to use whatever material he chooses in whatever way he chooses.

Yet there is another side to it. Hamilton's picture has enormous impact. It is a memorable and disturbing image which lingers in the mind. What makes it memorable is the sense of conflict that it gives—it makes a claim to complete liberty, and yet simultaneously reminds us of the obstacles to that liberty. This is true, to a greater or less degree, of nearly all the figurative works represented in the exhibition. One of the most disturbing of them all—even more disturbing than the picture by Hamilton—is "The Rape" by Magritte. Even after repeated viewing, this famous canvas retains its impact. The power of the statement which it makes about the terrors and attractions of sex springs from the wholly specific nature of the imagery which it employs. It could hardly be plainer or earthier.

The non-figurative works, by their very blandness, give one the real feeling that here, as elsewhere, it takes two to make a quarrel, that the superman can only assert himself to action if there is some challenge to his supremacy. We find, for example, that the organizers of the exhibition have classified Mathieu as a representative of the "Violence of Direct Expression". There is something both tranquillising and boring about the completely autonomous nature of Mathieu's artistic expression. This calligraphy may hold a charge of energy within itself, but no demand is made upon it, and therefore the energy remains locked up somewhere inside the picture. The spectator remains obstinately detached.

It is too early, of course, to make any judgment about the violence to be found in modern art—the exhibition is content to document and record. But one thing seems to be fairly certain. By setting themselves up as little gods, each creating a universe, artists are running a great risk. Every god of this sort needs his blasphemers. It is the curses of the impious which tell him he is still there. Will the audience continue to resist?

58. THE UNCOMMONNESS OF MEDARDO ROSSO

Medardo Rosso is one of those half-submerged figures in the history of art—acknowledged to be interesting and important, but little exhibited. The small but brilliant exhibition of his work which is now on show at the Museum of Modern Art in New York catches one almost totally unprepared. Rosso's achievement was an intensely personal one. His name is often coupled with that of Rodin, and it is true that he felt an intense rivalry towards the more famous French sculptor. Indeed, Rosso accused Rodin of piracy, and claimed that the "Balzac" contained borrowings which Rodin was reluctant to acknowledge. Then, again, Rosso is sometimes named as the real source of such more recent "humanist" Italian artists as Marini, Greco, and Manzù. Yet there is another side to him. There is the fact that the wild men of the Italian Futurist Movement admired him intensely. Stranger still, there is the fact that, at moments, he has distinct affinities with Brancusi. One of the difficulties about assessing Rosso is that his achievement is a very fragmentary one. His development as an artist is rather lacking in logic, some of his most important works have been destroyed (due both to bad luck and the extreme fragility of the materials which he used). For the last part of his life he worked very little. In any case, he seems never to have been prolific. And there is another difficulty still. Rosso is a very uncommon kind of artist—one whose achievement quite visibly transcends the intellectual basis of his work. A visitor to the New York exhibition is likely to be first enchanted, then repelled, and then enchanted again.

Rosso was born in 1858 at Turin. He trained at the Brera Academy, from which (in 1883) he was expelled. In spite of this evidence of rebelliousness, his early work belongs very clearly in the tradition of sentimental realism which flourished in Italy at this time. This tradition was something which remained with him. The one constant factor in his work is the liking for the "sweet" subject, for the anecdote, for emotion. English country houses of the Victorian period are full of statuary by now-forgotten Italian artists in which all these qualities are well to the fore. Anyone who looks at Rosso's work objectively must, I think, acknowledge that it, too, is tainted with the qualities we dislike in those sugary confections. Then, too, Rosso was much attracted by that *morbidezza* which we find in much Italian sculpture of the time. Those familiar busts of veiled girls are paralleled by his own "Donna Velata". On his anecdotal side, Rosso fails to sustain comparison with Daumier. Taken as images of humanity, or as projections of social attitudes, his "Kiss under the Lamp-post", or even the much stronger "Bookmaker" or "Man in Hospital" has little of Daumier's compassionate indignation.

The thing that rescues Rosso's work, and which frequently draws it up to great heights, is its astonishing technique and its originality of form. Rosso's great gift was his sensibility to light, light which dissolves the image, which smoothes it away—light which becomes what it caresses. Rosso was willing to risk the utmost distortion, the most daring transitions, in order to express this feeling. His work is often totally illogical. All the forms are daringly truncated. We are not allowed to choose our own viewpoint. We must look from one spot, and one only. Then the seemingly chaotic object before us suddenly resolves into a superbly realized image. Often Rosso used a special technique of wax over plaster in order to get his effects. In the New York exhibition it is possible to see how well this fragile medium suited him. The pieces in wax have a translucency which draws the eye on into the form—we see not only the epidermis but the structure beneath.

But even in other materials the magic works. One of the most impressive and certainly one of the most extreme works on show in New York is the "Yvette Guilbert", which is made of terracotta. Rosso's image challenges Lautrec's. Lautrec caricatures the singer. Rosso presents us with a haunting, unseizable, yet somehow monumental image. One side of the face is almost unmodelled; it has dissolved away in the gas-light of the theatre. The mouth is a slash, the famous ribbon round the neck is another slash. But the main forms are large and grand—the features seem like casual, accidental scribblings on a surface which rejects them.

The parallel with Brancusi can be seen clearly in another sculpture—the "Madame X" of 1896. Here is something which shows a startling resemblance to Brancusi's "Muse"—the same studied simplicity, the same pure oval. Yet Rosso started, I imagine, from a very different point. Brancusi wants to show us the "typical" form, the image in which all other possible images are contained. Rosso is obsessed by the action of a particular sort of light, a light which will never act again as it does now, at this moment.

The closer Rosso comes to complete chaos, the more dazzling the result. For me his masterpiece is the "Baby Chewing Bread" from the Hirshorn Collection. Void and solid are ignored. The piece is a flow of lava. From this lava the germ emerges. If one ran one's fingers over it the tactile sensations would certainly bear no relation to what one sees—and yet it works triumphantly.

59. MLLE. POGANY REVISITED

Among the most significant masters of the past hundred years—or so it seems to me—there are only a very few who triumph by their tenacity, by their gift for exploring an idea to its uttermost limits. Among these are Seurat and Constantin Brancusi. Both are artists who give me great pleasure. Unfortunately, British public galleries are not rich in works by either of them. At the National Gallery there is, of course, Seurat's sublime "Baignade à Asnières", which makes such a fascinating comparison with the Poussins only a room away. And at the Tate there is Brancusi's "Mlle. Pogany".

This sculpture is a version of an idea which pre-occupied Brancusi for 20 years—from 1913 to 1933. There are fairly numerous other versions in stone and in bronze, most of them more elaborate than this, in that they include the hands. Indeed, the version in the Tate, which dates from about 1920, is labelled not "Mlle. Pogany" but "Study for 'Mlle. Pogany' ". Beautiful as it is, no one would rank it among the most important of Brancusi's sculptures. Yet there is enough there to hint at the reasons why this Rumanian of peasant stock is probably the greatest sculptor that the twentieth century has so far produced.

From the very beginning Brancusi was a paradox. As Ionel Jianou remarks in his recent book about him, Brancusi believed that " Heaven, God, the occult forces which animate the world were really present in everyday life". His whole attitude towards his materials was that of the peasant craftsman—caressing, smoothing, perfecting. It is well known that Brancusi never used assistants. He did everything himself. The impulses behind each new creation were often very complex. "The Seal", for example, was in part inspired by the gesture of a girl sitting by a waterfall. It was the movement by which she finally set herself free from an unhappy love affair. And yet, for Brancusi, this gesture finally embodied itself in an abstraction made from the smooth sea-creature.

No romantic story of this sort attaches to the creation of "Mlle. Pogany". And yet the sculpture remains at the centre of an extraordinarily complex web of relationships. There is, first of all, the way in which it is linked to other studies of women by Brancusi—"The Sleeping Muse", for example, the "Portrait of Mrs. Eugene Meyer", "The Princess", "The White Negress". These have none of the "creatureliness" of Brancusi's studies of animals. Instead, Brancusi considers human beings, sometimes in their legendary but more often in their social relationships. The series of sculptures devoted to the theme of "Mlle. Pogany" is the one where these social aspects are the most prominent.

In the first place, Brancusi was attempting something which apparently ran completely counter to the whole main trend of his art—a portrait-bust. And, astonishing though it may seem, he was successful even in the matter of catching a likeness. The portrait is said to have much resembled the sitter. Even the Tate version, which is among the most abstract, still retains certain essentials of what must have been a very striking appearance—the neat small head, the sharp nose, the sweep of the eyebrows, the curls at the nape. In earlier versions, such as that of 1913 in the Museum of Modern Art in New York, the lady has huge Sumerian eyes and a tiny mouth. Jean Arp, a sculptor much influenced by Brancusi, once wrote a poem about the piece, in which he called Mlle. Pogany "*une parente de Lady Shub-ad la belle Summérienne et de Nefertiti*". He also described her, a line later, as "*la féerique grand-mère de la sculpture abstraite*". A formidable heritage, and an equally formidable responsibility.

But, in fact, one of the fascinating things about the sculpture in all its versions is the fact that it belongs to its own time. Mlle. Pogany is a Paul Poiret beauty. One does not have to look at her for very long to see emerging the outlines of a 1913 fashion drawing. We surmise that she wore a hobble skirt. Her sinuous elegance has, concealed within itself, sly references to Art Nouveau. The last cocottes must have looked a little like this. Brancusi has known exactly how to exploit this ephemeral material, and in this he is as much of a pop artist as any of the young tigers who have recently been hogging the headlines. Part of the fascination of the piece is the way in which smartness and fashionableness are suddenly made to work for a living. This is, of course, not entirely unprecedented in art. Anyone who cares to look at the splendid series of coins issued by the Greek city of Syracuse in the fifth century B.C. will see something of the same kind taking place. Here the nymph Arethusa, patroness of the city, is shown wearing the elaborate coiffures favoured by the young beauties of the time.

But what is particularly fascinating is the way in which Brancusi juggles with two entirely different concepts of "modernity". The Rumanian peasant was a sophisticate, after all. One kind of modernity is the kind we see in fashion—the rush to put a new face on things, to be in tune with the times. It is interesting, for example, that in making "Mlle Pogany" Brancusi comes quite close to some of the experiments which the Italian Futurists were making at the same period. But he is, I think, more intelligent than they, because he realizes that there is a tension between this kind of novelty and the sort which he himself wants to create. The novelty of smartness is something that manifests itself by contrast—we define it in terms of what has gone before, in a series of negatives. We are always saying what it *isn't*. Brancusi wants to produce a new creation with positive values of its own, where no such negatives are needed in the description. And this is what he achieves with "Mlle. Pogany". To infuse the momentary with all the weight and spiritual force of genuine classicism is a very considerable feat. It is done without sentimentality, without archaizing, and, above all, without making the subject look ridiculous. Brancusi makes us realize that there is something eternal about this pretty woman, who presents herself to us in the fashions of her day.

60. THE POET AND THE PAINTER

At the end of this month, a retrospective exhibition of the work of Joan Miró opens at the Tate. News of this made me turn again to a poem which is said to have been inspired by one of Miró's paintings: the beautiful "Angel Surrounded by Paysans" by Wallace Stevens. This poem is typical of Stevens's method of writing. He takes the abstract shapes he finds in the painting, and transforms them radically, just as he so often transformed the things he found in nature. The result has its own truth to the work which is its source, without being in any way a description. Stevens sees one form in the middle of the composition as being especially significant, and it is this which becomes the "angel" and addresses us:

> Am I not,
> Myself, only half of a figure of a sort,
> A figure half seen, or seen for a moment, a man
> Of the mind, an apparition apparelled in
> Apparels of such lightest look that a turn
> of my shoulder and quickly, too quickly,
> I am gone?

In comparing this to a typical Miró (in so far as one medium can be compared with another) one sees what is gained, and also what is lost by the metamorphosis. The poet is more definite than the painter. Sinuous and subtle as he is, Stevens cannot leave us to choose between possibilities, as the painter does. He must settle for one way of looking, an anthropomorphic way, and the words must guide us into seeing as he does. On the other hand, this greater explicitness brings with it something which Miró often lacks—a quality which I can only call "moral density". By which I mean that Stevens manages to show us something of our own impermanence, and to convince us that this impermanence, steadily regarded, yields its own value and meaning:

> Yet I am the necessary angle of earth,
> Since, in my sight, you see the earth again . . .

This is something which the painting may hint at, yet cannot say outright.

Yet, while it is true to say that modern poets take a more informed interest in the visual arts than most people, the marriage between painting and poetry is not always such a happy one. It is fair to say, I think, that there is a tradition when it comes to writing poems about works of art—a tradition which has been handed down to us from the great Romantic poets. One progenitor is Keats, with the "Ode to a Grecian Urn" and the sonnet on the Elgin marbles. Another is Browning. This ancestry suggests that poems about works of art will tend to join the anecdotal to the exclamatory. Thus, a contemporary poet writes about Caravaggio's "Conversion of St. Paul":

> O wily painter, limiting the scene
> From a cacophony of dusty forms
> To the one convulsion, what is it you mean
> In that wide gesture of the lifting arms?

It is unfair to quote out of context, especially as the poet gives us concrete details elsewhere in the poem, but I find in these few lines a good example of the way that the words so often begin to move away from the ostensible subject—a necessary closeness and intimacy is lost.

But why do I find this closeness, this intimacy, so essential? It may well be argued that for the poet the work of art, any work of art that he happens to choose, is merely an excuse, a germ from which the poem can grow. And this is true, of course, when we look at a poem like Yeats's "Lapis-Lazuli". Yet it seems to me that a close study of painting, especially of modern painting, has a good deal to offer the poet. On the whole, when faced with the great question of modernity, poets and painters have been forced to give diametrically opposite answers. For the painters, modernism has been a necessity—no painter can afford to rebel against it, and in many ways its disciplines have been fruitful ones. Poetry has regarded modernism not as a necessity but as a burden.

Partly this is due to the nature of the poet's medium—the fact that he works in words. The materials of the artist are without overtones—that is, if he wants them to be so. But words carry with them into the work of art the overtones of the workaday world. Because they have another function, they can never be used with the same purity, the same astringency that an artist like Mondrian can achieve with paint. Attempts to model poetry directly on the methods of modern artists—to use words as "colours" on a sheet of paper—have all proved failures.

In these circumstances, what can the poet hope to gain from a study of the sister art? Would he not do better to concentrate on innovations which are part of the very texture of the language, if innovate he must? Critics have always asserted that one of the best of all disciplines for a creative writer is translation from one language into another. Will not the effort of translation from one art into another be just as beneficial? To try to render one sort of sensibility in terms of another—this is a challenge difficult enough to be worth meeting. The paintings of an artist like Delacroix (also in the news as the subject of an exhibition) long ago proved that there were special pleasures to be gained from the transmutation of literature into painting, that literary painting need not be bad painting nor incomplete painting. Nor need painterly poetry be incomplete.

There is, however, yet another paradox to be faced. The whole tendency of modern painting has been hostile to the idea of representation. Much of the best of it has forsworn representation altogether, and even the recent return to the figurative has shown us images used in a special way, at one remove, so to speak. But the whole tendency of poetry has been on the whole towards the concrete. The poet who tries to render the work of art honestly must either (as Stevens does) recast it image for image—allegorize it almost—or must try to seize upon its existence as an object, to write poetry which not only describes, but *is*. And this, in a curious way, is what Stevens manages, too. Perhaps the last word ought to rest with another great Symbolist poet, Rainer Maria Rilke, who slyly says of an archaic Apollo:

> there's nothing in his head that could prohibit
> the splendour of all poems from centering
> upon us with an almost fatal shining. . . .

But then that "almost fatal shining" is what we demand of every great work of art, whether visual or verbal.

61. JUSTIFYING THE FORMAL DECISIONS

Colette, in one of her pieces about the theatre, says that: "In art, inhumanity does not constitute a deficiency." On the other hand, in a broadsheet issued by an *avant-garde* publishing house in America, I find the following: "Needed: somebody to write a good article on how, looking at formal works, one becomes bored and looks for subject-matter. Concentrating on subject-matter one becomes bored and wishes for a little more formal invention. Finally, it's only the interplay and the intertwining that allows the mind to experience the work, without becoming conscious of too much pre-classification and pre-conceptualizing."

Is it possible to reconcile these two points of view? Before I answer the question I want to strike out upon a slightly different track. At the moment, the Tate has on loan an immense *papier découpé* by Matisse—one of whose late works, made when the artist was too old and ill to paint. It is called "The Parakeet and the Mermaid", and there, sure enough, amid a rhythmic pattern of leaves and fruit, one sees the silhouettes of the bird and of the mermaid. What it reminds me of is that famous series of tapestries in the Cluny Museum, on the theme of the *Lady and the Unicorn*. Matisse is reinventing the art of the Middle Ages—his huge picture has the decorative sweetness of a *mille-fleurs* tapestry. I think Colette, with her passion for flowers and beasts, would have approved of it. Indeed, it seems to me that she and Matisse had a kind of sensibility which was in many ways identical. There is both an abstract and therefore paradoxical practicality, a detached passion for the earthiness of things.

Colette's marvellous descriptions do, in fact, produce in me an effect of the picture by Matisse which I have just been describing. Both she and he are sensual yet impersonal, and I think that "impersonality" is really what Colette means when she talked of "inhumanity". Yet each, of course, fulfils the prescription of the other writer I have quoted; each is a master of the intertwining of the formal and the real.

And yet, I must confess, I don't find the Matisse wholly satisfactory as a work of art. There is something missing. It is strange that such a big picture, so loosely and openly composed, should yet seem so claustrophobic. Finally, it seems to me a celebration of the senses which is also a hymn to ennui, to the boredom which the senses bring with them. And this, oddly enough, returns me to the theme with which I began.

What we have tended to forget, in the battle between abstract and figurative art, is the idea of embodiment. By this I mean the fact that, for the old masters, the subjects they painted were important not so much for their own sake, but because they focused the spectator's attention upon certain general ideas. If we look at the French painters who were to some extent the predecessors of Matisse—not the Impressionists, who came immediately before him in the historical sequence, but at painters like Georges de la Tour and the brothers Le Nain, who had all Matisse's fascination with the earthiness of life—we begin to see the difference.

To me, a picture like Georges de la Tour's famous "Le Nouveau Né" at Rennes (which was recently on loan to the Vermeer Exhibition) is infinitely more moving than "The Parakeet and the Mermaid" could ever be. The reason is not that the de la Tour has religious overtones, that this ordinary nativity is also a symbol of Christ's Nativity. It is simply that in the de la Tour there is a concentration which I cannot find in the Matisse. The seventeenth-century artist simplifies his forms almost as much as Matisse does—we are never more conscious of the interplay between formal design and subject matter than when we look at the work I have mentioned. But we are also aware of something else, not only of the intertwining, but of the linking together. The subject-matter, and the attitude which the painter takes up towards it, justify the formal decisions which he makes. To some, this notion of justification may seem merely priggish. It is the fact that one has to mention this which points towards the root of the trouble.

Matisse—the Matisse of the picture I have been talking about—is the victim of freedom, which means (I think) the victim of self-consciousness. One might also feel the same about Colette, on reading a great deal of what she wrote. Indeed, it is just this freedom that Matisse symbolizes in the flowing composition, which moves in an endless, unbroken wave from one side of the canvas to the other. The silhouettes, the repeated forms of the leaves and the fruits—these tell us that the painter lives in a world where no one thing is more important than another.

It suddenly occurs to me that this may sound like an impassioned plea for committed art. Not at all. Commitment is always guilty of "pre-classification and pre-conceptualizing", and the results are usually as dire as these ugly coinages suggest. What one regrets, in essence, is the inability of the contemporary artist to come to the point. In music, the interplay of one theme with another is usually followed by a resolution of some kind, and if it isn't we tend to feel disappointed—"cheated" perhaps is not too strong a word. I have said before, in this series of essays, that it is not the complexity of modern art which I find disconcerting, but its lack of complexity. I want to add another occasional source of discomfiture—occasional, but still frequent enough to be worth noticing—and this is the artist's inability to choose among priorities, or even (it seems) to convince himself that priorities exist.

62. WAS BRAQUE A GREAT CLASSICAL ARTIST?

When he died, just over a week ago, Braque's place in the history of modern painting had long been known. He was not, in a sense, an artist who had further surprises to offer. No one would have thought of applying to him a verdict such as the one which William of Malmesbury passed on William Rufus: "*Tanta vis erat animi, ut quodlibet sibi regnum promittere anderet.*" True enough, his painting was always distinguished by great "energy of mind". But it had long ago become evident that he no longer "dared to promise himself any kingdom whatever". He had conquered the only one he ever wanted.

This, in a sense, sounds like the definition of a great classical painter. Many people have already been content to apply the adjective "classical" to Braque, and it would be easy to follow unthinkingly in their footsteps. Failing this, it would be easier still to say that the whole question was beside the point: that Braque was indisputably a man of genius, and that this is what matters. Yet in using the words "classical" and "romantic", we perform a useful, if somewhat primitive, piece of analysis. And the act of analysis helps to break down our initial resistance to the work of art. It brings each individual picture nearer to us.

But in Braque's case, it becomes more and more evident that the question should be rephrased, and that we should ask ourselves not *was* he a classical artist, but *could he be* one. The reason for this is that, during the past 100 years or so, the concept of classicism has broken up under our feet. In 1846 Sir Henry Rawlinson wrote to Layard, who was then in the course of excavating the Assyrian sculptures at Nimrud: "I admit a certain degree of excellence in the conception and execution of some of the sculptures, but when we come to value, *a certain degree* won't do. We have specimens of the very highest art—and anything short of that is, as a work of art . . . valueless, for it can neither instruct nor enrapture us. I hope you understand this distinction and when I criticize design and execution, will do so merely because your winged God is not the Apollo Belvedere."

I quote this letter because it seems to me that it sums up, and in an unselfconscious way that is especially valuable, the essence of the classical position. Classicism, in fact, presupposes a single standard to which everything must be referred. The classical artist assumes that circumstances in no way alter cases; that his art must be the product of a single aim, an immutable ideal.

On the question of aim, we can call Braque himself as a witness. He said: "I no more made up my mind to become a painter than to go on breathing. In fact I cannot think of any deliberate action which I have taken at any stage of my life. I enjoyed painting, and I worked hard. . . . But I never had a definite aim in mind. 'An aim is a servitude' is, I think, what Nietzsche wrote, and it is true. It is a very bad thing to realize that one is a painter. The only intention I ever had was to live up to myself each day. But in the fulfilment of myself it happened to be that what I produced resembled a picture."

This sounds like the statement of the quintessential romantic. The last sentence, in particular, sums up the beliefs of the whole Romantic Movement. And yet—and yet Braque's actual works, hanging on the wall, do not strike us in this fashion. It is their balance, their repose, the impression they make of being at ease with themselves and with the world which attract us. And these are the very qualities which we are still drawn to think of as classical, though the classical ideal itself may have gone for ever.

The contrast becomes the more marked if we look at some artists who did "realize that they were painters". Mondrian is a good example. No one, I hope, will now deny that he was a great master. No one, at any rate, could contest the purity of style, or the singleness of aim which we find in his mature works. Yet, although his geometry evokes the idea of measure, he remains an extreme artist—one who is exploring the frontiers, not cultivating the centre.

Precisely the opposite is true of Braque. For all his assertion of the primacy of instinct, his instinct led him to the *just milieu.* The great canvases of the "Studio" series impress us primarily by the way in which all the sensations which they evoke are kept in balance with one another. They alter our conception of space without alarming us: in fact, they persuade us so gently and pleasurably into a new realm of experience, a realm where space is felt as well as seen, that we remain grateful to them for ever after. The humble objects which inhabit the picture are transformed into a kind of dance of the senses, a dance in which the spectator participates as the partner of the artist. And thus we get the idea of "measure" in another way; not only a feeling of power held in reserve, but a feeling of rhythm, and motion, and music. If we turn from these pictures to the things which earlier and simpler times would have recognized as classical, in fact, if we turn to the Parthenon itself, do we not feel the same sensations?

It was Braque's triumph to persuade us that the classical ideal could be reborn in changed circumstances. His art seems a little larger every time we look at it.

63. THE CLASSICAL IDEAL

René Char is not usually thought of as a classical poet, but there are two aphorisms of his which seem to me to contain a definition of classicism. One of these runs: "*L'essentiel est sans cesse menacé par l'insignificant. Cycle bas.*" The other: "*L'obsession de la moisson et l'indifference a l'Histoire sont les deux extrémités de mon arc.*" In these words one catches a hint of the attitudes of certain modern artists who have perhaps deserved the adjective "classical". Among them I would place such figures as Mondrian, Giacometti, Brancusi, and Nicolas de Stael. The de Stael exhibition now on at the Gimpel Fils gallery has already been reviewed at length in these columns, and there would be no point in repeating the discussion here. But one point at least is worth stressing, and that is the radical nature of de Stael's humanism, at least in his later years. It is this which gives his classicism its fullness, that peculiar weight which marks him off from his imitators.

In saying this, I am of course conscious that I apparently contradict my earlier pairing of de Stael with Mondrian. Yet they are, I think, artists who are to be regarded as the two sides of the same medal. In Mondrian's career we see a heroic struggle to abandon a literary way of painting—Mondrian's early works have a distinctly Expressionist air about them. In de Stael, the journey—the essential journey—is from the tension, the anguished energy of the abstract works of around 1948, to the serenity of the late landscapes. Yet here, too, we feel external associations dropping away; in some mysterious fashion these late paintings are more absolute, more self-contained than the earlier ones.

This absolute quality is sometimes attributed to the power which de Stael's paintings have to be abstract and figurative at the same time; that is, the shapes and colours are so nicely adjusted to each other that we can see them either as pattern or as representation. A good many painters since de Stael have sought for the trick of doing this. Some of them have even found it. The fact that their works remain so immeasurably inferior to his proves the falsity of this explanation. De Stael, like Mondrian, has proved to be an artist whose influence is usually dangerous and frequently fatal. A school of prettily decorative painters have done their best to sicken us of de Stael's characteristic simplifications, his broad square touches, his thick creamy paint. The formula remains a formula. Yet in a picture like the large "Marine" in the Gimpel exhibition, we find something where all these imitable hallmarks are to be found, but which breathes an almost frightening serenity.

One way of defining a classical work of art, I suppose, would be to say that it is one which stresses the potential, the moment before movement, before action. This definition is unsatisfactory in the sense that it apparently excludes such centrally classical works as the sculptures of the Parthenon. The Centaurs and Lapiths of the metopes, the riders of the frieze, are indeed in motion, and that motion is often violent. Always present, however, is an underlying rhythm, a feeling of mathematical order. In fact, this is the thing which the modern spectator finds it hard to forgive the Greek sculptors of the fifth century. The marbles in the Elgin Room at the British Museum keep us chillingly at arm's length. We are required to consider, to reflect; we are not invited to participate or to identify ourselves with the action before us. The work of art is complete; not only perfect, but deliberately *perfected*.

It might seem that it is at this point that de Stael differs from the classicism of the Greeks. His sensual touch, his rich *matière*, invite us to a wholly different sort of relationship. But this, in turn, is outweighed by another aspect of de Stael—one which critics have not emphasized enough. I mean his Russianness, even his Byzantinism. True enough, de Stael, though born in Russia, was not of Slav stock. True, he left Russia at the age of five, and never went back. Yet his sense of colour is quite extraordinarily Russian. In a picture like the "Sicile, Agrigente" at Gimpels, we find colour used as an icon-painter would use it, expressively rather than naturalistically.

Father Gervase Mathew, in his brilliant new book, *Byzantine Aesthetics*, reminds us that the Byzantines thought of form as something which is apprehended through colour. In his late pictures, de Stael constructs his form in precisely this way. In him, as in Byzantine and Russian painting, colour is the agent by which the old classical rules of form are translated and set to work on a flat surface. Father Mathew quotes a passage from Plotinus which seems to me apposite: "The arts give no bare reproduction of the thing seen, but go back to the ideas from which nature itself derives, and furthermore much of their work is all their own; they are holders of beauty and add where nature is lacking. Thus Pheidias wrought Zeus upon no model among things of sense, but by apprehending what form Zeus must take if he chose to become manifest to sight." I think there could be no better description of what de Stael was about in his last years. At that time he was truly in pursuit of the essential, and obsessed with the harvest but indifferent to history.

64. RELIGIOUS ART IN THE TWENTIETH CENTURY

As part of the current Venice Biennale, the Museo Correr is exhibiting the sketches and projects by Giacomo Manzù for the bronze doors at St. Peter's in Rome. These reliefs have already been widely illustrated in England, but, as far as I know, little serious discussion has been given to them. Yet Manzù's work raises once again, in especially acute form, the whole question of the validity of religious art in the twentieth century. Manzù is an artist who is modern but not hermetic. His art draws nourishment from the Italian past without being overwhelmed by it. And these doors are deeply meditated—Manzù first started work on them in 1947. It may therefore seem churlish to say that this ambitious enterprise is a failure. Yet to pass from the room where the Manzù reliefs are shown, and to walk through the galleries of the museum itself until one reaches the sublime "Christ Lamented by Angels" by Antonello da Messina, is to realize the extent to which Manzù has failed in the task which he set himself. The Antonello is wholly explicit. The angels who surround the body of Christ are not even particularly restrained in their grief, and the Flemish influence in Antonello's style sees to it that the body of Christ is far gawkier than Bellini or Mantenga would have made it. Yet the word which immediately comes to mind as one stands before the picture is "dignity". It has dignity because the supernatural event is so much present to the artist; he records it, but it is not thrust at you. Going again to Manzù's reliefs one is conscious of the element of rhetoric in them.

Yet I do not think that rhetoric itself is the reason for the failure. One of the most interesting and revealing of the series is the "Death of the Virgin", a work in which Manzù borrows the pose of the Virgin from the famous "St. Teresa" by Bernini. No one could say that Bernini lacks the rhetorical touch. Yet, when we see his "St. Teresa", we are carried along by the sheer afflatus of the thing. In Manzù there is a shrillness, a touch of uncertainty. One might even localize it in the way in which the two reclining figures are presented to us. With the Bernini, the setting is carefully contrived, the sculpture is held in a framework which focuses our attention, the arrow held by the angel leads our eyes inward. Manzù's Virgin floats in shallow relief on the bronze ground, while two angels plummet towards her in a tangle of draperies—one already grasps her by the arm. The drapery is, in fact, the whole point of the composition, as it is about most of the other reliefs which belong to the door. The flesh—the Virgin's face, the arms of the angels—is deliberately slurred to give full value to the cloth. And the drapery has a special quality because of the technique the sculptor has used in making his sketch—the medium is paper, folded and glued, then cast in bronze (in other works, string has been used as well as paper). This technique imparts a curious air of impermanence; every fold is about to move into a different position. But all this agitation and spontaneity exist within what is really a Donatellesque convention; the convention of shallow relief. The spectator admires the way in which all these ideas have been brought together, but the borrowings do not blend. Brittleness and bravura are not the ideal qualities for evoking a meditative religious response.

I use this adjective "meditative" because it seems to me that this, so far as Christianity is concerned, is the very thing that religious art is about. Byzantine icons, for example, follow inflexible rules. The artist subordinates himself because he is making something which exists, not in and for itself but as an aid to prayer. By focusing on the picture, the Christian tries to reach the divine; he looks *through* the image as well as *at* it. With later religious works—Michelangelo's *Pieta* in St. Peter's, for example—our reaction is a little different. We see the artist struggling towards a goal—of liberation, of communion, of ecstasy. And we identify ourselves with him as he struggles. Later still, as the Baroque and the Counter-Reformation develop in conjunction with each other, we find religious works which offer the spectator yet another kind of experience, perhaps no less valid. Tiepolo is the last of the great Baroque masters, and we cannot, when we look at his religious pictures, claim that their piety is insincere. Indeed, not a few of his works of this sort are very moving. We soar, joyfully, amid a throng of saints and angels.

Modern art has displaced this kind of mediation by quite another. What has replaced the idea of the divine is the idea of the creative act itself. Man, rightly or wrongly, has ceased to look for divinity outside his own person, and what he looks for is proof that his own capacities are infinite. Hence, I think, the continued emphasis on "spontaneity" in painting and sculpture. Hence, too, the growing tendency of artists to make "museum objects"—sculptures and paintings which are not meant to be lived with from day to day, but which are meant to be objects of pilgrimage, which cry out to be enshrined. One sees this clearly in sculptors of a very different tendency from Manzù—in, for example, the latest work by Aduardo Paolozzi. The numinous quality in such works (that is, where they possess it genuinely and do not merely pretend to it) does not depend on appeal to dogma or to organized religion. The work itself generates tensions within the spectator, who is driven to contemplate his own inner nature.

The idea which I have just sketched is, of course, a very sweeping one. Yet if there is anything in it at all—and I am convinced there is something—then it is easy to see why the artist who undertakes a religious commission finds himself in difficulties. For artists cannot escape from their own time—the *Zeitgeist* is a powerful master. One course of escape is towards journalism. The artist is tempted to turn the religious myth into a commentary on the times. Thus, in the sketch for the "Death of Gregory VII" Manzù equips the young bystander with a German helmet, a detail which Breughel might perhaps have triumphed with, but which in our own day and age seems to narrow the theme instead of enlarging it. Another course of escape is towards the vaguely symbolical—what I once heard called the "this-beautiful-adornment-for-our-church" approach. Hence such lovely but somehow slightly irrelevant things are John Piper's stained-glass window for Coventry Cathedral. Finally, there are the moments when traditional iconography coincides with something which is truly personal to the artist. It is then that a work is produced which seems to demolish all my arguments—I am thinking now of Henry Moore's deeply moving Northampton Madonna.

65. THE ARTIST'S FANTASY

In the film devoted to the work and personality of Salvador Dali, shown on B.B.C.-2 the other day, the commentator, Jane Arden, noted Dali's dependence on other people—his whole way of life, so it seemed to her, required that everyone he met should co-operate in acting out his own personal fantasies. This set me off thinking, not so much of Dali, as of the part which fantasy plays in the lives of all artists.

As it happens, I have just encountered a delightful and extremely amusing documentation of one artist's fantasies, and their relationship to his own everyday life. A week from today, an exhibition of drawings by the Victorian artists George and John Hayter opens at the Christopher Powney Gallery in Berkeley Square. These two painters seem to have lived utterly blameless lives—no scandals, no dramas, only the humdrum business of painting pictures for the Academy. Of the two brothers, John is the less known. Biographical dictionaries tell us almost nothing about him—only the fact that he was quite astonishingly prolific. It now emerges that he left something very personal behind him—not an autobiography, like Benjamin Robert Haydon's, but a long series of sketch drawings in pen-and-ink. The drawings are of good quality—an odd mixture of Keene and Flaxman and Delacroix—but it is the content which is so interesting.

When one looks at the series, one is at first charmed by the glimpses of Victorian domestic life—a child reading, a mother talking to her children, a young girl seated at a table, with a lighted candle in front of her. But as one examines the drawings in more detail, one begins to realize that not all of them are wholly realistic. What about this one, for example, of an heroic bowman in medieval dress, marked "self"? And this other, with a muscular naked figure in the immediate foreground, behind whom are a Victorian lady and her child. The second drawing is marked "self—nature". It seems a little unlikely.

But indeed, as one begins to realize, this swaggering muscleman always has the same head—a square head, mustachioed, a little bald—the Victorian *paterfamilias* in person. He has no luck, but he is always sublimely unconscious of how odd he must appear. While he shoots that arrow in the air, a large, melancholy looking dog is busy walking off with his quiver. And so on, through the series, the grandiloquent gestures are always neatly punctured. And yet, I must hasten to emphasize, the drawings are not caricatures. They are not even especially "humorous". Their real quality is a wise detachment. It looks to me as if John Hayter was indulging his own very genuine fantasies, yet at the same time he was busy reminding himself that they *were* fantasies, and not reality.

Very occasionally, artists do attain this previous detachment. Usually they are great artists—one might almost say that Hayter is, among the company he keeps, exceptional because his talent is so minor. I am thinking of such things as Goya's San Lucar sketchbooks, which tell the story of his affair with the Duchess of Alba, and also of drawings by Picasso, especially those made recently in which the artist seems to lament his own failing powers—the drawings in which he appears as a little erotic goblin, vainly trying to seduce a beautiful young girl.

Artists are, I think, very fortunate in this—that if they are capable of self-revelation, that revelation can be made so much more directly. No literary work could be so transparent. In Hayter's sketches we are conscious of a very special kind of honesty—a determination not to blur things, to show even the ambiguous clearly. Words are, it seems to me, the allies of self-consciousness. When the image remains an image, and does not have to be translated, then the artist is able to get at the undistorted truth.

Think, for a moment, about the kind of society lived in—that comfortable, gentle, slightly complacent society of the early Victorian middle-class. As I have said, we see it very clearly in these drawings. Certain tricks of style do serve to remind us that this was nevertheless a society where powerful feelings stirred beneath the apparently placid surface. People tended to cultivate their emotions. A certain storminess of line, on the one hand; and on the other a touch of classicism—the flowing draperies of the Victorian matron do not always conceal the fact that the artist saw her as a Guinevere or a Demeter. But it was also—do we need to be reminded of this?—a world in which certain topics were not mentioned.

And here, suddenly, are quite a few of these forbidden topics. They parade before us openly, in the drawings made by this highly respectable and conventional man. The likelihood is that, sane and detached as he so evidently was, he still had no notion of how much he was revealing. No notion of the erotic force of certain lines, for example. If someone had tried to explain to him the narcissism of those muscular figures, he would have refused to listen. After all, people in those days had not the tools to deal with such things—they lacked both the vocabulary and the framework of argument. A Victorian like Hayter can tell us in pictures what no Victorian could have put into words—for the most part, there *were* no words.

And perhaps we still lack them. Fantasy has always been the strongest and surest bridge between the artist and his audience. We have, after 50 years of modernism, become very blasé about the recognition of a shared "exterior" reality. What does it matter to us, we say, if appearances are cleverly copied? But we cannot resist a shared dream. Or even, for that matter, a shared nightmare. And when the artist has the wit (or, rather, the degree of sanity) which allows him to make it plain to us that he knows the dream for what it is, even if he cannot completely interpret it, we are apt to be enslaved. I am certain that I shall see many more important exhibitions this year, but few that will give me more pleasure.

66. THE WORK OF ART AS A SPRING-BOARD FOR FANTASY

In an extremely effective bare setting at 76 Berwick Street in Soho there is at the moment an exhibition which entitles itself "Random Sculpture". What lurks behind this intriguing phrase is an exhibition of "found objects". The source of these objects is not the natural, but the industrial environment. To me the effect is disconcerting. Invited to a dinner with the famous, one discovers that all the guests come from Madame Tussaud's. Shut up with a whole roomful of Mona Lisas, one finds that not one of them possesses a secret. What I am trying to say is that these objects have, for me, an unmistakable aura of the *ersatz*. By chance they resemble modern sculpture. Yet I feel that the resemblance in some strange way amounts to imitation—and that the objects have all the deadness of copies. Or perhaps it is simply the disappointment and frustration which we all feel when holding converse with an echo. Things of this sort have nothing of their own to give—they can only provide a slavish reflection of our own thoughts and feelings.

The idea of treating artifacts as works of art—and thereby, according to one theory, *making* them into works of art—is not by any means a new one. It is years now since Marcel Duchamp sent his celebrated *urinoir* to an exhibition. All the same, it is an idea we have never quite come to terms with. In discussing it, we begin to question many of the basic assumptions of modern art. There come to mind, for some reason, the opening lines of a charming poem by the American, Louis Zukofsky:

> Daruma
> *found object*
> that is art
> for good luck

Where did the good luck go? Found objects often seem to me not only blank, but baleful things.

But let me go back to the beginning again. It is generally agreed, I think, that one of the tests of a great work of art is the quality of our response to it. If then we manage to drum up a similar response to an object which is not made to elicit it, we are (it is arguable) cheating ourselves, or else being cheated. One reply to this—the one which would certainly be made by Mrs. Pauline Brooke, who is responsible for the exhibition in Berwick Street—is that the creative act is here the act of choice. By selecting this object, and, moreover, by mounting it in such a way that its qualities are emphasized, the artist (and how quickly one slips into using the term!) has already justified her existence. She has imposed order where none existed. If we are prepared to look outside the tradition of our own civilization, there is even a respectable, scholarly background to this sort of activity. I am thinking of the Chinese, who will sometimes accept a piece of veined marble as the landscape drawing which, cut in a certain way and polished, it so closely resembles. Add a calligraphic inscription, containing an appropriate literary allusion or two, affix a seal—and, hey presto, another masterpiece!

Yet, instead of reassuring me, this comparison makes me feel more uneasy than ever. I have just, as it happens, been rereading Herman Hesse's novel *Das Glasperlenspiel*, known in its English version as *Magister Ludi*. The book, as most people will remember, centres upon the "bead-game" or "bead-play" which gives it its title. Hesse imagines a race of mandarins whose highest occupation is this marvellous game, where all arts and sciences, reduced to symbolic form, are pressed into service. Yet he is careful to point out that nothing is added to these arts and sciences by their employment in the game. Indeed, artistic creation has almost come to a stop, and the only original thinkers left are those which explore remote fields of learning to see how the knowledge gleaned there can be fitted into the all-devouring game. Hesse describes the game as very beautiful, and we believe him; he also hints that it is sterile, and we believe this also.

The parable of *Das Glasperlenspiel* does not, of course, refer only to the arts. But since the book has so much to say regarding artistic activity, it is impossible not to apply it. In fact, it does seem to me that a great change has come over our attitudes both to creativity and to the object of art, almost without our noticing it. What we now look for is a certain kind of contemplation—the work of art exists not for its own sake, but as a spring-board for fantasy. It is thus, for example, that "free abstraction" is so readily accepted by many people. What they like about it is its permissiveness. By not settling for any one object or image, the artist permits every spectator to choose his own. The effects of the more recent Op Art are curiously similar. All these optical tricks—these spinning discs, these weaving bending lines—are slightly hypnotic in their effect. The sensitive and willing subject is thrown into a light trance state, and the unconscious rises more freely to the surface of the mind.

Yet what is there to object to in this greater level of participation—this partnership, so it might seem, between the spectator and the artist? Simply, in my opinion, that it is not really a partnership at all. So many contemporary works of art have retreated to the status of the *objet trouvé* in this respect, if in no other—they offer the spectator only his own reflection. What he will find in the work of art is precisely what he brings to it, however much or little that may be. The artist, in seeming to collaborate with us, is merely fencing us off. This may seem a harsh verdict. Let me modify it a little. There is certainly every sign that ours is a mandarin civilization. All mandarin civilizations have a fascination with the idea of the contemplative, of the soul achieving knowledge of itself through meditation. In other times, much art has been made as an instrument towards this end—the marvellous ceramics of the Sung Dynasty, for example. But we must be careful to differentiate the contemplative from that idle fantasy which runs across the surface of our thoughts, changing nothing and demanding nothing. It is this fantasy which makes every object a mere counter in the intellectual bead-game. This piece of scrap metal looks like a piece of modern scuplture, therefore it *is* a piece of modern sculpture. Not necessarily—any more than it is necessarily true to say that a piece of sculpture which looks like scrap metal is therefore no better than scrap. We must learn to respect the power of our own humanity: its need to create as well as to choose, to act as well as to contemplate.

67. TRIUMPH OF MANNER OVER CONTENT

The "Young Contemporaries" exhibition is with us again in Suffolk Street. Once more the critics and the trend-spotters wander round those large, light, but somehow melancholy rooms at the top of a steep staircase. Once more they wrestle with a catalogue which is perhaps more logically arranged than last year, but still devilish difficult to find one's way about in. One good thing the catalogue does have, and that is the Introduction written by Joseph Rykwert, the critic member of this year's selection committee. Mr. Rykwert does not go in for fanfares. Very gently, he predicts the death of "Pop"—indeed, he seems to look forward with some relish to its public obsequies. He deplores the cult of originality at all costs; he murmurs that "dealers and critics have recently come to think of art schools as forcing frames to feed an insatiable market with novelties".

In all this he shows himself a man of excellent sense. It is where Mr. Ryckwert starts to talk of the "real problems" which face the young artist that he begins to worry me, or at least that I begin to wish that he had been given the space to say more. As Mr. Rykwert sees it, the crucial problem for the young artist is "the relationship of his message, whether public or personal, to the formal integrity of each individual work he produces". Decidedly, the exhibition makes one think there was need to elaborate.

For the thing about the "Young Contemporaries" is its strangely blinkered quality. Many of the paintings, and even some of the sculptures, have about them a crispness, a confidence, a completeness of vision which is at first sight very impressive. It is only gradually that one begins to wonder. We all, I imagine, expect very young artists to be derivative. For a little while, until their own personalities take on shape and strength, we expect to find unassimilated tricks of style, borrowings which have not been fully transformed. What is frightening is that these borrowed garments fit their young wearers so well.

Basically speaking, there is not much variety. There are the austere geometric exercises in the wake of Vasarely. There are one or two attempts to "do a Poliakoff". There are distinct traces of the influence of the brothers Cohen. There are tributes to Peter Phillips, to Peter Blake and to Allen Jones—and also, in a few paintings, to Kitaj. In almost every case, manner triumphs easily over content. This produces an especially odd effect in the case of those paintings which are figurative or semi-figurative. At first, the impersonation often seems quite as good as the real thing.

Bryan Ingham's "Family Group" catches Peter Blake's manner so hallucinatingly well that one begins to believe in some sort of ventriloquism of the brush. But then one begins to see a difference. Peter Blake is a nostalgic artist. His pictures—even those which supposedly copy old-fashioned picture-postcards on a gigantic scale—express a mixture of amusement and melancholy. What Mr. Ingham is being nostalgic about, on the other hand, is Mr. Blake himself. The message the picture carries is nothing to do with its ostensible subject, but about how nice it would be to be "an artist like that".

I pick on Mr. Ingham rather unfairly, not only because he is so obviously talented, but because he has another, rather different, picture in the show. This, a still life, has elements of Peter Blake in it, but also takes hints from Ben Nicholson. The mixture is piquant, unexpected, and personal. The picture says something about scrubbed tables and kitchen utensils which is fresh, even if not very profound. Looking at it, one feels a sudden relief that the artist has jibbed, has refused to settle for the clearcut choices which surround him.

In effect, the thing about painting just now seems to be its obsession with the idea of alternatives. Art students are especially sensitive to this—everything tells them that they must choose, must pick a manner and stick to it, otherwise they'll never come to anything. This, of course, is in turn the consequence of the passion for labels which has long possessed the minds of those who write about art. But the trouble with labels is that it is inconvenient to have too many of them. Four or five basic categories is about as many as we can cope with at once. The result is, I think, that young painters, and especially young figurative painters, find themselves forced into a kind of strait-jacket.

Curiously enough, it does not seem to me so harmful for an abstract artist to begin by choosing a manner, almost in cold blood. If he has any talent, his own sensibility will soon begin to corrupt the formula, and in the early stages he may not even notice the change in his own work. With non-figurative painting, definitions, and therefore choices, are difficult. It is natural that an artist with this kind of bent should begin by looking at the work of a painter he admires, and saying "That's the kind of thing I'd like to do".

With a figurative painter, things ought to be different. The whole revival of figuration is comparatively new still, and what brought it about in the first place was the sudden yearning which artists felt for something intractable and unyielding, for the brute fact. The best side of the "Pop" movement was its determination to get facts back into pictures. The artist hooted derisively at the idea of "fine art" because he had found an army of allies, and those allies were the banal objects which surrounded him. To these he gave a loving and concentrated attention. But what happens when the succeeding generation convinces itself that objects are all very well—so long as you depict them only according to the hallowed formulae? The whole idealist heresy comes back with a rush, the concept triumphs over the image. This is what I want Mr. Rykwert to tell me about—what happens when the message is simply that there is no message, when "formal integrity" is simply a matter of choosing what label one will wear?

68. THE NUMINOUS IN MODERN ART

One of the fascinating things about modern art is the obsession which it has with the idea of the numinous. People tend to discuss *avant-garde* sculpture and painting in entirely contradictory ways. On the one hand, they would like to feel in it the touch of some mysterious power. They treat the artist as if he were the vehicle for a voice beyond himself—with that mingling of contempt and awe men have always reserved for oracle and their priests. If one follows this theory of art to its logical end, paintings and sculptures are like the pieces of pumice which one picks up after a volcanic explosion. From these tortured, twisted forms it is possible to guess at the magnitude of the eruption which produced them. The assumption is that works of art possess no intrinsic interest but are merely clues. The spectator turns detective. And like all detectives, he does not value the evidence for its own sake, but only for the conclusions which it enables him to reach. On the other hand, we still find ourselves talking about modern art as if it obeyed the old rules—as if the objects before us were the results of an attempt to extend our experience within a given framework, the framework of the classical norm.

An opportunity to see these two attitudes in direct conflict with one another is provided by Michael Ayrton's current exhibition at the Grosvenor Gallery. Mr. Ayrton is one of the few modern artists of any stature who is still fascinated by classical myth. In this exhibition he explores two themes in depth. One is the figure of the minotaur, the other is that of the oracle or sibyl. We have here, then, direct reference to classical prototypes, combined with an equally overt allusion to the mysteriousness which I have mentioned above. The minotaur is the creature of the maze or labyrinth, the sibyl is she who utters prophecies in ignorance of what they mean. One cannot help feeling that Ayrton has failed to resolve the complexities of his material. The sculptures which form the bulk of the show make gestures—gestures towards the severity of classical art, gestures towards the modern dissolution of form. So often his sibyls seated on their tripods seem like stubborn trees bending before a wind which will eventually break them. There is a sort of frozen mannerism about the outlines, about the relationship of the tiny heads to the twisted yet swollen bodies. They are descriptions of inspiration, not embodiments of it.

Yet the use of classical myth does provide Ayrton's exhibition with a welcome solidity. Whatever one's doubts about the individual pieces, the show as a whole gives evidence of a powerful and sophisticated intelligence—the sort of intelligence which, in other circumstances, might have created one of the great sculptural momuments of the renaissance. The elegant collage landscapes, for example, do provide us with a setting which oracles and minotaur might have inhabited. We are told—almost too plainly—how everything fits, at what point the myth is to be regarded as universal, as an allegory of our own lives.

Other artists, perhaps less sophisticated and intellectual than Ayrton, attempt to give us the *frisson* of the mythical, without actually settling for a particular theme. They try to convince us that what they make—these objects which may be figurative, or may be merely objects—allude to some buried meaning. Taking clues from primitive art, they create a series of fetishes, of tribal totems. They ask us to judge, not by any canon of proportion, not by the way in which form answers form to create an aesthetic experience but by the closeness of the picture or of the sculpture before us to some notion of the inexpressible. In effect, they try to persuade us that the strangeness of the thing answers to some strangeness in ourselves. The elaborate wooden sculptures of Louise Nevelson, for example, tackle the notion of the labyrinth from quite a different direction from the one which Ayrton chooses. He tries to persuade us that a story many times told can still be galvanized to life again, though all the religious and social concepts which formed it have gone. She, on the other hand, argues that the constructions she creates, visibly irrational as they are, chime with an equivalent irrationality in ourselves.

I cannot myself feel that either argument is convincing. The employment of myth as Ayrton tries to use it seems to me to rest on a misconception—or rather on two misconceptions, both fatal. One is simpler and more particular than the other. Ayrton evidently feels that the impact of places—of Crete and South Italy—can be personified. But this kind of personification is really too primitive a procedure for the twentieth century, with its deficient sense of allegory. In the well-known Pompeian fresco of Hercules and Telephus, now in the Museo Nazionale Archaeologico in Naples, the wilds of Arcadia are personified in the figure of the nymph of the place, who dominates the painting. But it is only by an effort of the scholarly imagination that we can accept the convention, and the scholarly imagination, or at least to bridle their action. The other misconception which I find in Ayrton's work is simply that he mistakes name for thing—that he commits the common error of supposing that because the modern psychologists have labelled common patterns of human action by the names of Greek myths, so the evocation of these myths will necessarily summon up before us a given pattern of behaviour. The result is that his minotaurs and his sibyls remain literary.

On the other hand, one respects Ayrton's obstinate clinging to known myths the more when one turns to a sculptor like Nevelson, or indeed to the work of artists like Paolozzi or Dalwood on this side of the Atlantic. This is not to say that their work is inexpressive. Indeed, it is often the very opposite—powerfully suggestive, but with the suggestions at work in so many different directions that the spectator feels dissatisfied. An artist like Ayrton does not trust our imaginative faculty enough—we feel stifled by the learned apparatus with which he decks out his creations. But at least he is not naive about the way the imagination goes to work. We read meanings into the work of an artist like Nevelson—but we soon tire ourselves out with choices. Where it is possible to interpret a work of art in several entirely contradictory senses, it is likely that its effect will be centrifugal—that we will follow this will o' the wisp or that, without ever being drawn in towards some central, inescapable meaning, some powerful emotion. It becomes an amusement to see in how many ways the work of art can be turned to account.

The strange thing about these two different sorts of failure—honourable failure, let it be said—is that they both seem to spring from a single weakness, which is the reluctance of the artist to integrate himself with the society in which he lives. Ayrton rejects society for the consolations of scholarship. Nevelson, Paolozzi, Dalwood and their peers are indulgent to private fantasy. It may seem perverse to say that the most mysterious and numinous works are those which most completely express the society which formed them, which surrender themselves most completely to the desire to communicate plainly and unambiguously ideas and emotions which the artist feels to be the rightful property of all. Yet we have only to turn and look at the classical ideal in a new light to see that this is true. What more mysterious, yet more essentially public works of art, than the sculptures which Phidias designed for the Parthenon?

69. THE SPECTATOR'S COLLABORATION IN CONTEMPORARY ART

The Marcel Duchamp exhibition is almost with us. One of the great enigmas of the century is about to be canonized at the Tate. But Duchamp is (it seems now that he always was) a highly relevant enigma, a sphinx capable of giving us an answer which is both useful and practical. Or, rather, he is a sphinx who asks the right questions. One of these questions, quite simply, is: "What is a work of art?" With his famous "ready-mades", Duchamp seemed to put forward the idea that the artist's power of choice is, in fact, much more important than his power to make things in the physical sense.

But Duchamp, I think, sees the "conventional" work of art as in fact the product of a series of choices—a sum total of yeses and noes. He is prepared to simplify the whole process—to single one thing out and affirm that it *is* a work of art. At the moment when he makes his affirmation the object becomes what he says it is, regardless of any state it might have existed in before. It seems to me that this side of his work is the really important and challenging one. It is not enough to say, as some critics have done in the past, that he taught us to discover the aesthetic quality of ordinary objects by removing them from their usual surroundings and presenting them as works of art. The point is not to be found in this—the banal comment on what the spectator sees; it lies far more in the comment on what the artist does, the whole moral and philosophical basis of his activity.

The gesture which Duchamp made has led to other gestures—interesting in themselves, but perhaps no more radical than his. The other day, for instance, I received notice of a "Happening" which was to take place in New York. Those who wished to attend were asked, first of all, to go to different points on the New York subway system. Here, on successive days, a man would be ready to stamp the card which they presented to him. These journeys, and anything which happened on the way, were officially included in the total work of art.

All this, perhaps, makes certain kinds of modern art sound like Humpty Dumpty. It *is* because it (or someone) *says* it is.

We are commanded to take everything on trust. A Campbell's soup-can is mysteriously transformed because Andy Warhol has signed it. This Brillo box is different from that—which it closely resembles—because it is a copy made by someone who calls himself an artist. As I list some of the activities of modern artists, I can hear the outcry begin. Even the sympathetic spectator begins to murmur that this is all puerility. The unsympathetic one wants to know why he too cannot make works of art. "Suppose", he says, "I nominate that lamp post, and the drunk leaning against it—are these works of art?"

And yet there is no reason why one should be afraid to answer such a question. The answer is "yes". The man who asks has already, in some degree, allowed himself to become an artist. By which I mean that the question, however hostile its intention, proposes that these two objects—the drunk and the lamp post—be separated from their environment, cherished for their own sake, cherished for what they are.

The isolation of things is, I believe, very important. When we are thinking of a work of art, we may make a primitive definition as a preliminary. A work of art is something which we look at by itself, a centre which draws some things towards it and fends off others, but which always remains *sui generis*. What it looks like is entirely secondary to this—the next stage. And a stage farther still is the whole question of how it was made, and what intention lies behind it.

"Intention" is, of course, one of the main stumbling blocks for the art critic who attempts to deal with modern art. The healthy critical impulse is to judge things in isolation; but more and more art seems to frustrate this. We discover we can judge success or failure of the work only if we know what intention subsumes it. What is decorative on one level may be tragic on another. In this case one is forced to argue that the object is not in fact the total work of art, but only a part of it—the whole is formed by matching the object to the intention; the thing we see before us completed by something entirely bodiless and abstract—an idea, or a set of ideas. Only thus can we isolate the work, mark it off from its surroundings in the way that I have been talking about.

But let me change the point of view, and consider the idea of the artist's intention, not in particular, but in general. A large number of modern paintings and sculptures are neither one thing nor the other. That is, they neither represent anything in the world around us, nor propose an abstract harmony. What, then, is their purpose? It is, I believe, to act as catalysts. The spectator finds himself precipitated into the state of being which the painter or sculptor has ordained for him. The work of Henry Moore often seems to me to match this definition pretty precisely—and few people nowadays complain of having difficulty with Moore.

Is there any reason, however, why our catalysts should be made rather than chosen? Here is a query to which it is very difficult to give a satisfactory answer. One reply seems to be that the "chosen" object is, for various reasons, feebler. It has less warmth, less complexity. But to say that something is less efficient is not the same as saying that it cannot be used. The real barrier, the real difficulty, seems to arise when—having flung the work of art back into the common stock of objects—we still persist in treating the artist as a special kind of person.

The blurring of the barrier between the artist and the spectator has, I believe, been one of the most conspicuous features of contemporary painting and sculpture. The artist has gradually come to demand that the spectator do more and more. The spectator (as with some kinetic works) is asked to collaborate by setting the work of art physically in motion. Or else, as I have suggested, the work of art is activated when the spectator agrees to pursue a particular chain of thought, or to apply the information which he has, or can acquire. The situation, as we now have it, suggests that the work of art is very often to be regarded as a collaboration—the spectator of the moment becomes in a very real sense the part-author of what he is looking at, and the artist takes up a detached, spectatorial attitude. One solution, then, to the problem which I posed at the beginning of this article is that a work of art is the framework for a game; a chessboard where there are no winners or losers. Duchamp, who is a passionate chess-player, might, I suspect, agree with me. He would also agree, no doubt, that such a definition still falls short—but have not all the previous definitions of art done so, too? It is this very uncertainty which gives art its dynamic.

70. AESTHETIC OBJECTS: THE DRUNK AND THE LAMP-POST AGAIN

The other day I was amused and flattered to find that something I said in one of my articles on this page had attracted the attention of Paul Jennings. His column "Oddly Enough" in *The Observer* of two or three Sundays ago was based on my perhaps mischievous proposition that the modern artist, simply by choosing or nominating something in his environment, could turn it into a work of art. My example was the man who elects a lamp-post and the drunk leaning against it—this prompted Mr. Jennings to a pleasing fantasy concerning an artist who eventually emerged triumphant, "bursting into fame, or whatever it is now, with his epoch-making exhibition, 'Twenty Sober Men and Lamp-posts' ". Ought I to feel abashed for having given this particular aesthetic notion an airing? Not at all.

The reasons may require a little explanation—but not, I hope, too much. Let me begin by citing something which Cyril Connolly quoted in *The Sunday Times* that very Sunday. It was an explanation (by the phenomenologist Dufrenne) of the independent life led by works of art, once these had left the hands of those who created them: "An aesthetic object appears *in* the ordinary world of space and time, and yet is not wholly *of* it, it is 'privileged' over the other objects about it in space, as the painting lords it over the gallery wall, and refuses to sink into its background."

I want to ask this—what, precisely, is an "aesthetic object"? The modern situation makes it more and more difficult to be sure. Here are some examples of the kind of difficulty I have in mind—the questions raised by things which are currently on view at a couple of leading art galleries. At the Hanover Gallery, for instance, there is an immense thumb in red plastic by César. The thumb is utterly naturalistic. Only its size and its colour mark it off from the real thing—otherwise no transformation has taken place. At the Robert Fraser Gallery, in the current New Idioms show, there is a work called "Van Gogh's Chair", by Clive Barker. It consists of a chair with a pipe and a half opened packet of tobacco on it. The chair, the pipe, and the tobacco are precisely equivalent to their "real" counterparts, with this exception—all three of them are made of shiny chromium-plated steel.

There are two arguments you can put forward about these objects. One is the argument I should choose to support; the other is the one which (I imagine) has the allegiance of Mr. Jennings. And both are obvious enough. For me, the thumb and the chair are indeed "real" objects, chosen and alienated, "privileged" as the phenomenologist would have it. The badges of this privilege are, in both cases, a change of material and of colour; and, in one case, there is a change of scale as well. Which is more important—the act of choice, the singling out? Or these comparatively simple transformations? Surely it's the act of choice that counts. The artist chooses his own thumb, or the chair he sits on, and the rest follows. The changes are something mechanical. They make it plain to us, the audience, what happened, but they don't alter the nature or significance of the artist's action in any way.

The opposing argument is simpler still—that objects such as the ones I've been describing are not works of art at all, but things of an entirely different nature. Hoaxes. Aridly intellectual paradoxes. Fashionable ornaments. But wait a moment! Ask the man who puts forward this view my original question—what is an aesthetic object? Or, in plainer terms, what is a work of art? He will, I believe, find himself unable to answer in general terms. He can only make his definition by pointing to specific examples: this picture by Rembrandt is a work of art, and so is that piece of sculpture by Michelangelo. And asked *why* these are works of art, he can only reply (whatever elaboration he chooses) that they are works of art because we all assume them to be so, or else that they provide him with the subjective emotions and sensations which he assumes he ought to have when in the presence of the work of art. (And what taught him to recognize those emotions, those sensations?—Society, the environment he lives in.)

This is to introduce into contemporary aesthetics an idea which somewhat resembles the "general will" of the eighteenth-century political philosophers. This, in turn, leads us inexorably to the notion that objects are sometimes works of art, and sometimes not, depending on the circumstances. To take a reasonably neutral example, after two polemical ones—a Japanese tea-bowl may rank as a great work of art in the eyes of an oriental observer, but may be merely a rather lumpish piece of crockery to a western one.

The truth is, I think, that we are in the midst of a great change in sensibility—the "general will" that I've talked about is perhaps in the process of shifting from one side of the question to the other. The act of choosing (choosing drunks and lamp-posts) is still something which has to be made manifest by some further process of embodiment. Or, at the very least, the object chosen has to be removed from its usual context and deposited somewhere else; has to be put on a pedestal, either actually or metaphorically. A coat-stand is only a work of art when you show it as such in the Tate Gallery. But once it's there, how are you going to prove that it *isn't* a work of art? Especially if other people are prepared to recognize it as such? One may argue that the coat-rack hasn't got an iota of the emotional charge we find in the Rembrandt or the Michelangelo. But this isn't the point—after all, aestheticians and philosophers are always reminding us what a treacherous guide mere emotion is.

The dilemma is a genuinely crucial one. It calls to my mind a very remarkable novel, *Magister Ludi*, by Herman Hesse. I think I have mentioned it previously in these columns. Essentially what Hesse imagines, and then proposes to us, is a society where all the arts and all the sciences have been brought within the compass of a celestial, an unimaginably complex game. The game proceeds almost entirely in the abstract; it is an activity of the mind. The mind glories in its own power—a few signs and symbols are enough to guide it.

Modern art resembles this game because it grows increasingly abstract—abstract even in the sense that real objects tend to acquire a purely abstract significance. Press such a development far enough, and my point is made—the mere act of choice is enough to "create" a work of art, and the work of art can be anything at all you happen to choose. Of course, you couldn't sell your choice, or exhibit it. But not even Mr. Jennings is going to tell me that sales and exhibitions are necessary criteria. Or is he? At any rate, one thing is plain, he has his notions, his fancies—and I have mine.